HOSPITALITY AND TOURISM MARKETING

HOSPITALITY AND TOURISM MARKETING

Ajay Kaul

ABD PUBLISHERS
Jaipur ■ New Delhi

ABD PUBLISHERS

Regd. Off. "Bony Residency", Gate No. 2
Opp. Tilak Public School, Vishweswariya Nagar,
Gopalpura Road, Jaipur - 302018, India
Ph: 0141 - 2761280, Telefax: 2761381
Email: abdpublishersjpr@gmail.com

Delhi Office: 102, 1st Floor, Satyam House,
4327/3, Ansari Road, Darya Ganj,
New Delhi - 110002, India
Ph: 011-45652440

visit us: www.oxfordbookcompany.com

Distributed By
KEYA INTERNATIONAL PRESS LLP
E-mail: keyainternationalpressllp@gmail.com

Published in India, 2026

ISBN: 9788183769105

Typeset by Shivangi Computer, Jaipur

Printed and bound in India by Thomson Press Ltd.,
New Delhi

Contents

Preface

Hospitality and Tourism Marketing book you down the intriguing, discovery laden road to learning marketing. It is our goal is to help you master the basic concepts and practices of modern hospitality marketing in an enjoyable and practical way. Achieving this goal involves a constant search for the best balance among the "three pillars" that support the book-theories and concepts, practices and applications and pedagogy.

The hospitality and travel industry are undergoing rapid changes. The applications you learn today may not apply five years from now. Thus, it important that you have an understanding of the marketing concepts. This will allow you to analyze future situations and make the proper decisions. Practices and applications are provided to give you examples of how we currently apply the concepts to industry situations. Finally, we hope you will feel is interesting and makes learning fun.

— ***Ajay Kaul***

Chapter 1

Tourism and Hospitality Industry

Tourism is a powerful economic force providing employment, foreign exchange, income, and tax revenue. The generators of economic impact for a city, a state, a province, a country, or a destination area are visitors, their expenditures, and the multiplier effect.

The economic impact of tourism spending is a function of the numbers of domestic and international visitors and their expenditures. Because of the economic importance of tourism, the World Tourism Organization maintains statistics by region and country on tourism arrivals and both tourism expenditures and receipts.

Tourism destinations are becoming increasingly competitive as more and more destinations look at tourism to become the new economic generator replacing declining activity in agriculture, mining, and manufacturing. As a consequence of pervasive anxiety caused by these events, people cut back on their travel; economic forecasts were put on hold; airline, lodging, tour operators, and travel agent revenue declined; and widespread layoffs occurred throughout the industry.

We realised very directly and in a personal manner the real economic impact of tourism. However, over the long run, it is believed that travel will recover and the 2020 forecasts will be realised. Negative factors such as the Iraq conflict, terrorism, SARS, and a weak economy made 2003 another difficult year for international tourism. SARS brought the steady growth of Asia and the Pacific to an abrupt halt in April and May, and while tourists quickly started to return after the virus was contained, the region could not make up the losses in the remainder of the year. The war and the economy dampened tourism demand in other key regions. According to WTO preliminary results, the total number of international arrivals reached 694.0 million in 2003, a decrease of 1.2 per cent from 2002.

Europe is the main tourist receiving region, followed by Asia and the Pacific, and the Americas. In 2003, Europe accounted for almost 58 per cent of the arrivals, Asia and the Pacific 17.2 per cent, and the Americas 16.2 per cent. International arrivals were most impacted by the unexpected drop of 12 million in Asia and the Pacific due to the SARS panic.

The Americas recorded a decrease of 2.5 million, while Europe was basically flat, recording an increase of 0.4 per cent. The Middle East and Africa were the surprise regions in 2003 as they recorded healthy increases in tourism arrivals of 10 per cent and 5 per cent respectively. An initial analysis of this data shows that international receipts increased by $40.2 billion, and measured in U.S. dollars every region recorded an increase in receipts except

Asia and the Pacific. The series has always been reported in U.S. dollars; however, in this case, it does not present as accurate a picture as it should and illustrates the impact exchange rates can have. When one examines the increase of receipts from $474.2 billion in 2002 to $514.4 billion in 2003, it should be taken into account that this is largely because of the strong depreciation of the U.S. dollar versus many other currencies, especially the euro. In 2003, a euro bought almost 20 per cent more U.S. dollar than in 2002.

Thus, receipts earned in euro destinations, which account for over a quarter of worldwide receipts, when expressed in dollar terms, are magnified. Consequently, expressing worldwide receipts in a currency other than the U.S. dollar would present a different picture. WTO has computed worldwide receipts in euros and found that worldwide receipts decreased by 50 billion from euro 502 billion in 2002 to euro 455 billion in 2003. WTO states that a way to compensate for this distortion caused by exchange rates is to express the evolution of receipts in weighted local currencies. At the same time, it is preferable to take inflation into account by using constant prices instead of current prices. Calculated this way, international tourism receipts were estimated to have decreased by about 2 per cent in 2003, while 2002 was still just positive at 0.3 per cent.

When one reviews the period 1996 to 2000, they find that international tourism receipts grew faster than arrivals. In the last three years, receipts have grown at a lower rate, reflecting unsettled times and a slow economy. In difficult times, travelers are resourceful and will keep traveling, but will economize by traveling with friends, taking shorter trips, staying in less expensive accommodations, eating out less, and so on. All of these actions reduce tourism receipts. The Americas' share is 22.5 per cent and Asia and the Pacific share is 17.2 per cent. The shares of Africa and the Middle East were both at 2.7 per cent. Receipts per arrivals averaged $740. The Americas averaged the highest receipts per arrival at $1,030, followed by Asia and the Pacific at the average of $740, Europe with $700, and Africa and the Middle East both at $460.

EXPECTATIONS FOR 2007 AND BEYOND

Prospects for 2007 and the future appear to be very positive as short-term data confirm the upward trend in arrivals that started in late 2003. Asia and the Pacific are showing a strong rebound from 2003. United States international arrivals are recording monthly double-digit increases. Business travel is showing signs of recovery. Low-cost airlines are continuing to increase their capacity and expand their coverage.

As expected 2004 saw a return to growth in the travel industry with a record 760 million international arrivals for a 10 per cent increase over 2003. However, rising oil prices are a major concern. *Tourism 2020 Vision* is the World Tourism Organization's long-term forecast and assessment of the development of tourism through the first twenty years of the new millennium. An essential outcome of *Tourism 2020 Vision* is quantitative forecasts covering a 25-year period, with 1995 as the base year and forecasts for 2000, 2010, and 2020.

WTO's *Tourism 2020 Vision* forecasts that international arrivals are expected to reach over 1.56 billion by the year 2020. Of these worldwide arrivals in 2020, 1.18 billion will be intraregional and 377 million will be long-haul travellers. The total tourist arrivals by region shows that by 2020 the top three receiving regions will be Europe, East Asia and the Pacific and the Americas, followed by Africa, the Middle East, and South Asia. East Asia and the Pacific, South Asia, the Middle East, and Africa are forecasted to record growth at rates of over 5 per cent, compared to the world average of 4.1 per cent. The more mature regions of Europe and the Americas are anticipated to show lower-than-average growth rates.

Europe will maintain the highest share of world arrivals, although there will be a decline from 60 per cent in 1995 to 46 per cent in 2020. By 2010, the Americas will lose its number-two position to the East Asia and Pacific region, which will receive 25 per cent of world arrivals in 2020, with the Americas decreasing from 19 per cent in 1995 to 18 per cent in 2020.

Long-haul travel worldwide will grow faster, at 5.4 per cent per year over the period 1995–2020, than intraregional travel, at 3.8 per cent. Consequently, the ratio between intraregional and long-haul travel will shift from around 82:18 in 1995 to close to 76:24 in 2020.

Comparing International and Despite the importance of international tourism for many countries, domestic tourism is even more important. The World Tourism Organization estimated that international travel involved receipts of US$514.4 billion in 2003. In contrast, the World Travel and Tourism Council estimated that in 2004, both international and domestic travel together generated about US$3,133.2 billion.

As can be seen from these estimates of the magnitude of international and domestic travel, the latter is much greater than the former. This fact surprises many people who primarily think of tourism as being exotic, international travel. In the United States the travel industry received $545.5 billion from domestic and international travelers in 2002. Of these total international visitors spent $83.5 billion traveling in the United States for 15.3 per cent of the total. Domestic travel expenditures were $462.0 billion for 84.7 per cent of the total.

EMPLOYMENT

The World Travel and Tourism Council estimates that in 2005 employment in the travel and tourism economy was 221,568,000 jobs or 8.3 per cent of total employment, which is 1 in every 12.0 jobs. By 2015, this should grow to 269,556,000 jobs, 8.9 per cent of total employment or 1 in every 11.2 jobs. The 74,223,000 travel and tourism industry jobs accounted for 2.8 per cent of total employment in 2005 and are forecast to rise to 85,521,000 jobs or 2.8 per cent of the total by 2015.

Tourism provides both direct and indirect employment. Firms such as hotels, restaurants, airlines, cruise lines, and resorts provide direct employment because their employees are in contact with tourists and provide the tourist experience. Employees of firms providing goods and services to the direct employment firms, such as aircraft manufacturers, construction firms, and restaurant suppliers, create indirect employment. The impact of this can be illustrated using a United States example. In 2003, the TIA published its annual study, *Tourism Works for America,* which contains employment estimates.

Employment by sector, shows that in 2002, travel and tourism directly generated nearly 7.2 million jobs in the U.S. economy. Travellers in the United States produce secondary impacts over and above that of their original expenditures. These secondary outputs and earnings supported by this "indirect" and "induced" spending add an additional 9.7 million jobs to the U.S. economy.

With the almost 6.3 million jobs in 2002 generated directly by domestic travel spending, and the 900,000 employment opportunities generated by international travel to the United States, total U.S. employment created by the travel and tourism industry was 16.9 million in 2002.

The complexity of accurately measuring the vast economic impacts of the tourism industry has created a movement to link tourism expenditure accounting with that used for the national system of accounting in most countries. Earlier attempts to include tourism in the standard industry classification codes proved unsuccessful because of the diversity and overlapping nature of many tourism expenditures. In order to overcome these difficulties, a system of tourism satellite accounting has been proposed and implemented.

Economics is concerned with the attainment of an optimum return from the use of scarce resources. Whether it is a person seeking psychological benefit from travel, or a business interested in providing tourists goods and services at a profit, or a host community government viewing tourism in terms of the economic benefits resulting from tourist expenditures, the principle is the same. Economic agents seek to allocate the limited supply of tourism resources as they seek to meet the demands of tourists. The demands are the result of their physical/functional needs and their psychological wants.

As such, the problem that economics attempts to solve is how to achieve an economical optimal allocation of scarce tourism resources, when facing the constantly shifting demand for these resources.

GOALS

As indicated, at least three major goals can be identified in tourism:

1. Maximize the amount of psychological experience for tourists.
2. Maximize profits for firms providing goods and services to tourists.
3. Maximize the direct and indirect benefits of tourist expenditures on a community or region.

These goals are often compatible; maximizing psychological experience creates happy clientele, which causes them to return, to spend money, and to make every one in the industry and the region satisfied. In certain situations, they can also be incompatible. A short-run profit-maximizing goal may cause the development of facilities beyond the capacity of the site, thus leading to overuse and a decline in psychological enjoyment. Extreme emphasis on tourism as an element in economic development might have the same result. There can also be clashes between the use of resources for tourism and for other kinds of development.

CONSTRAINTS

The second half of the optimizing situation is occupied by those factors that place obstacles in the way of goal attainment. We assume that it is desirable to have unlimited amounts of psychological enjoyment, profits, and local impacts. But that is not possible, because something always gets in the way. Tourism, being extremely broad and diverse, must deal with a large number of constraints. To make an analysis of relationships, it will be necessary to classify them.

DEMAND

Every firm providing goods and services to tourists is constrained by the demand functions of its customers. These relate quantity purchased to price, wealth, and income.

SUPPLY OF ATTRACTIVE RESOURCES

Possibly one of the most important constraints faced by the industry as a whole is the limited amount of resources available for tourist enjoyment. This is particularly true when geographic distribution of these sites is considered. Some areas are simply better attractions for tourists than others are.

TECHNICAL AND ENVIRONMENTAL CONSTRAINTS

Each particular site or situation has certain technical and environmental constraints. They involve such things as the relationship between sewage effluent disposal and the environment, numbers of fish and numbers of fishermen, number of people who can walk in a given area without causing unacceptable damage, number of elephants supportable on a wildlife range, impact on lions' behaviour of tourists observing them from a car, number of campsites possible in a given area without harming the environment, and so on.

TIME CONSTRAINTS

The amount of vacation time available limits what the vacationer can do. The length of the tourist season influences profitability of tourist-oriented businesses and the impact of tourist expenditures on the local economy.

INDIVISIBILITIES

Many times it is necessary to deal either with all of something or with nothing. It is not possible to fly half an airplane, even though the seats are only half filled. It may not be profitable to build a hotel under a given size. A road has to be built all the way from one point to another.

LEGAL CONSTRAINTS

Several types of legal constraints affect tourism. Activities of the government tourist bureau might be one. Laws concerning environmental problems could be another.

Zoning and building codes may influence the construction of facilities. Laws concerning contractual relations may limit activities.

SELF-IMPOSED CONSTRAINTS

Conflicting goals need to be reconciled, which leads to self-imposed constraints. The conflicts may arise within a firm or among firms, government agencies, and so on, that are seeking to develop a particular area or concept.

LACK OF KNOWLEDGE

Many activities are limited because little is known about particular situations. Business people are used to living with a certain amount of uncertainty, but there are inevitable limits to the amount they are willing to countenance. Ignorance influences governmental operations as well.

LIMITS ON SUPPORTIVE RESOURCES

There are always limits to the amount of money, managerial talent, workers, construction materials, social capital, and so on. And these, in turn, limit chances to provide psychological enjoyment, take advantage of profit-making opportunities, or develop local attractions. Many times these individual constraints interact, creating compound constraints on given activities.

OPTIMIZING THE EXPERIENCE

Maximization of the tourist experience is subject to a number of constraints and is manifested in the demand function. Demand for tourist experience is peculiar in the sense that the product being purchased is not easy to identify directly and is frequently purchased sight unseen. The tourist is particularly constrained by time and budget. To optimize the experience, it is necessary to determine the combination of destinations preferred and then the possibilities within the money and time constraints.

This explains some of the popularity of package tours, where both time and cost can be known in advance. There are some exceptions. Retired persons and young people often have time but limited resources. A few people have neither constraint.

OPTIMIZING RETURNS TO BUSINESSES

Because goods and services provided to tourists are really inputs to the process of producing the experience, demand for them is derived from demand for tourism as a whole. Some goods and services are complementary, and their demand is interrelated in a positive fashion. Others are substitutes and are characterized by limited area competition.

Packaged tours have the characteristic of putting all parts and services together, so they become complementary. Competition occurs among tours. Tour operators can maximize profits by selling tours of different value and costs, in order to cater to as many people as possible along the demand curve. The number of people to be accommodated can be determined from the marginal cost of the tour and the marginal revenue to be derived from a given price level. Goods and services sold to tourists are subject to severe peaking in demand. That is, the heaviest tourist season is usually limited. During that period, demand is intense and must be met with facilities that are excess in the off-season. This means that investment necessary to provide the excess capacity must be paid for from revenues received during the peak period. During off-peak periods, only variable cost is of interest, but because demand is low, some capacity will not be utilized.

As owners of the facilities, firms are concerned with providing adequate long-run capacity and with choosing those investments that will give optimum returns. In the tourist industry, a number of interrelationships must be considered. Sometimes, low benefit-cost investments are made so that higher-yielding investments can succeed. Consequently, it is not always true that investors choose the highest-yielding opportunities.

Generally, it is considered the long-run business of the firm to remove constraints on operations. But tourism has a number of constraints to expansion. These include demand for the tourist experience and environmental constraints.

OPTIMIZING FOR THE LOCAL ECONOMY

Tourism affects a region during periods of intense investment activity and afterward when the investments are producing. The effects depend on linkages among economic units. Money spent for investment will go to construction and a few other industrial sectors. These will have links to economic units varying from households to manufacturing plants. Money spent by tourists will also be introduced through a few sectors that will also be linked to the economy.

The multiplier effects in both cases are dependent upon the strength of the linkages. The multiplier reflects the amount of new economic activity generated as basic income circulates through the economy. Some sectors have strong links to other sectors in an economy and a large multiplier effect. Others have weak links and small multipliers. It is possible to have a thriving tourist industry and abject poverty in the local populace if there are no links. For example, linkages will be strong and the income multiplier high if the year-round resorts in a particular destination area hire all local labour; buy their flowers, fruit, vegetables, and poultry products from local farmers; hire local entertainers; and buy furnishings for guest rooms from local manufacturers. Linkages would be weak if most of these goods and services were imported from another state or country.

TOURISM EXPORTS AND IMPORTS

The host region is defined loosely as a county, a state, or a nation, depending on the level at which the problem is being considered. For a county-level government, the income of the county is of primary interest. A state government would perceive the maximization of the combined income of the entire state to be its objective, and so on.

Regardless of which definition of host region is being considered, expenditures in this area by tourists coming from another region represent injections into the area's economy. Japanese tourists traveling to the United States presumably earned their income in Japan. When spending money in the United States as tourists, they are "injecting" money into our economy that wasn't here before. As such, expenditures by foreigners in this country represent tourism exports for the United States.

This may be somewhat confusing because we are accustomed to thinking of something leaving the country as an export. When we export computers or cars, for example, these commodities are sent out of the United States. In the example of the Japanese tourists, the tourists are coming into this country. So how is it an export?

There seems to be a contradiction in terminology. As the astute student would note, however, when tourists come into this country, they are purchasing travel experiences. When they leave, they take these experiences back with them. Thus, we have exported travel experiences, which are, after all, what tourism is all about. When U.S. tourists travel to Japan and spend money there, this becomes a tourism import to the U.S. economy. Japanese money spent in the United States is a tourism import for the Japanese economy. In tourism exports, the flows of tourists and payments are in the same direction, whereas in commodity exports, the two flows are in opposite directions. Therein lays the confusion. However, if one were to look at the *direction of payment flow* to determine what an export is, there is no contradiction between the two cases. When payment flows into the United States, something has been exported— travel experiences, for instance, or commodities. Both payment flows are in the same direction.

BALANCE-OF-PAYMENTS EFFECTS

Tourism is one of the world's largest international industries. As such, it has a noticeable impact on the balance of payments of many nations. We have heard much about the balance-of-payments problems of the United States, and, indeed, tourism imports do affect the balance of payments and economic conditions generally.

We define tourism imports as those expenditures made by American tourists in foreign countries. An easy way to remember this is to ask, "Who got the money?" If, for example, Great Britain received American funds, it makes no difference whether an American bought some English china or an American tourist visited England. Our balance-of-payments situation directly affects the gross national product of the United States.

By looking at the formula, we can see that if imports exceed exports, then the difference will be a negative number, and Y will thus be smaller. Thus, it is advantageous to us in our American economy to attract more visitor spending in the United States. These "tourism exports" are like credits and help our economy.

It is economically better to have foreign visitors come to the United States than it is to have U.S. citizen's travel abroad. However, this should be tempered with the realisation that the situation is not entirely positive or negative. Expenditures by U.S. tourists abroad make possible purchasing power in foreign countries for those countries to buy American-made products. For example, most airlines of the world use American-made equipment. Purchase of these aircraft, parts, supplies, repair services, and so forth makes an important contribution to the export trade of the United States; thus, we cannot charge the U.S. international traveller with a total negative balance of payments. The purpose of the foregoing discussion is simply to point out the relationships.

Tourism exports become very desirable as far as the gross national product and the prosperity of the country are concerned. Efforts on the part of national tourism offices to attract foreign visitors have a great impact on the balance-of-payments situation. Business firms that serve the foreign visitor, provide desired services, and stimulate sales materially help our national economy.

However, during periods when the U.S. dollar is high against foreign currencies, a dampening effect occurs on our tourism exports because this situation is seen as unfavourable by prospective foreign visitors. Conversely, if the dollar is low, more foreign tourists will visit the United States. This increases our tourism exports, improves our balance of payments, and raises the gross national product. These same relationships of comparable currency values exist between any country that exports tourism and the countries of its tourists' origin.

In 1998 the value of the Canadian dollar was low in comparison to the U.S. dollar and illustrated this principle. The number of Americans visiting Canada to take advantage of the exchange rate increased dramatically. This contributed positively to Canada's balance of payments.

INVESTMENT STIMULATION

The tourist industry has a unique structure. It is characterized by and, in fact, is an agglomeration of a large number of very small units, covering a variety of different service trades—the small restaurants, motels, guest houses, laundries, arts and crafts shops, and others. Thus, investment in infrastructure and sometimes expensive superstructure by the government stimulates investment in numerous smaller businesses. Because of the small size of these businesses, capital requirements are relatively low and investment generally proceeds at a rapid pace. In this respect, too, governments view tourism rather favourably.

The initial investment in tourism brings forth a large investment in supporting and tertiary industries. This also includes large investments in major hotels, restaurants, shopping Centres, marinas, airports, and so on.

TOURISM INCREASES TAX REVENUE

Tourists must pay taxes like most other people. Because they come from other regions or countries, their expenditures represent an increased tax base for the host government. In addition to the usual sales tax, tourists sometimes pay taxes in less direct ways.

Airport taxes, exit fees, customs duty, and charges assessed for granting visas are just a few examples of commonly used methods of taxing tourists. The wisdom of imposing such special taxes on tourists is questionable, because it merely serves to reduce demand. In some countries, for instance, the room rate at a hotel optimization can be different for tourists than for residents. This is a questionable practice, because it leaves the tourist with a feeling that he has been "taken." Apart from these special cases, the usual taxes collected from both tourists and residents increase because of tourism expenditures.

Is tourism, then, a panacea for all the economic woes of a region or country? It has been claimed that tourism increases incomes, employment, investment, tax revenues, and so forth, so it might indeed appear to be one. However, constraints limit the extent to which governments can maximize the benefit from these aspects of tourism.

These constraints are of two types: social and economic. The social constraints have already been discussed. The economic constraints are in the form of potential economic costs that the tourism industry may impose. These merit further scrutiny to gain a better understanding of the government's optimization problem.

INFLATIONARY PRESSURE

Tourists inject money into the destination economy. While this increases the income of the region, it also might cause inflationary pressures. Tourists typically have a higher expenditure capability than the residents do—either because tourists have higher incomes or because they have saved for the trip and are inclined to "splurge" while on vacation. Hence, they are able to somewhat bid up the prices of such commodities as food, transportation, and arts and crafts. This causes inflationary pressures, which can be detrimental to the economic welfare of residents of the host community. This is particularly true when inflation affects the prices of essentials such as food, clothing, transportation, and housing. Land prices have been known to escalate rapidly in tourist destination areas. The prices that foreigners are willing to pay for "vacation homes" in the area can decrease the demand for "first homes" by residents. Lundberg notes that as the tourist industry developed in an area, land prices rose sharply. In a particular underdeveloped area, the amount of investment in land constituted just 1 per cent of the total investment for a hotel project. By contrast, this ratio increased to 20 per cent in an area where tourism was already overdeveloped. With such increases in land prices, it can be expected that local residents are effectively "chased out" of the housing market in a tourism-developing section.

DIRECT EFFECT

In addition to the direct impact of tourism expenditures on an area, there are also indirect impacts. The indirect or multiplier impact comes into play as visitor spending circulates and recirculates. The direct effects are the easiest to understand because they result from the visitor spending money in tourist enterprises and providing a living for the owners and managers and creating jobs for employees.

INDIRECT EFFECT

This visitor expenditure gives rise to an income that, in turn, leads to a chain of expenditure- income-expenditure, and so on, until leakages bring the chain to a halt. Consequently, the impact of the initial income derived from the tourist's expenditure is usually greater than the initial income, because subsequent rounds of spending are related to it. For example, a skier purchases a lift ticket for $40. This money received by the ski area will be used to pay the wages of the lift operators.

The lift operator spends the money on groceries; the grocer uses the money to pay part of his rent to the local landlady; the landlady uses it to pay for her dry cleaning; the dry cleaner spends it in a restaurant for a dinner; the restaurant owner spends it for steaks shipped in from Kansas City; and the cycle stops as the money is lost to the local economy. This last transaction is known as *leakage* from the economy. The combination of the direct and indirect effects of an expenditure pattern determines the impact.

In a typical situation, not all of the income generated in each round of expenditure is respent. Some portion tends to be saved, and some portion tends to be spent outside the local economy. The greater the proportion of income spent locally, the greater will be the multiplier. The degree to which a local area is able to retain tourist income depends on how self-sufficient the local economy is. If the local economy is able to produce the goods and services tourists buy, the greater will be the multiplier effect. The more goods that have to be imported from outside the region, the smaller the multiplier will be. From the discussion, it is clear that when a tourist's spending injects funds into the economy of a host area, an economic effect occurs that is a specified number of times what was originally spent.

Initially, this effect is thought of as an *income multiplier,* as tourist expenditures become income directly and indirectly to local people. However, there are additional economic phenomena. Increased spending necessitates more jobs, which results in an *employment multiplier.* Because money changes hands a number of times during a year, there is a transactions multiplier. This is of particular interest to governmental tax officials where sales taxes are imposed. As business grows in a tourist destination area, more infrastructure and superstructure are constructed. This results in a *capital multiplier.* Examples are provided here of how an employment multiplier and an income multiplier were determined.

EMPLOYMENT MULTIPLIER

The employment multiplier varies from region to region depending on its economic base. In a study entitled *Recreation as an Industry,* by Robert R. Nathan Associates, county employment multipliers calculated for the Appalachian region provide a good illustration of what typical multipliers are and how they work.

The multipliers estimated in this study were based on county employment data. They represent the approximate measure of the direct and indirect employment associated with each addition of direct employment to the export sector of a county. Multipliers were estimated for 375 counties and three independent cities. The smallest multiplier was 1.13, and the highest was 2.63.

Thus, the county with the smallest multiplier value would provide other employment opportunities for approximately 0.13 person for each person directly employed in servicing export demand, and the county with the highest multiplier value would provide other employment opportunities for approximately 1.63 persons for each person directly employed in servicing export demand.

In general, county employment multipliers vary directly with the population or total employment size of the counties: As county population size grows, so does the multiplier value. This relationship is as might be expected, insofar as import leakages would tend to be less where diversity of occupations is greater, and diversity is positively associated with county population or total employment.

INCOME MULTIPLIER

Jobs mean income, which stimulates the economy of the area in which the development occurs. How much stimulation occurs depends on several factors. The management of a hotel, for example, takes two actions with the revenue earned: It spends parts of the money on goods and services, and it saves part of such funds. Economists refer to such actions as marginal propensity to consume and marginal propensity to save—removing funds from the local economy. Such removal of these marginal funds can be made in two ways: they can be saved and not loaned to another spender, or they can be used to purchase imports.

In either case, so doing removes the funds and thus does not stimulate the local economy. Economic research is needed in a tourist destination area to determine what these income relationships are. If the results of such economic research were made available, many beneficial results might be possible. For example, governmental bodies might be more inclined to appropriate additional funds for tourism promotion to their areas if they knew more about the income that was generated by tourist expenditures.

Also, improved and added developments of facilities to serve tourists might be more forthcoming if prospective investors could have more factual data upon which to base decisions. To understand the multiplier, we must first make some approximation as to what portion of the tourist dollars received in a community is spent and what portion is saved . To illustrate this, suppose that we had a total of $1,000 of tourist spending in a community and that there was an MPC of 1/2.

The expenditure pattern might go through seven transactions in a year. The other formula for the multiplier is 1/MPS. Leakage, as defined, is a combination of savings and imports. If we spend the money outside our country for imports, obviously it does not stimulate the economy locally. If it is put into some form of savings that are not loaned to another spender within a year, it has the same effect as imports—not stimulating the economy.

Thus, to get the maximum benefits economically from tourist expenditures, we should introduce as much of the tourist funds as possible into the local economy for goods and services rather than save the proceeds or buy a large amount of imports. Here, also, more economic research is needed. Some studies have indicated that the multiplier might be as high as 3 in some areas, but economic research in other localities indicates that it may be more typically lower than this.

ECONOMIC BENEFITS WIDELY DISTRIBUTED

Using a conceptual approach, you should realise that tourism is characterized by the existence of a large number of very small businesses that support and are ancillary to the industry.

The receipts from tourism quickly filter down to an extremely broad cross section of the population, so that the entire community shares the economic benefits.

STRUCTURAL CHANGES

In countries that primarily rely on a single industry, such as agriculture, the introduction of tourism has often led to a decrease in the agricultural base of the country. Agriculture is an extremely low productivity industry in the developing countries.

The promise of much higher wages in the tourism industry draws people away from farming. Agricultural output declines as a result, just when the demand for food increases because of the influx of tourists. The inflationary pressure on food prices is further aggravated and can lead to considerable social upheaval. In the mid-1970s, some Caribbean countries experienced a wave of protests and even direct attacks on tourists, as the resident population expressed its dissatisfaction over rising prices.

Another major implication of the structural change is that instead of diversifying its economic base, the country's tourism sector merely "cannibalizes" its other major economic sector. Diversity is the foundation of economic stability. When one sector experiences a slump, another sector booms, thus reducing the probability of a severe depression and, indeed, reducing its impact if a depression does occur. Thus, tourism, instead of diversifying an economy, sometimes replaces agriculture as a "subsistence" sector.

FORMS OF TOURISM

ADVENTURE TOURISM

Adventure tourism is a type of tourism involving exploration or travel to remote areas, where the traveller should expect the unexpected. Adventure tourism is rapidly growing in popularity as tourists seek unusual holidays, different from the typical beach vacation. Adventure tourism typically involves traveling into remote, inaccessible and possibly hostile areas. It may include the performance of acts that require significant effort and grit and may also involve some degree of risk. Adventure Tourism becoming more and more Famous specially among youth. India is not a country but a world in itself. Here one can find World's biggest river for rafting and endless mountains for trekking. It is a country who has something for every kind of Adventure lover. For Mountainerring and Trekking one can go to Sikkim, the home of mighty Kunchnjanga and situated within eastern himalayas. Jummu and Kashmir the heaven on earth.

The place for Ski lovers and wonderful for backpackers. Himachal one of the best sites for Pargaliding in World and famous for beautiful gentle hills and Where glaciers are not far from mainland. Uttranchal a place where every single person wants to go, famous for valley of flowers and for Shiva Dhams and Last but not least Leh and Ladakh the cold deasert of India a place where one cannot find Trees and find really cold and different culture much closer to Tibtian culture and a starting point for Extreme tourism lovers who want to travel beyond the main land towards zanskar and nubra valleys. For Rafting India is heaven the rivers like Ganga, Teesta, and Brahamaputra provide rafters a real thrill and challenge. Rafting is becoming very popular among the corporates combined with Stay in riverside resorts and team building exercises.

MOUNTAINEERING

Mountaineering is the sport, hobby or profession of walking, hiking and climbing up mountains. It is also sometimes known as alpinism, particularly in Europe. It may be said to consist of two main aspects, rock-craft and snow-craft, depending on whether the route chosen is over rock or over snow and ice. Both require great gymnastic and technical ability, but experience is also a very important part of the latter. Training in these areas for several months enhances a person's abilities and increases their chances for survival while climbing.

AGRITOURISM

Agritourism is a style of vacation in which hospitality is offered on farms. This may include the opportunity to assist with farming tasks during the visit. Agritourism is often practiced in wine growing regions, as in Italy, France and Spain. In America, Agritourism is wide-spread and includes any farm open to the public at least part of the year. Tourists can pick fruits and vegetables, ride horses, taste honey, learn about wine, shop in gift shops and farm stands for local and regional produce or hand-crafted gifts, and much more. Each farm generally offers a unique and memorable experience suitable for the entire family.

Agritourism is being developed as a valuable component of a business model to support many agricultural entities when the farm products they produce are no longer economically competitive otherwise. To help promote the single agritourism operations, farms get together and form festivals or tours, such as Agri-tours, a two-weekend festival in September celebrating the lower Ottawa Valley's unique farms. This festival includes over a dozen non-traditional farms that specialize in everything from deer and pheasant, to apples and wine. People are more interested in how their food is produced and want to meet the producers and talk with them about what goes into food production.

Children who visit the farms often have not seen a live duck, or goat, and have not picked an apple right off the tree. This form of expanded agri-tourism has given birth to what are often called "entertainment farms." These farms cater to the pick-your-own crowd, offering not only regular farm products, but also food, mazes, open-pen animals, train rides, picnic facilities and pick-your-own produce. Dude ranches offer tourists the chance to work on cattle ranches and sometimes include cattle drives.

CULTURAL TOURISM

Cultural tourism and ecotourism, the number of living cultural areas is continually droping off. For an indigenous culture that has stayed largely separated from the surrounding majority culture, tourism can present both advantages and problems on to it. On the positive side are the unique cultural practices and arts that attract the curiosity of tourists and provide opportunities for tourism and economic development. On the negative side is the issue of how to control tourism so that those same cultural amenities are not destroyed and the people do not feel violated.

DESTINATION PLANNING RESOURCES

It is important that the destination planner takes into account the diverse definition of culture as the term is subjective. Satisfying tourists' interests such as landscapes, seascapes, art, nature, traditions, ways of life and other products associated to them -which may be categorized cultural in the broadest sense of the word, is a prime consideration as it marks the initial phase of the development of a cultural destination.

The quality of service and destination, which doesn't solely depend on the cultural heritage but more importantly to the cultural environment, can further be developed by setting controls and policies which shall govern the community and its stakeholders. It is therefore safe to say that the planner should be on the ball with the varying meaning of culture itself as this fuels the formulation of development policies that shall entail efficient planning and monitored growth.

While satisfying tourists' interests and demands may be a top priority, it is also imperative to ruminate the subsystems of the destinatons. Development pressures should be anticipated and set to their minimum level so as to conserve the area's resources and prevent a saturation of the destination as to not abuse the product and the residents correspondingly. The plan should incorporate the locals to its gain by training and employing them and in the process encourage them to participate to the travel business. Keep in mind that the plan should make travellers not only aware about the destination but also concern on how to help it sustain its character while broadening their travelling experience.

HERITAGE TOURISM

Cultural heritage tourism is a branch of tourism oriented towards the cultural heritage. Culture has always been a major object of travel, as the development of the Grand Tour from the 16th century onwards attests. In the 20th century, some people have claimed, culture ceased to be the objective of tourism: tourism is now culture. Cultural attractions play an important role in tourism at all levels, from the global highlights of world culture to attractions that underpin local identities.

According to the Weiler and Hall, culture, heritage and the arts have long contributed to appeal of tourist destination. However, in recent years 'culture' has been rediscovered as an important marketing tool to attract those travellers with special interests in heritage and arts. According to the Hollinshead, cultural heritage tourism defines as cultural heritage tourism is the fastest growing segment of the tourism industry because there is a trend towards an increase specialization among tourist. This trend is evident in the rise in the volume of tourists who seek adventure, culture, history, archaeology and interaction with local people.

Cultural heritage tourism is important for various reasons; it has a positive economic and social impact, it establishes and reinforces identity, it helps preserve the cultural heritage, with culture as an instrument it facilitates harmony and understanding among people, it supports culture and helps renew tourism. Cultural heritage tourism has a number of objectives that must be met within the context of sustainable development such as; the conservation of cultural resources, accurate interpretation of resources, authentic visitors experience, and the stimulation of the earned revenues of cultural resources. We can see therefore, that cultural heritage tourism is not only concerned with identification, management and protection of the heritage values but it must also be involved in understanding the impact of tourism on communities and regions, achieving economic and social benefits, providing financial resources for protection, as well as marketing and promotion.

Heritage tourism involves visiting historical or industrial sites that may include old canals, railways, battlegrounds, etc. The overall purpose is to gain an appreciation of the past. It also refers to the marketing of a location to members of a diaspora who have distant family roots there. Heritage tourism is distinct from visiting a family member in a faraway place because the connection to the original homeland is removed; a recent Irish immigrant to the US, for example, may return home to see relatives but would probably not be considered a heritage tourist.

On the other hand, an Irish-American whose family emigrated in the 19th century, also going to Ireland but rather to see the country generally, would be partaking in heritage tourism. This is particularly relevant to European areas where large numbers of people emigrated to North America in the 19th century and early 20th century. People from Quebec have been moving back and forth to France for centuries in fairly significant numbers, as have their counterparts with ties to the British Isles and other countries for more recent immigrants. Other examples include Black/African Americans who visit Africa and Hispanics who visit Spain. The purpose can be education, fun, marriage, employment, etc.

Permanent emigration tied to heritage tourism is less common but increasing. Diagonalization and immigration form the major background of much contemporary heritage tourism. Falling travel costs have also made heritage tourism possible for more people. Another possible form involves religious travel or pilgrimages. Many Catholics from around the world come to the Vatican and other sites such as Lourdes or Fatima. Large numbers of Jews have both visited Israel and emigrated there. Many have also gone to Holocaust sites and memorials. Islam commands its followers to take the hajj to Mecca, thus differentiating it somewhat from tourism in the usual sense, though the trip can also be a culturally important event for the pilgrim. Heritage Tourism can also be attributed to historical events that have been dramatised to make them more entertaining. For example a historical tour of a town or city using a theme such as ghosts or vikings.

ECOTOURISM

Ecotourism means ecological tourism, where ecological has both environmental and social connotations. It is defined both as a concept-tourism movement and as a tourism section. Born in its current form in the late 1980's, Ecotourism came of age in 2002, when the United Nations celebrated the "International Year of Ecotourism". The meeting was a watershed event, but it was not created with those who had pioneered the niche. There are various definitions as this is a vibrant movement and ecotourism may be defined by its lack of definition.

Generally speaking, ecotourism focuses on local cultures, wilderness adventures, volunteering, personal growth and learning new ways to live on the planet. It is typically defined as travel to destinations where the flora, fauna, and cultural heritage are the primary attractions. Responsible ecotourism includes Programmes that minimize the adverse effects of traditional tourism on the natural environment, and enhance the cultural integrity of local people. Therefore, in addition to evaluating environmental and cultural factors, initiatives by hospitality providers to promote recycling, energy efficiency, water reuse, and the creation of economic opportunities for local communities are an integral part of ecotourism. Many global environmental organizations and aid agencies favour ecotourism as a vehicle to sustainable development.

Ideally, true ecotourism should satisfy several criteria, such as:

- Conservation of biological diversity and cultural diversity, through ecosystems protection
- Promotion of sustainable use of biodiversity, by providing jobs to local populations
- Sharing of socio-economic benefits with local communities and indigenous people by having their informed consent and participation in the management of ecotourism enterprises.
- Increase of environmental and cultural knowledge
- Minimisation of tourism's own environmental impact
- Affordability and lack of waste in the form of luxury
- Local culture, flora and fauna being the main attractions

For many countries, ecotourism is not so much seen as a marginal activity intended to finance protection of the environment than as a major sector of national economy and as a means of attracting tourists. For example, in countries such as Costa Rica, Ecuador, Nepal, Kenya, Madagascar and Antarctica, ecotourism represents a significant portion of the gross domestic product.

The concept of ecotourism is widely misunderstood and, in practice, is often simply used as a marketing tool to promote tourism that is related to nature. Critics claim that ecotourism as practiced and abused often consists of placing a hotel in a splendid landscape, to the detriment of the ecosystem. According to them, ecotourism must above all sensitize people with the beauty and the fragility of nature.

They condemn some operators as "green-washing" their operations — that is, using the label of "ecotourism" and "green-friendly", while behaving in environmentally irresponsible ways. Although academics argue about who can be classified as an ecotourist, and there is precious little statistical data, some estimate that more than five million ecotourists — the majority of the worldwide population — come from the United States, with other ecotourists coming from Europe, Canada and Australia. Currently there are various moves to create national and international ecotourism certification Programmes, although the process is causing controversy. One example of ecoturism certificates has been put into place at Costa Rica, though the Programmes has been dismissed as green-washing by others. One criticism against ecotourism is that the air travel to often remote places is not included in the "environmental impact calculation". A journey to a place 10,000 kilometers away and home consumes about 700 litres of fuel per person. Another problem is that some of the destinations visited by ecotourists are extremely sensitive to environmental impact from human use and can be damaged even by careful travellers. A new form of tourism is called Clean Tourism.

ECOLOGICAL MASS TOURISM

When people think about the word 'Ecological Mass Tourism' they normally link it with negative thoughts of mass tourism that is associated with environmental degradation. The truth is we believe that Ecological Mass Tourism is beneficial for everyone, but in essence we must first understand what Ecological Mass Tourism actually encompasses: Mass Tourism: "refers to the steady stream of large numbers of tourists to holiday destinations."

Ecotourism "nature based tourism involving the education and interpretation of the natural environment and is managed to be ecologically sustainable. This definition also recognises that 'natural environment' includes cultural components and that 'ecologically sustainable' involves an appropriate return to the local community and long term conservation of the resource" Ecotourists: are tourists who participate in different sorts of nature based tourism.

Furthermore "most ecotourists are often found to be residents of the developed world with above average incomes and educations." By integrating all 3 words into 1 we have constructed our definition of Ecological Mass Tourism or for short. Ecological Mass Tourism or : are large numbers of educated tourists and ecotourists participating within the realms of diversified forms of managed ecotourism. EMT also attracts tourists who not only participate in ecotourism, but also recognise its cultural components and its involvement with giving a fitting return to the local community and long term conservation of the resource. In properly defining EMT we believe that it is beneficial to all parties involved, and more importantly it can also be perceived to be sustainable. In addition to this EMT also has the ability to be managed properly and has definite infrastructure, cultural and social benefits linked Ecological Mass Tourism does not go against the principle of mass tourism on the basis that it contains financial, cultural and social benefits associated with its concept.

HERITAGE TOURISM

Cultural heritage tourism is a branch of tourism oriented towards the cultural heritage. Culture has always been a major object of travel, as the development of the Grand Tour from the 16th century onwards attests. In the 20th century, some people have claimed, culture ceased to be the objective of tourism: tourism is now culture. Cultural attractions play an important role in tourism at all levels, from the global highlights of world culture to attractions that underpin local identities.

According to the Weiler and Hall, culture, heritage and the arts have long contributed to appeal of tourist destination. However, in recent years 'culture' has been rediscovered as an important marketing tool to attract those travellers with special interests in heritage and arts. According to the Hollinshead, cultural heritage tourism defines as cultural heritage tourism is the fastest growing segment of the tourism industry because there is a trend towards an increase specialization among tourist.

This trend is evident in the rise in the volume of tourists who seek adventure, culture, history, archaeology and interaction with local people. Cultural heritage tourism is important for various reasons; it has a positive economic and social impact, it establishes and reinforces identity, it helps preserve the cultural heritage, with culture as an instrument it facilitates harmony and understanding among people, it supports culture and helps renew tourism. Cultural heritage tourism has a number of objectives that must be met within the context of sustainable development such as; the conservation of cultural resources, accurate interpretation of resources, authentic visitors experience, and the stimulation of the earned revenues of cultural resources. We can see therefore, that cultural heritage tourism is not only concerned with identification, management and protection of the heritage values but it must also be involved in understanding the impact of tourism on communities and regions, achieving economic and social benefits, providing financial resources for protection, as well as marketing and promotion.

Heritage tourism involves visiting historical or industrial sites that may include old canals, railways, battlegrounds, etc. The overall purpose is to gain an appreciation of the past. It also refers to the marketing of a location to members of a diaspora who have distant family roots there. Heritage tourism is distinct from visiting a family member in a faraway place because the connection to the original homeland is removed; a recent Irish immigrant to the US, for example, may return home to see relatives but would probably not be considered a heritage tourist.

On the other hand, an Irish-American whose family emigrated in the 19th century, also going to Ireland but rather to see the country generally, would be partaking in heritage tourism. This is particularly relevant to European areas where large numbers of people emigrated to North America in the 19th century and early 20th century. People from Quebec have been moving back and forth to France for centuries in fairly significant numbers, as have their counterparts with ties to the British Isles and other countries for more recent immigrants. Other examples include Black/African Americans who visit Africa and Hispanics who visit Spain.

The purpose can be education, fun, marriage, employment, etc. Permanent emigration tied to heritage tourism is less common but increasing. Diagonalization and immigration form the major background of much contemporary heritage tourism. Falling travel costs have also made heritage tourism possible for more people. Another possible form involves religious travel or pilgrimages. Many Catholics from around the world come to the Vatican and other sites such as Lourdes or Fatima. Large numbers of Jews have both visited Israel and emigrated there. Many have also gone to Holocaust sites and memorials. Islam commands its followers to take the hajj to Mecca, thus differentiating it somewhat from tourism in the usual sense, though the trip can also be a culturally important event for the pilgrim. Heritage Tourism can also be attributed to historical events that have been dramatised to make them more entertaining. For example a historical tour of a town or city using a theme such as ghosts or vikings.

MEDICAL TOURISM

Medical tourism is the act of traveling to other countries to obtain medical, dental, and surgical care. The term was initially coined by travel agencies and the media as a catchall phrase to describe a rapidly growing industry where people travel to other countries to obtain medical care while at the same time touring, vacationing and enjoying the attractions of the countries which they are visiting.

A combination of many factors has led to the recent increase in popularity of medical tourism: the high cost of healthcare in industrialized nations, the ease and affordability of international travel, and the improvement of technology and standards of care in many countries of the world. A large draw to medical tourism is the convenience in comparison to that of other countries. Some countries that operate from a public health-care system are so taxed that it can take a considerable amount of time, sometimes even years, to get needed medical care. The time spent waiting for a procedure, such as a hip replacement, can be a year or more in Britain and Canada; however, in Bangkok or Bangalore, a patient could feasibly have an operation the day after their arrival.

The real lure to medical tourism is saving money on costly procedures. According to research found in an article by UDaily: the cost of surgery in India, Thailand or South Africa can be one-tenth of what it is in the United States or Western Europe, and sometimes even less. A heart-valve replacement that would cost US$200,000 or more in the U.S., for example, goes for $10,000 in India—and that includes round-trip airfare and a brief vacation package. Similarly, a metal-free dental bridge worth $5,500 in the U.S. costs $500 in India, a knee replacement in Thailand with six days of physical therapy costs about one-fifth of what it would in the States, and Lasik eye surgery worth $3,700 in the U.S. is available in many other countries for only $730. Cosmetic surgery savings are even greater: A full facelift that would cost $20,000 in the U.S. runs about $1,250 in South Africa."

Medical tourists are generally residents of the industrialized nations of the world. The countries to which they travel are typically less developed and have a lower cost of medical care. This is, in some cases, due to Favourable currency exchange ratios. Currently, many of the procedures accessed are considered "elective procedures," such as cosmetic surgery. Because elective procedures are rarely covered through health insurance plans, there may be greater incentive to find such care at lower costs.

The list of countries currently promoting medical tourism include: Bolivia, Brazil, Cuba, Costa Rica, Hungary, India, Israel, Jordan, Lithuania, Malaysia, The Philippines, and Thailand with the Joint Commission International accredited Bumrungrad Hospital. Belgium, Poland and Singapore are also breaking into the business. South Africa is taking the term "medical tourism" very literally by promoting their "medical safaris": Come to see African wildlife and get a facelift in the same trip. However, feelings towards medical tourism are not always positive. In places like the US, where most have insurance and access to quality health care, medical tourism is viewed as risky.

While the tourism component might be a big draw for Southeast Asia countries that focus on simple procedures, India is positioning itself the primary medical destination for the most complex medical procedures in the world. India's commitment to this is demonstrated with an ever growing number of hospitals that are attaining the US Joint Commission International accreditation. Singapore has made international news for providing complex neurosurgical procedures. Currently Singapore boasts the largest number of US Joint Commission accredited hospitals in the region. There are companies emerging to offer global healthcare options that will allow North American patients to take full advantage of dramatic reductions in air travel and access world class healthcare at a fraction of the cost. Companies that focus on 'Medical Value Travel' typically will have experienced nurse case managers to assist patients with pre- and post-travel medical issues. They will also help provide resources for follow-up care upon the patient's return. While these services will initially be of interest to the self-insured patient, several studies indicate that the rapid growth of Health Savings Accounts will also drive interest to healthcare in other countries.

POP-CULTURE TOURISM

Pop-culture tourism is the act of traveling to locations featured in literature, film, music, or any other form of popular entertainment. Popular destinations have included the Iowa cornfields featured in Field of Dreams, New Zealand after The Lord of the Rings was filmed there, and The Louvre in which the book and movie The Da Vinci Code takes place.

Prince Edward Island, in which the Canadian novel Anne of Green

Gables takes place, is a popular attraction for tourists, notably from Japan. Pop-culture tourism is in some respects akin to pilgrimage, with its modern equivalents of places of pilgrimage, such as Elvis Presley's Graceland and the grave of Jim Morrison in Père Lachaise Cemetery.

PILGRIMAGE TOURISM

A pilgrimage is a term primarily used in religion and spirituality of a long journey or search of great moral significance. Sometimes, it is a journey to a sacred place or shrine of importance to a person's beliefs and faith. Members of every religion participate in pilgrimages. A person who makes such a journey is called a pilgrim. Secular and civic pilgrimages are also practiced, without regard for religion but rather of importance to a particular society. For example, many people throughout the world travel to the City of Washington in the United States for a pilgrimage to see the Declaration of Independence and the Constitution of the United States. British people often make pilgrimages to London for public appearances of the monarch of the United Kingdom. Pop culture has also sought to redefine pilgrimages, defining a demoscene party as a pilgrimage.

DEPENDENCE ON TOURISM

Permitting tourism to become the subsistence industry is not desirable for a number of reasons. First, tourism is by its very nature subject to considerable seasonality. While seasonal fluctuations in demand can sometimes be reduced, they cannot be eliminated. Thus, when tourism is the primary industry in an area, the off-season periods inevitably result in serious unemployment problems. Such areas find that the seasonal character of tourism leaves severe economic and social effects on the host region.

Another very important reason relates to the source of demand for tourism. The demand for tourism depends largely on the income and the tastes of tourists, both of which are beyond the control of the host region. When the American economy goes through a slump, demand for travel to a foreign destination by Americans will fall off. A destination area can do precious little, in this case, to increase the level of demand. If the tastes of the people in the tourist-generating area change—that is, they decide to travel to a new destination—tourism in the old area will decline, causing economic and social problems.

Again, the destination can do little or nothing to avoid this. In fact, as Plog points out, there is reason to believe that such a decline in an area's popularity may be largely inevitable. Quite clearly, then, tourism should not be allowed to grow to an extent that the destination area becomes totally dependent on it. In other words, total dependence on a single industrial sector is undesirable. If it cannot be avoided, then dependence on domestic agriculture is in many ways preferable to dependence on tourism. The country has presumably adapted itself economically and socially to dependence on agriculture over several centuries. The demand for agricultural output is also unlikely to suffer from a secular decline, because people must eat. Also, it is the residents, not foreigners as in tourism, who directly benefit from agricultural production.

INVESTMENT PRIORITIES

Sometimes, governments of developing countries take an overly optimistic view of tourism. They undertake aggressive investment Programmes to develop tourism, assigning it top priority in their development plans. In extreme cases, such an approach can lead to the neglect of more fundamental investment needs of the country. For example, funds can be channeled into tourism development at the cost of education, health, and other social services—aspects of the social well-being of the population that should be of primary concern for a developing country.

Not only is undue glamorization of tourism unwise because it usurps this position, but such a strategy only speeds up the process of dependence on tourism, which, as discussed earlier, is itself undesirable. Moreover, investment in tourism at the cost of health and education Programmes also slows down the rate at which the local population is assimilated into the modern market economy of the country. Under certain circumstances, it may actually retard development rather than enhance it.

The conclusion is that although tourism has tremendous potential as a tool in economic development, it is no panacea. Governments should attempt to optimize the benefits that tourism provides, being ever mindful of the costs that it can impose. It should be noted also that the probability and the intensity of the economic costs of tourism are greater for developing nations than for wealthy ones. Wealthy nations, by definition, possess robust economies that can more easily absorb the cost of tourism. Typically, such economies are well diversified, and government investment Programme are not so central to development efforts. The social benefits and costs of tourism should be viewed similarly. While the host community seeks to maximize the benefits, it must weigh these against the social costs. The social costs are likewise higher in both probability and magnitude when tourism is being considered for development in an area that still possesses a traditional social structure.

QUANTITY DEMANDED AND PRICE ELASTICITY

For some products, even a large change in price over a certain range of the demand curve results in only a small change in quantity demanded. In this case, demand is not very responsive to price.

For other products, or for the same product over a different range of prices, a relatively small change in price elicits a much larger relative change in quantity demanded. Demand can be classified as inelastic or elastic on the basis of the relative responsiveness of quantity demanded to changes in price.

Specifically, price elasticity of demand may be defined as the percentage change in demand resulting from a given percentage change in price. Most tourism products are price elastic. During 1992, when U.S. airlines began offering half fares, the number of air travellers increased to record-high levels.

INCOME ELASTICITY OF DEMAND

As income rises, more travel is demanded at any given price. Thus, the relationship between income and demand is positive. The responsiveness of demand to changes in income is called income elasticity of demand. It is defined as the percentage. Tourism makes a major economic contribution to the world economy.

Despite this economic significance, tourism managers have for some time been met with complaints such as "All the type about tourism's contribution to economic growth and job creation is a gross exaggeration." As well, members of the industry itself want to be sure that the economic impact figures are indeed accurate so that they can better plan their investments and improve their productivity and performance. In an attempt to ensure the accuracy and reliability of the measures of tourism's economic impact, the World Tourism Organization in collaboration with the World Travel and Tourism Council and with the support of the Canadian Tourism Commission have undertaken to develop a tourism accounting system that is not only rigorous, but consistent with the national accounts of every country. This system has been named Tourism Satellite Account.

TOURISM SATELLITE ACCOUNT

A Tourism Satellite Account is a system developed by the United Nations to measure the size of economic sectors that are not defined as industries in national accounts. Tourism, for example, is an amalgam of industries such as transportation, accommodation, food and beverage services, recreation, and entertainment and travel agencies.

Tourism is a unique phenomenon as it is defined by the consumption of the visitor. Visitors buy goods and services associated with both tourism and nontourism alike. The key from a measurement standpoint is to associate their purchases to the total supply of these goods and services within a country. The TSA is a new statistical instrument designed to measure these goods and services according to international standards of concepts, classifications, and definitions that will allow for valid comparisons with other industries and eventually from country to country and between groups of countries. Such measures will also be comparable with other internationally recognized economic statistics.

In addition, a TSA possesses the following characteristics:

- Provides credible data on the impact of tourism and the associated employment
- Is a standard framework for organizing statistical data on tourism
- Is a new international standard endorsed by the U.N. Statistical Commission
- Is a powerful instrument for designing economic policies related to tourism development
- Provides data on tourism's impact on a nation's balance of payments
- Provides information on tourism human resource characteristics

While it may be obvious, it is useful to stress why a TSA is needed. In brief, there is an acute shortage of information on the increasing role of tourism in national economies worldwide, hence the need for reliable data relative to the importance and magnitude of tourism, using the same concepts, definitions, and measurement approaches as other industries. With the TSA, governments, entrepreneurs, and citizens will be better equipped for designing public policies and business strategies for tourism and for evaluating their effectiveness and efficiency.

Development of a TSA framework has been fueled by the recognition that its implementation will serve to increase and improve knowledge of tourism's importance relative to overall economic activity in a given country. It will also provide an instrument for designing more efficient policies relating to tourism and its employment aspects; and it will create awareness among the various players directly and indirectly involved with tourism of the economic importance of this activity, and by extension its role in all the industries involved in the production of goods and services demanded by visitors.

THE NATURE OF A TSA

A TSA is characterized by the manner in which it seeks to balance measures of tourism demand versus supply. Tourism measurements, in order to be credible and comparable with other industries in a country's economy, must follow concepts and definitions consistent with internationally accepted macroeconomic guidelines, such as the System of National Accounts.

The fundamental structure of the TSA therefore relies on the balance existing within an economy between, on one hand, the demand for goods and services generated by visitors and by other consumers and, on the other hand, the overall supply of these goods and services. The idea is to analyse in detail all aspects of demand for goods and services that are associated with tourism within the economy, and to measure the relationship with the supply of such goods and services within the same economy.

More specifically, a TSA measures:

- Tourism's contribution to gross domestic product
- Tourism's ranking compared to other economic sectors
- The number of jobs created by tourism in an economy
- The amount of tourism investment
- Tax revenues generated by tourism industries
- Tourism consumption
- Tourism's impact on a nation's balance of payments
- Characteristics of tourism human resources

Because of its comprehensive nature, a TSA provides decision makers with a valuable tool for planning and policy making. In particular, it provides them with reliable data of tourism's impact on the economy and employment. As well, it permits the measurement of both domestic and nonresident tourism—and the employment associated with each. A TSA, however, can do much more. Following are some examples. A TSA can provide information on how much tourism is worth to the national economy, and how it compares to other industries and other countries. By demonstrating and using the size of tourism, tourism officials and private-sector businesses will have more influence on policy makers at all levels of government. As well, it can make clear which industries benefit from tourism and by how much— in particular, industries not traditionally associated with tourism.

For instance, business enterprises can identify the role tourism plays in their success and develop business strategies accordingly. A TSA is able to provide information regarding how much tax revenue is generated by tourism. This information is useful in convincing municipal, provincial, or federal levels of government to invest further in tourism. In addition, it provides data on visitor demand and how this demand is met by domestic supply. A TSA enables the establishment of a tourism economic impact model, which can be used to estimate the effect on the economy and on employment of various tourism expenditure shocks. Such an impact model provides a better understanding of tourism employment and where each industry ranks compared to other tourism industries. It should be emphasized that the ongoing development of TSAs as national promotion tools has been a process dating back to at least 1993. The most recent focus of this development was a major international TSA conference held in Vancouver, Canada, in 2001. This and other conferences have brought together the following organizations: World Tourism Organization, World Travel and Tourism Council, Organization for Economic Cooperation and Development, United Nations, Eurostat, and a number of government statistical agencies, national tourism administrators, and central banks. The collaboration demonstrates the general principle that in order to develop a national TSA, it is essential to involve a number of key actors within a country.

The most significant of these are:

- National statistical offices, national tourism administrations, central banks, and associations of national tourism enterprises.
- Information-producing units such as tourism enterprises and establishments, and other public departments.
- Users of the tourism information that is generated, the NTAs themselves, the units responsible for preparing the national accounts and the balance of payments, and others.
- The participation and collaboration of tourism enterprises and, more specifically, their corresponding national associations.

SOURCES OF DATA USED IN A TSA

Canada, as an Example

The data used in the calculation of a TSA in Canada come from a diverse number of surveys produced by Statistics Canada. The preparation of tourism demand estimates involve several surveys that record information on tourism consumption of Canadians traveling in and outside Canada and nonresidents traveling to Canada.

These include:

- Canadian Travel Survey
- International Travel Survey of Canadian Residents
- Canadian Resident Questionnaire for same-day automobile travel between the

  United States and Canada:
- United States Resident Questionnaire for same-day automobile travel between the United States and Canada
- Government Travel Survey of U.S. visitors to Canada
- Government Travel Survey of visitors to Canada

Much of the information for the supply-side estimates are drawn from the worksheets used in the making of the input-output tables by industry, commodity, and employment of the System of National Accounts. Data from reference publications, and relevant business surveys and administrative data, are used to obtain as much detail as possible on revenues generated from the sale of tourism commodities.

In conclusion, a TSA recognizes that tourism is not an industry in the traditional sense—that is, identified in the System of National Accounts—because industries are classified according to the goods and services they produce, while tourism is a consumption-based concept that depends on the status of the customer. Furthermore, tourists buy many of the same products as other consumers, including items not normally associated with tourism—clothes, groceries— while Canadians at home buy tourism goods and services for nontourism reasons—restaurant meals, postcards, recreational services.

The TSA brings together these diverse aspects of tourism by providing a tourism dimension to the framework of the System of National Accounts. It makes it possible to separate and examine the demand and supply sides of tourism within an integrated system that describes the production and demand aspects of the whole economy. The recognition of these factors has led to the situation where more than ten countries have a TSA and more than thirty are in the process of developing a TSA. These include Austria, Canada, Chile, the Dominican Republic, France, Mexico, New Zealand, Norway, Singapore, Sweden, the United States, Spain, and Italy. Domestic and international tourism are major economic strengths to many of the world's countries, states, cities, and rural areas. Thus, those who live there are affected by the economic results of tourist spending. This stage explained why these resulting effects vary greatly and what brings about a large measure of benefits or possible detriments to a community.

The main economic phenomena described are various multipliers, balance of payments, investments, tax consideration, employment, economic impact generators, travel expenditures, dependence on tourism, price and income elasticity as related to buying travel experiences, and optimization. The stage also discussed a new method of measuring tourism economic impact, satellite accounting. Many people do not understand or appreciate the economics of tourism.

The following list summarizes the principal economic effects:

1. Expenditures by foreign visitors in one's country become exports. The economic effects are the same as those derived from exporting tangible goods. If there is a Favourable exchange rate, the country that has the devalued currency will experience a higher demand for visitor services than before devaluation.
2. If citizens of one country spend money in foreign countries, these expenditures become imports for the tourists' originating country.
3. Sums of the values of national exports and imports are used when calculating a nation's balance of payments. A positive balance results when exports exceed imports, thus increasing a nation's gross national product.
4. Tourism developments typically require large investments of capital. Thus, local economies where the developments take place are stimulated by such investments.
5. Tourists pay various kinds of taxes directly and indirectly while visiting an area. Thus, tax revenues are increased for all levels of government.
6. Because tourists usually spend more per day at a destination than they do while at home, these extra expenditures may cause inflationary pressures and rising prices for consumer goods in the destination area.
7. Tourism expenditures injected into the economy produce an income multiplier for local people. This is because of the diversity of expenditures made by those receiving tourist payments. Tourist receipts are used to buy a wide variety of

goods and services over a year's time. The money turnover creates additional local income.

8. The amount of income multiplication, however, will depend on how much leakage takes place. Leakages are a combination of imported goods and services purchased by tourism suppliers, and savings made of tourist receipts not loaned to another spender within one year of receipt. Thus, the more tourist goods that are supplied locally, the higher will be the multiplier.
9. Income multiplication caused by tourist expenditures necessitates hiring more people. Thus, they also affect an employment multiplier.
10. As increased spending produces more financial transactions, they create a transactions multiplier. These are of particular interest to governments that have a sales or value-added tax on such transactions.
11. As a tourist area grows, more capital is invested in new facilities. This results in a capital multiplier.
12. It is an unwise policy for a society to place too much dependency on tourism as a subsistence industry.
13. Although tourism often has an excellent potential in economic development, it is not a panacea for economic ills. Its economic benefits should be optimized rather than maximized.
14. We believe that tourism products are mainly price elastic, meaning that as prices rise, the quantity demanded tends to drop.
15. In general, we believe that tourism is income elastic. This means that as family income rises, or a particular market's income rises, and tourism prices do not rise proportionally, the demand for travel to that particular area will increase.

HOSPITALITY

Hospitality is the act or practice of being hospitable, that is, the reception and entertainment of guests, visitors, or strangers, with liberality and goodwill. Hospitality frequently refers to the hospitality industry jobs for hotels, restaurants, casinos, catering, resorts, clubs and any other service position that deals with tourists. It's important for people to know what you stand for. It's equally important that they know what you won't stand for. The twenty-first century began with a flurry of high-profile scandals involving managers in a wide variety of industries, ranging from high-tech firms to pharmaceutical manufacturers.

Many very successful business-people found themselves behind bars for their ethical transgressions. The topic of business ethics is receiving increasing coverage in all media, including newspapers, business periodicals, television, radio, and even the Internet, while the pressures on businesses to perform continue to increase. With continued technological advancement, political upheaval, increased global competition, changing demographics, and pressure from stockholders, maintaining one's ethical integrity will become both more difficult and more important.

In 1993 a large group of hospitality industry executives were asked, "What skills and abilities do students need to obtain to be successful in the hospitality industry?" The number one answer was "business ethics." There is little evidence to suggest the answer would be any different today. One thing is clear: Ethical behaviour is important, and all of you will be facing situations in which you will need to make difficult decisions that you will base on your ethical beliefs and value systems.

ENVIRONMENTALLY RESPONSIBLE HOTELS

One component of ecotourism travelers can consider is environmentally responsible hotels. The concept of "green hotels"—hotels, motels, bed and breakfasts, lodges, and inns that use energy and other natural resources in environmentally responsible ways—is one that can be adopted not only by ecotourists but by anyone who travels, whether for business or pleasure. Hotels that adopt green practices help reduce the negative impact that hotel use has on the environment when they utilize renewable resources whenever possible, make efficient use of nonrenewable resources, and ensure that any by-products that result from their operations are reused or recycled.

Examples of green practices some hotels have adopted include rerouting waste water to irrigate their golf courses and salvaging the sludge to use as fertilizer; reducing laundry water temperatures from 90 °C to 60 °C, replacing incandescent lights with compact fluorescent lamps, installing low-flow shower head and low-flow toilets, offering a sheet and towel reuse Programmes whereby guests have their linens exchanged every two to three days instead of daily, installing solar panels to heat water, implementing a hotel-wide recycling Programmes, and replacing individual soaps and lotions with wall dispensers. Adoption of green practices typically helps hotels realise considerable savings that can range from several thousand to hundreds of thousands of dollars per year.

Although the number of hotels adopting green practices is growing, many have not yet embraced the concept. All travelers can support green hotels, encourage nongreen hotels to adopt environmentally responsible practices, or engage in such practices themselves whenever they are hotel guests. Tourism event organizers can also distinguish themselves by explaining the criteria of where they stage events. Sadly, most ecotourism events have been held at hotels which have not distinguished themselves with green building, eco-efficient technology or community-friendly relations.

HOSPITALITY AS A SOCIOLOGICAL PHENOMENON

As hospitality is a sociological phenomenon, and because its norms differ in each society, there might be:

- Christian view of hospitality,

Paul of Taurus urged hospitality on Christians, telling them that some people have thus entertained angels. Offering hospitality to pilgrims was a major duty of a monastery.

- Middle Eastern rules of hospitality,
- Greek hospitality.

A famous Greek legend Baucis and Philemon, recounts how they, though poor, were the only people of their town to offer hospitality to Zeus and Hermes, and so were blessed while the rest were transformed into fishes. Smoke weed everyday. Further, Zeus was the patron of hospitality and guests, ready to avenge any wrong done to a stranger

- And any other hospitality norms that differ in various world cultures,
- And very contemporary, in virtual communities.

CONTEMPORARY USAGE

Contemporary usage seems rather different from historical uses that lend it personal connotations. Today's hospitality conjures images of throwing good parties, gracious hosts entertaining, etiquette, Martha Stewart or even talk shows, or, the hospitality services industry as it relates to the entertainment and tourism business. On the other hand, hospitality used to be, and may still be, a serious personal duty or responsibility. Hospitality is a prosaic word, even trivial, that everyone can relate to, perhaps even more concretely so outside of North American culture. It seems perhaps even a candidate for having something like a universal meaning or agreement, if not positive value. In the western context, with its dynamic tension between Athens and Jerusalem, two phases can be distinguished with a very progressive transition: a hospitality based on an individually felt sense of duty, and one based on "official" institutions for organized but anonymous social services: special places for particular types of "strangers" such as the poor, orphan, ill, alien, criminal, etc. Perhaps this progressive institutionalization can be aligned to the transition between Middle Ages and Renaissance.

OTHER CONCEPTIONS OF HOSPITALITY

In Middle Eastern Culture, it was considered a cultural norm to take care of the strangers and aliens living among you. These norms are reflected in many Biblical commands and examples, for instance: Perhaps the most extreme example is provided in Genesis. Lot provides hospitality to a group of angels; when a mob tries to rape them, Lot goes so far as to offer his own daughters as a substitute, saying "Don't do anything to these men, for they have come under the protection of my roof.". The obligations of both guests and hosts are stern. The bond is formed by eating salt under the roof, and is so strict that an Arab story tells of a thief who tasted something to see if it was sugar, and on realising it was salt, put back all that he had taken and left.

Cultural Value or Norm

Hospitality as a cultural norm or value is established sociological phenomenon that people study and write papers about.

STAR

Stars are often used as symbols for classification purposes. In particular, a set of one to five stars is employed to categorize hotels. In some countries, there is an official body with standard criteria for classifying hotels, but in many others there is none. There have been attempts at unifying the classification system so that it becomes an internationally recognized and reliable standard but large differences exist in the quality of the accommodation and the food within one category of hotel, sometimes even in the same country.

A "Five Star Hotel"

However, regardless of what public or private agency performs the classification, the term five star hotel is always associated with the ultimate luxury . The lack of standardisation has allowed marketing-driven inflation, with some hotels claiming six stars; at one point the Burj al-Arab marketed itself as "the world's first seven-star hotel". Well-established prestige hotels are usually content to claim the traditional five.

Rating by Stars

The five categories can be described as follows:

- *(one star)—Low budget hotel; inexpensive; may not have maid service or room service.
- **(two stars)—Budget hotel; slightly more expensive; usually has maid service daily.
- ***(three stars)—Middle class hotel; moderately priced; has daily maid service, room service, and may have dry-cleaning, Internet access, and a swimming pool.
- ****(four stars)—First class hotel; expensive has all of the previously mentioned services; has many "luxury" services .
- *****(five stars)—Luxury hotel; most expensive hotels/resorts in the world; numerous extras to enhance the quality of the client's stay.

The AAA and their affiliated bodies use diamonds instead of stars to express hotel and restaurant ratings levels. Traditional systems rest heavily on the facilities provided, which is often disadvantageous to smaller hotels whose quality of accommodation could fall into one class but the lack of an item such as an elevator would prevent it from reaching a higher categorization.

PRESENT TRENDS

Hotel rooms that can access everything from your favourite food to your musical preferences— while running on technology that's clever enough to repair itself—might sound like a page torn right out of a pulp sci-fi novel. Hotels are doing it today, and many more are on the verge of implementing these innovative technologies. If you're a guest at one of these forward-looking properties, get ready for a completely different kind of experience—one in which technology anticipates your every need and gives it to you without you ever having to ask.

And it isn't just hotels that are leveraging these new tools to their advantage; so are theme parks, restaurants, and casinos. The overall effects of these new tools on the hospitality business promises to be far-reaching. From the perspective of a hotel, casino, or restaurant, these important advances have the potential to create more efficient and profitable businesses, and make your business more appealing to guests.

NO MORE QUESTIONS AT CHECK-IN

Remember all those queries when you pick up your room key, such as, What kind of newspaper do you prefer? Would you like a poolside or oceanside room? Asking such questions eats up hotel employees' valuable time and, after a while, guests get tired of answering them. New customer relationship management tools allow a hotel to gather guest preference information from various systems at property level and distribute them throughout the company. So your hotel knows what you like, right away.

For example, one hotel chain asks guests signing up for its loyalty Programmes to fill out a preferences questionnaire that is entered into its CRM system at the property level. The information can be made available for any hotel in the chain that the guest checks in to, while the CRM system itself is still maintained locally, at the property level.

When the day of arrival comes, the preference data is pushed to the property and generates an activity list to prepare the guest's room. At the same time, historical transaction data about the guest is made available, which can help predict the behaviours and likely service consumption the guest will have. "If the guest typically orders room service shortly after checking in to their room, then you can proactively suggest—or offer—the in-room dining specials for that day, even take their order at the front desk to shorten the wait for their dinner" says Bill Frizzell, the industry technology strategist for the Microsoft Worldwide Hospitality Team. "This has been a long sought-after capability for the industry," he adds. "Defining a single view of the guest, without duplicate stores of information, is the key to understanding their habits, trends, and behaviours."

TVs that deliver music, movies—and much more. Today's leading-edge hotels have in-room systems that do far more than allow guests to watch their Favourite first-run movie. They can also control in-room music, provide gaming options, display your bill—even control the thermostat and lights. The Hotel 1000 in Seattle, Wash., for instance, has centered the room around the availability of Favourite media and services on a number of widescreen plasma monitors located throughout its rooms and suites. You can control content, multi-area volume of the sound system, and interact with your profile through these devices. And because it's a multi-use property—part residence, part hotel—the same entertainment offerings are available for their property owners.

That lessens the typical multi-use management burden of maintaining multiple service offerings per type of area on the property.

FIND YOURSELF

People in the hospitality industry have found a variety of uses for new radio frequency identification technology—from helping guests find each other at a ski resort to allowing them to pay for a meal. That's because, increasingly, this technology is gaining traction with hotels and resorts in the form of cashless payment systems that can be used on-property and, more and more often, off-property as well.

For example, at Wild Rivers, a water theme park in Irvine, Calif., RFID locator bracelets can be preloaded and used to pay for food and beverages . The RFID systems, developed by Guest Technologies, have yielded an almost immediate return on investment. After the system was introduced at Wild Rivers, guest spending quadrupled, with the average family of four spending twice their normal amount on meals. Another key capability of this offering is location-based services, where groups of individuals can be instantly found at the property, simultaneously allowing for more freedom and security in these safety-conscious times. "Imagine taking a group of seven 12 year-olds to a water park for a birthday party," says Frizzell. "You can go to any information kiosk in the park and instantly find where all of the kids you are responsible for are, and what activities and payments they have made, using their RFID bracelet. All of this is enabled through the implementation RFID and location-based services, using Microsoft technologies and Microsoft MapPoint Location Server."

BACK-OFFICE SYSTEMS

Hotel guests might not have noticed this but applications that handled property management, food and beverage, and sales and catering functions often couldn't communicate with one another easily. Now they can. A large, multi-property hotel chain in Las Vegas is currently integrating systems and platforms that were in application silos—meaning that they were running as stand-alone applications, not intended to share their information with other applications—to better integrate each other's data.

Through this interchange of data, they are better able to implement efficient business processes that rely on the delivery of data between these systems that were previously separated. For example, if you dine on-property the morning you intend to check out, you can get a final bill that is inclusive of your full folio of charges—even the breakfast you had five minutes ago. That's because there's no more "batching" of data to be sent to the property management system for posting to your guest folio. Instead, the interchange of your transaction to your folio is now happening at the time you make it. "To achieve this level of integration between property-level systems, hospitality organizations had to create specific interfaces between them," says Frizzell. "But these interfaces are not typically designed with flexibility and scaling of processes in mind, which had the unfortunate side effect of making the interfaces very brittle in use." Think of it this way: If you have 10 on-property systems that all needed to share the same base set of guest transaction data, it would result in 90 separate interfaces being built to accommodate the integration. Considering the inflexible nature of these point-in-time interfaces, keeping them running and orchestrated to perform the simple task of sharing data can easily become a huge financial and management burden.

But by implementing an "Information Hub" at the property level, all systems and applications that need to share data report that data in an open format, based on industry standards, to the hub. The hub is then responsible for routing the information to the various systems and orchestrating the intended business processes. In effect, the hub streamlines the exchange of data, reducing the number of integration interfaces from 90 to 10.

SELF-HEALING HOTEL TECHNOLOGY

A hotel's information technology systems are typically managed in a reactive way, which is to say that when something breaks down an IT person is called upon to fix it. But bringing systems off-line to repair them can affect the whole operation—think of the long check-in lines when the credit-card systems aren't working. The solution? A dynamic platform that constantly monitors a hotel's systems for problems and fixes them before they affect the whole property.

A large multi-concept fine dining chain has added a system to keep an eye on its restaurant-level systems and enterprise servers. This system controls everything from the deployment of operating systems to the handheld devices the company's employees use. System problems and failures are reported to the IT help desk as they occur, minimizing the time it takes to get mission-critical systems back online.

INDIVIDUAL ETHICS

Ethics is defined as "the system or code of morals of a particular person, religion, group, or profession." As such, ethical beliefs may vary from person to person. There are three basic individual approaches to ethics that are reflected in the behaviour of people. First is the moral rights approach, which judges the consistency of decisions and behaviours with the maintenance of certain fundamental personal and group liberties and privileges such as life, freedom, health, privacy, and property.

Second is the justice approach, which judges the consistency of decisions and behaviours with the maintenance of equity, fairness, and impartiality in the distribution of costs and benefits among individuals. Third is the utilitarian approach, which judges the effects of decisions and behaviours on providing the greatest good for the greatest number of people.

BUSINESS ETHICS

Business ethics in Western society emerged with the growth in capitalism in sixteenth-century Europe. Up to that time it was largely believed that it was immoral to produce goods for profit. With the Protestant Reformation came the belief that a diligent worker pleased God, and that the wealth that was acquired from business activities was a sign that God was pleased.

Good business people could be good human beings by satisfying the needs of customers and providing employment for workers. Today there is a common belief among many organizations that good ethics is good business. This idea has evolved into the concept of social responsibility, and some companies, such as HVS and the Ecotel concept, have stressed the importance of energy conservation, recycling, and minimal disturbance of ecological systems in property development. It is too soon to tell if there is a positive relationship between social responsibility and profits, but there are clearly increasing numbers of companies who want to be known as being socially responsible. It is important to note that operating within the legal system may not be an adequate basis for evaluating the ethics of a business decision.

Chapter 2

Market of Hospitality and Tourism

A market is a social arrangement that allows buyers and sellers to discover information and carry out a voluntary exchange of goods or services. It is one of the two key institutions that organize trade, along with the right to own property. Allowing markets to arrive at a pareto efficient outcome is one of the key components of capitalism. In everyday usage, the word "market" may refer to the location where goods are traded, sometimes known as a marketplace, or to a street market.

The function of a market requires, at a minimum, that both parties expect to become better off as a result of the transaction. Markets generally rely on price adjustments to provide information to parties engaging in a transaction, so that each may accurately gauge the subsequent change of their welfare. In less sophisticated markets, such as those involving barter, individual buyers and sellers must engage in a more lengthy process of haggling in order to gain the same information. Markets are efficient when the price of a good or service attracts exactly as much demand as the market can currently supply.

The chief function of a market, then, is to adjust prices to accommodate fluctuations in supply and demand in order to achieve allocative efficiency. An economic system in which goods and services are exchanged by market functions is called a market economy. An alternative economic system in which non-market forces determine prices are called planned economies or command economies. The attempt to combine socialist ideals with the incentive system of a market is known as market socialism. Although many markets exist in the traditional sense—such as a flea market—there are various other types of them and various organizational structures to assist their functions. A market can be organized as an auction, as a shopping centre, as a complex institution such as a stock market, and as an informal discussion between two individuals.

In economics, a market that runs under laissez-faire policies is a free market. It is "free" in the sense that the government makes no attempt to intervene through taxes, subsidies, minimum wages, price ceilings, etc. Markets may be distorted by a seller or sellers with monopoly power, or a buyer with monopsony power. Also, the level of organization or negotiation power of buyers, markedly affects the functioning of the market. Markets where price negotiations do not arrive at efficient outcomes for both sides are said to experience market failure.

Most markets are regulated by state wide laws and regulations. While barter markets exist, most markets use currency or some other form of money. Markets of varying types can spontaneously arise whenever a party has interest in a good or service that some other party can provide. Hence there can be a market for cigarettes in correctional facilities, another for chewing gum in a playground, and yet another for contracts for the future delivery of a commodity.

MARKET FAILURE

If advertising is poor, definitely there will be market failure. Market failure is a term used to describe a situation in which markets do not efficiently allocate goods and services. To economists, the term would normally be applied to situations where the inefficiency is particularly dramatic, or when it is suggested that non-market institutions would be more efficient and wealth-producing than their private alternatives.

On the other hand, the term "market failure" is also often used to describe situations where market forces do not serve the perceived public interest. However, the focus is on market failure as defined by mainstream economics. Economists use model-like theorems to explain or understand such cases.

The two main reasons that markets fail are:

- The inadequate expression of costs or benefits in prices and thus into microeconomic decision-making in markets.
- Sub-optimal market structures.

The existence of a market failure in a certain economic activity is often used as an argument that the activity in question should not be directed by market forces. This generally leads to a debate on the question of what - if anything - should be used to replace markets. The most common response to a market failure in the present day is to use the government to produce certain goods and services. However, government intervention may cause nonmarket failure by the intevention itself causing externalitites.

Types of Market Failures

Imperfect Competition

In economic theory, imperfect competition, is the competitive situation in any market where the conditions necessary for perfect competition are not satisfied.

Forms of imperfect competition include:

- Monopoly, in which there is only one seller of a good.
- Oligopoly, in which there is a small number of sellers.
- Monopolistic competition, in which there are many sellers producing highly differentiated goods.
- Monopsony, in which there is only one buyer of a good.
- Oligopsony, in which there is a small number of buyers.

There may also be imperfect competition in markets due to buyers or sellers lacking information about prices and the goods being traded. There may also be imperfect competition due to a time lag in a market. For example, in the 1990s, there was a shortage of computer programmers, but becoming a skilled programmer requires several years of experience. This drove up salaries. Another example is the "jobless recovery". There are many growth opportunities available after a recession, but it takes time for employers to react, leading to high unemployment. High unemployment decreases wages, which makes hiring more attractive, but it takes time for new jobs to be created.

Market Power

In economics, market power is the ability of a firm to alter the market price of a good or service. A firm with market power can raise price without losing all customers to competitors. When a firm has market power it faces a downward-sloping demand curve. In perfectly competitive markets, market participants have no market power. A firm with market power has the ability to individually affect either the total quantity or the prevailing price in the market. If the demand curve is downward sloping then the decrease in supply as a result of the exercise of market power creates an economic deadweight loss in comparison with a situation of perfect competition. This is often viewed as socially undesirable, and as a result, many countries have anti-trust or other legislation with the aim of limiting the ability of firms to accrue market power. Such legislation often regulates mergers and sometimes introduces a judicial power to compel divestiture.

A firm usually has market power by virtue of it controlling a large portion of the market. In extreme cases - monopoly and monopsony - the firm controls the entire market. However, market size alone is not a good indicator of market power. Highly concentrated markets may be contestable if there are no barriers to entry or exit, limiting the incumbent firm's ability to raise its price above competitive levels. Market power gives firms the ability to engage in unilateral anti-competitive behaviour. Some of the behaviours that firms with market power are accused of engaging in include predatory pricing, product tying, and creation of overcapacity or other barriers to entry. If no individual participant in the market has significant market power, then anti-competitive behaviour can take place only through collusion, or the exercise of a group of participants' collective market power. When several firms control a significant share of market sales, the resulting market structure is called an oligopoly or oligopsony. An oligopoly may engage in collusion, either tacit or overt, and thereby exercise market power. An explicit agreement in an oligopoly to affect market price or output is called a cartel. The behaviour of firms in perfect competition or monopoly can be treated as a simple optimization, but an oligopoly requires game theoretic analysis. Monopoly power is an example of market failure which occurs when one or more of the participants has the ability to influence the price or other outcomes in some general or specialized market. The most commonly discussed form of market power is that of a monopoly, but other forms such as monopsony, and more moderate versions of these two extremes, exist. Market participants that have market power are sometimes referred to as "price makers", while those without are sometimes called "price takers".

A well known example of monopolistic market power is Microsoft's market share in PC operating systems. The United States v. Microsoft case concerned the allegation that Microsoft illegally exercised its market power by bundling its web browser with its operating system. Some have suggested that Wal Mart exercises monopsonistic market power; its size allows it to extract extremely low prices from its suppliers.

Monopoly

In economics, is defined as a persistent market situation where there is only one provider of a product or service. Monopolies are characterized by a lack of economic competition for the good or service that they provide and a lack of viable substitute goods. Monopoly should be distinguished from monopsony, in which there is only one buyer of the product or service; it should also, strictly, be distinguished from the phenomenon of a cartel. In a monopoly a single firm is the sole provider of a product or service; in a cartel a centralized institution is set up to partially coordinate the actions of several independent providers.

STRATEGIES IN MARKETING

Marketing strategy is a powerful process that gives an organization a competitive advantage in the marketplace. While just defining a marketing strategy will not automatically create a competitive advantage, it will allow the organization to concentrate its resources on the greatest opportunities to increase sales and achieve a sustainable competitive advantage. The word strategy comes from the Greek word strategies meaning general. Strategy is what generals use to win battles. Thus properly understood, marketing strategy is a high-level exercise involving the "generals" of the organization in determining how to build on the firm's strengths while taking advantage of competitors' weaknesses. Marketing strategy is most effective when it is a vital component of corporate strategy, defining how the organization will engage customers, prospects and the competition in the market arena for consistent success.

A marketing strategy also serves as the foundation of a marketing plan. A marketing plan contains a set of specific actions required to successfully implement a specific marketing strategy. For example: "Use a low cost product to attract consumers. Once our organization, via our low cost product, has established a relationship with consumers, our organization will sell additional, higher-margin products and services that enhance the consumer's interaction with the low-cost product or service."

A strategy is different from a tactic. While it is possible to write a tactical marketing plan without a sound, well-considered strategy, it is not recommended. Without a sound marketing strategy, a marketing plan has no foundation. Marketing strategies serve as the fundamental underpinning of marketing plans designed to reach marketing objectives. It is important that these objectives have measurable results. A good marketing strategy should integrate an organization's marketing goals, policies, and action sequences into a cohesive whole. The objective of a marketing strategy is to provide a foundation from which a tactical plan is developed. This allows the organization to carry out its mission effectively and efficiently. Marketing strategies are partially derived from broader corporate strategies, corporate missions, and corporate goals. They should flow from the firm's mission statement. They are also influenced by a range of microenvironmental factors. Marketing strategies are dynamic and interactive. They are partially planned and partially unplanned.

Commercial Planning

In the modern world of business, it is useless to be a creative original thinker unless you can also sell what you create. Management cannot be expected to recognize a good idea unless it is presented to them by a good salesman. The success of a new product depends not only on the idea behind the product, but also on the marketing of the new product before, during and after the product launch.

Commercializing a product is commonly known as Commercial Planning. No concrete methods are currently available for New Product Launching. However, to launch a new product. This describes a set of activities and products, that are essential for launching a new product. New Product Launching is part of the New Product Development method.

Strategic Management

An organization's strategy must be appropriate for its resources, environmental circumstances, and core objectives. The process involves matching the company's internal resources and capabilities to the external business environment the organization faces.

Strategy formulation involves:

- Doing a situation analysis: Both internal and external; both micro-environmental and macro-environmental.
- Concurrent with this assessment, objectives are set. This involves crafting vision statements, mission statements, overall corporate objectives, strategic business unit objectives, and tactical objectives.
- These objectives should, in the light of the situation analysis, suggest a strategic plan. The plan provides the details of how to achieve these objectives.

This three-step strategy formulation process is sometimes referred to as determining where you are now, determining where you want to go, and then determining how to get there. These three questions are the essence of strategic planning. SWOT Analysis: I/O Economics for the external factors and RBV for the internal factors.

Strategy implementation involves:

- Allocation of sufficient resources
- Establishing a chain of command or some alternative structure
- Assigning responsibility of specific tasks or processes to specific individuals or groups
- It also involves managing the process. This includes monitoring results, comparing to benchmarks and best practices, evaluating the efficacy and efficiency of the process, controlling for variances, and making adjustments to the process as necessary.
- When implementing specific programmes, this involves acquiring the requisite resources, developing the process, training, process testing, documentation, and integration with legacy processes.

Strategy formulation and implementation is an on-going, never-ending, integrated process requiring continuous reassessment and reformation. Strategic management is dynamic. It involves a complex pattern of actions and reactions.

It is partially planned and partially unplanned. Strategy is both planned and emergent, dynamic, and interactive. Some people feel that there are critical points at which a strategy must take a new direction in order to be in step with a changing business environment. These critical points of change are called strategic inflection points.

Strategic management operates on several time scales. Short term strategies involve planning and managing for the present. Long term strategies involve preparing for and preempting the future. Marketing strategist Derek Abell has suggested that understanding this dual nature of strategic management is the least understood part of the process. He claims that balancing the temporal aspects of strategic planning requires the use of dual strategies simultaneously. Strategic Management is actually a solid foundation or a framework within which all the functioning managerial operations are bundled together. This is the highest level corporate activity that sets the terms and goals for a company that it should follow for prosperity.

Strategic management techniques can be viewed as bottom-up, top-down, or collaborative processes. In the bottom-up approach, employees submit proposals to their managers who, in turn, funnel the best ideas further up the organization. This is often accomplished by a capital budgeting process. Proposals are assessed using financial criteria such as return on investment or cost-benefit analysis.

The proposals that are approved form the substance of a new strategy, all of which is done without a grand strategic design or a strategic architect. The top-down approach is the most common by far. In it, the CEO, possibly with the assistance of a strategic planning team, decides on the overall direction the company should take. Some organizations are starting to experiment with collaborative strategic planning techniques that recognize the emergent nature of strategic decisions.

In most corporations there are several levels of strategy. Strategic management is the highest in the sense that it is the broadest, applying to all parts of the firm. It gives direction to corporate values, corporate culture, corporate goals, and corporate missions. Under this broad corporate strategy there are often functional or business unit strategies. Functional strategies include marketing strategies, new product development strategies, human resource strategies, financial strategies, legal strategies, and information technology management strategies.

The emphasis is on short and medium term plans and is limited to the domain of each department's functional responsibility. Each functional department attempts to do its part in meeting overall corporate objectives, and hence to some extent their strategies are derived from broader corporate strategies. Many companies feel that a functional organizational structure is not an efficient way to organize activities so they have re-engineered according to processes or strategic business units . A strategic business unit is a semi-autonomous unit within an organization. It is usually responsible for its own budgeting, new product decisions, hiring decisions, and price setting. An SBU is treated as an internal profit centre by corporate headquarters. Each SBU is responsible for developing its business strategies, strategies that must be in tune with broader corporate strategies.

The "lowest" level of strategy is operational strategy. It is very narrow in focus and deals with day-to-day operational activities such as scheduling criteria. It must operate within a budget but is not at liberty to adjust or create that budget. Operational level strategy was encouraged by Peter Drucker in his theory of management by objectives . Operational level strategies are informed by business level strategies which, in turn, are informed by corporate level strategies. Business strategy, which refers to the aggregated operational strategies of single business firm or that of an SBU in a diversified corporation refers to the way in which a firm competes in its chosen arenas.

Corporate strategy, then, refers to the overarching strategy of the diversified firm. Such corporate strategy answers the questions of "in which businesses should we compete?" and "how does being in one business add to the competitive advantage of another portfolio firm, as well as the competitive advantage of the corporation as a whole?" Since the turn of the millennium, there has been a tendency in some firms to revert to a simpler strategic structure. This is being driven by information technology.

It is felt that knowledge management systems should be used to share information and create common goals. Strategic divisions are thought to hamper this process. Most recently, this notion of strategy has been captured under the rubric of dynamic strategy, popularized by the strategic management textbook authored by Carpenter and Sanders. This work builds on that of Brown and Eisenhart as well as Christensen and portrays firm strategy, both business and corporate, as necessarily embracing ongoing strategic change, and the seamless integration of strategy formulation and implementation. Such change and implementation are usually built into the strategy through the staging and pacing facets. Management by Objectives is a process of agreeing upon objectives within an organization so that management and employees buy in to the objectives and understand what they are. Management By Objectives term was first popularized by Peter Drucker in 1954 in his book 'The Practice of Management'.

It is all too easy for managers to fail to outline, and agree with their employees, what it is that everyone is trying to achieve. MBO substitutes for good intentions a process that requires rather precise written description of objectives and timelines for their monitoring and achievement. The process requires that the manager and the employee agree to what the employee will attempt to achieve in the period ahead, and that the employee accept and buy into the objectives .

For example, whatever else a manager and employee may discuss and agree in their regular discussions, let us suppose that they feel that it will be sensible to introduce a key performance indicator to show the development of sales revenue in a part of the firm. Then the manager and the employee need to discuss what is being planned, what the time-schedule is and what the indicator might or might not be. Thereafter the two of them should liaise to ensure that the objective is being attended to and will be delivered on time.

Organizations have scarce resources and so it is incumbent on the managers to consider the level of resourcing but also to consider whether the objectives that are jointly agreed within the firm are the right ones and represent the best allocation of effort. Also, reliable Management information systems are needed to establish relevant objectives and monitor their "reach ratio" in an objective way.

MBO is often achieved using set targets. MBO introduced the SMART criteria: Objectives for MBO must be SMART . However, it has been reported in recent years that this style of management receives criticism in that it triggers employees' unethical behaviour of distorting the system or financial figures to achieve the targets set by their short-term, narrow bottom-line, and completely self-centered thinking.

Marketing Strategy Tools and Models

Ansoffs Matrix

A common tool used within marketing was developed by Igor Ansoff in 1957. His model gives organisation five strategic business options.

1. *Market Penetration:* This involves increasing sales of an existing product and penetrating the market further by either promoting the product heavily or reducing prices to increase sales.
2. *Product Development:* The organisation develops new products to aim within their existing market, in the hope that they will gain more custom and market share. For Example Sony launching the Playstation 2 to replace their existing model.
3. *Market Development:* The organisation here adopts a strategy of selling existing products to new markets. This can be done either by a better understanding of segmentation, *i.e* who else can possibly purchase the product or selling the product to new markets overseas.
4. *Diversification:* Moving away from what you are selling to providing something new *e.g.* Moving over from selling foods to selling cars.
5. *Consolidation:* Where the organisation adopts a strategy of withdrawing from particular markets, scaling back on operations and concentrating on its existing products in existing markets.

Product Life Cycle

The product life cycle concept suggests that a product passes through four stages of evolution. Introduction, growth, maturity and decline. As a product evolves and passes through theses four stages profit is affected, and different strategies have to be employed to ensure that the product is a success within its market. As a new product much time will be spent by the organisation to create awareness of it presence amongst its target market. Profits are negative or low because of this reason. Growth: If consumer clearly feels that this product will benefit them in some ways and they accept it, the organisation will see a period of rapid sales growth. Maturity: Rapid sales growth cannot last forever. Sales slow down as the product sales reach peak as it has been accepted by most buyers. Decline: Sales and profits start to decline, the organisation may try to change their pricing strategy to stimulate growth, however the product will either have to be re-modified, or replaced within the market.

Value Chain Analysis

Michael Porter in 1985 introduced in his book ' The competitive advantage' the concept of the Value Chain. He suggested that activities within the organisation add value to the service and products that the organisation produces, and all these activities should be run at optimum level if the organisation is to gain any real competitive advantage. If they are run efficiently the value obtained should exceed the costs of running them *i.e.* customers should return to the organisation and transact freely and willingly. Michael Porter suggested that the organisation is split into 'primary activities' and 'support activities'.

Primary Activities

- *Inbound logistics*: Refers to goods being obtained from the organisations suppliers ready to be used for producing the end product.
- *Operations*: The raw materials and goods obtained are manufactured into the final product. Value is added to the product at this stage as it moves through the production line.
- *Outbound logistics*: Once the products have been manufactured they are ready to be distributed to distribution centres, wholesalers, retailers or customers.
- *Marketing and Sales*: Marketing must make sure that the product is targeted towards the correct customer group. The marketing mix is used to establish an effective strategy, any competitive advantage is clearly communicated to the target group by the use of the promotional mix.
- *Services:* After the product/service has been sold what support services does the organisation have to offer. This may come in the form of after sales training, guarantees and warranties.

With the above activities, any or a combination of them, maybe essential for the firm to develop the competitive advantage which Porter talks about in his book.

Support Activities

The support activities assist the primary activities in helping the organisation achieve its competitive advantage.

They include:

- *Procurement:* This department must source raw materials for the organisation and obtain the best price for doing so. For the price they must obtain the best possible quality
- *Technology development:* The use of technology to obtain a competitive advantage within the organisation. This is very important in today's technological driven environment. Technology can be used in production to reduce cost thus add value, or in research and development to develop new products, or via the use of the internet so customers have access to online facilities.
- *Human resource management*: The organisation will have to recruit, train and develop the correct people for the organisation if they are to succeed in their objectives. Staff will have to be motivated and paid the 'market rate' if they are to stay with the organisation and add value to it over their duration of employment. Within the service sector *e.g.* airlines it is the 'staff' who may offer the competitive advantage that is needed within the field.
- *Firm infrastructure:* Every organisations needs to ensure that their finances, legal structure and management structure works efficiently and helps drive the organisation forward.

As you can see the value chain encompasses the whole organisation and looks at how primary and support activities can work together effectively and efficiently to help gain the organisation a superior competitive advantage.

SWOT Analysis

A tool used by organisations to help the firm establish its Strengths, Weaknesses, Opportunities and Threats . A SWOT analysis is used as a framework to help the firm develop its overall corporate, marketing, or product strategies. Note: Strengths and Weaknesses are internal factors which are controllable by the organisation. Opportunities and threats are external factors which are uncontrollable by the organisation.

Strength examples could include:

- A strong brand name.
- Market share.
- Good reputation.
- Expertise and skill.
- Weaknesses could include:
- Low or no market share.
- No brand loyalty.
- Lack of experience.
- Opportunities could include:
- A growing market.
- Increased consumer spending.
- Selling internationally.
- Changes in society beneficial to your company.

Threats could include:

- Competitors
- Government policy *e.g.* taxation, laws
- Changes in society not beneficial to your company

A SWOT analysis is an excellent tool to use if the organisation wants to take a step back and assess the situation they are in. Issues raised from the analysis are then used to assist the organisation in developing their marketing mix strategy. A SWOT analysis must form the part of any prudent marketing strategy.

Generic Strategies

For an organisation to obtain a sustainable competitive advantage Michael Porter suggested that they should follow either one of three generic strategies.

Strategy One: Cost Leadership

This strategy involves the organisation aiming to be the lowest cost producer within their industry. The orgainisation aims to drive cost down through all the elements of the production of the product from sourcing, to labour costs. The cost leader usually aims at a broad market, so sufficient sales can cover costs. Low cost producers include Easyjet airline, Ryan air, Asda and Walmart. Some organisation may aim to drive costs down but will not pass on these cost savings to their customers aiming for increased profits clearly because their brand can command a premium rate.

Strategy 2: Differentiation

To be different, is what organisations strive for. Having a competitive advantage which allows the company and its products ranges to stand out is crucial for their success. With a differentiation strategy the organisation aims to focus its effort on particular segments and charge for the added differentiated value. If we look at Brompton folding cycles their compact design differentiates them from other folding bike companies. New concepts which allow for differentiation can be patented, however patents have a certain life span and organisation always face the danger that their idea that gives the competitive advantage will be copied in one form or another.

Strategy 3: Niche Strategies

Here the organisation focuses its effort on one particular segment and becomes well known for providing products/services within the segment. They form a competitive advantage for this niche market and either succeed by being a low cost producer or different within that particular segment. Examples include Roll Royce and Bentley.

Are you 'Stuck in the Middle'

The danger some organisation face is that they try to do all three and become what is known as stuck in the middle. The have no clear business strategy, be all to all consumers, which adds to their running costs causing a fall in sales and market share. 'Stuck in the middle' companies are usually subject to a takeover or merger.

Industry Analysis Model

Porters fives forces model is an excellent model to use to analyse a particular environment of an industry. So for example, if we were entering the PC industry, we would use porters model to help us find out about:

- Competitive Rivalry
- Power of suppliers
- Power of buyers

- Threats of substitutes
- Threat of new entrants.

The five main factors are key factors that influence industry performance, hence it is common sense and practical to find out about these factors before you enter the industry.

Competitive Rivalry

A starting point to analysing the industry is to look at competitive rivalry. If entry to an industry is easy then competitive rivalry will likely to be high. If it is easy for customers to move to substitute products for example from coke to water then again rivalry will be high.

Generally competitive rivalry will be high if:

- There is little differentiation between the products sold between customers.
- Competitors are approximately the same size of each other.
- If the competitors all have similar strategies.
- It is costly to leave the industry hence they fight to just stay in

Power of Suppliers

Suppliers are also essential for the success of an organisation. Raw materials are needed to complete the finish product of the organisation. Suppliers do have power.

This power comes from:

- If they are the only supplier or one of few suppliers who supply that particular raw material.
- If it costly for the organisation to move from one supplier to another
- If there is no other substitute for their product.

Power of Buyers

Buyers or customers can exert influence and control over an industry in certain circumstances.

This happens when:

- There is little differentiation over the product and substitutes can be found easily.
- Customers are sensitive to price.

- Switching to another product is not costly.

Threat of Substitutes

Are there alternative products that customers can purchase over your product that offer the same benefit for the same or less price?

The threat of substitute is high when:

- Price of that substitute product falls.
- It is easy for consumers to switch from one substitute product to another.
- Buyers are willing to substitute.

Threat of New Entrant

The threat of a new organisation entering the industry is high when it is easy for an organisation to enter the industry *i.e.* entry barriers are low. An organisation will look at how loyal customers are to existing products, how quickly they can achieve economy of scales, would they have access to suppliers, would government legislation prevent them or encourage them to enter the industry.

So to summaries porters five forces model is essential to carry to help you understand your industry in depth before you enter it.

Diffusion of Innovation

This extension of the product life cycle was developed by Everett M. Rogers in 1962 and simply looks who adopts products at the different stages of the life cycle. Rogers identified five types of purchasers as the product moves through its life cycle stage.

He suggested:

1. Innovator who make up 2.5% of all purchases of the product, purchase the product at the beginning of the life cycle. They are not afraid of trying new products that suit their lifestyle and will also pay a premium for that benefit.
2. Early Adopters make up 13.5% of purchases, they are usually opinion leaders and naturally adopt products after the innovators. This group of purchasers are crucial because adoption by them means the product becomes acceptable, spurring on later purchasers.
3. Early Majority make up 34% of purchases and have been spurred on by the early adopters. They wait to see if the product will be adopted by society and will purchase only when this

has happened. They early majority usually have some status in society.

4. Late Majority make up another 34% of sales and usually purchase the product at the late stages of majority within the life cycle.
5. Laggards make up 16% of total sales and usually purchase the product near the end of its life. They are the 'wait and see' group. They wait to see if the product will get cheaper. Usually when they purchase the product a new version is already on the market. Some may call Laggards, bargain hunters!

Boston Consultancy Group

This product portfolio matrix classifies product lines into four categories. The BCG models suggests that organisations should have a healthy balance of products within their range. The Boston Consultancy Group classified these products as following:

Question Mark/Problem Child

These are products with low market share but operate in high market growth rates. The company puts a lot of resources in this product in the hope that it will eventually increase market share and generate cash returns in the future.

Star

Stars have high market shares that operate in growing markets. The product at this stage should be generating positive returns for the company.

Cash Cow

Cash Cow are products at the mature stage of the lifecycle, they generate high amounts of cash for the company, but growth rate is slowing. There are chances that the product may slip into decline, appropriate marketing mix strategies should be employed to try to prevent this from happening.

MANAGING INCOME

Accounting is the measurement, disclosure or provision of assurance about financial information that helps managers, investors, tax authorities and other decision makers make resource allocation decisions.

The names come from the use of financial accounts. Financial accounting is one branch of accounting and historically has involved processes by which financial information about a business is recorded, classified, summarized, interpreted, and communicated. Accounting is also widely referred to as the "language of business". Auditing, a related but separate discipline, has two sub-disciplines: Internal and External auditing. External auditing is the process whereby an independent auditor examines an organization's financial statements and accounting records in order to express an opinion — that conveys reasonable but not absolute assurance — as to the truth and fairness of the statements and the accountant's adherence to Generally Accepted Accounting Principles in all material respects.

Internal auditing is an examination in which management, and not the external public, is the main beneficiary. It is carried out usually by auditors employed by the company, but sometimes by external service providers. The internal auditor's role is broader, and basically depends on what kind of assurance management wants.

It usually certifies the efficiency and effectiveness of processes, departments, projects or internal controls. The Institute of Internal Auditors is generally accepted as the custodian of Internal Auditing best practice. At the heart of accounting is the measurement of financial transactions which are transfers of legal property rights made under contractual relationships. Non-financial transactions are specifically excluded due to conservatism and materiality principles. Practitioners of accountancy are known as accountants.

There are many professional bodies for accountants throughout the world. Many allow their members to use titles indicating their membership. Examples are Chartered Certified Accountant, Chartered Accountant and Certified Public Accountant. Accountancy attempts to create accurate financial reports that are useful to managers, regulators, and other stakeholders such as shareholders, creditors, or owners. The day-to-day record-keeping involved in this process is known as bookkeeping.

At the heart of modern financial accounting is the double-entry bookkeeping system. This system involves making at least two entries for every transaction: a debit in one account, and a corresponding credit in another account. The sum of all debits should always equal the sum of all credits. This provides an easy way to check for errors. This system was first used in medieval Europe, although claims have been made that the system dates back to Ancient Greece. According to critics of standard accounting practices, it has changed little since. Accounting reform measures of some kind have been taken in each generation to attempt to keep bookkeeping relevant to capital assets or production capacity. However, these have not changed the basic principles, which are supposed to be independent of economics as such. In recent times, the divergence of accounting from economic principles has resulted in controversial reforms to make financial reports more indicative of economic reality.

Accountancy's infancy dates back to the earliest days of human agriculture and civilization, when the need to maintain accurate records of the quantities and relative values of agricultural products first arose. Simple accounting is mentioned in the Christian Bible in the book of Matthew, in the Parable of the Talents. Twelfth century writer Ibn Taymiyyah mentioned in his book Hisba, detailed accounting systems used by the Muslims as early as in the mid-seventh century.

The accounting practices were influenced by the Roman and the Persian civilizations that Muslims interacted with. The most detailed example of a complex governmental accounting system is the Divan of Umar, the second Caliph of Islam in which all revenues and disbursements were recorded. The Divan of Umar has been described in detail by various Islamic historians and was used by Muslim rulers with mofidications and enhancements until the fall of the Ottoman Empire.

Applied Modern Accountancy in Hotel

The first book on accounting was written by a Croatian merchant Benedetto Cotrugli, who is also known as Benedikt Kotruljeviæ, from the city of Dubrovnik. During his life in Italy he met many merchants and decided to write, Della Mercatvra et del Mercante Perfetto in which he elaborated on the principles of modern, double-entry book-keeping. He finished his lifework in 1458. However, his work was not published until 1573, as a result of which his contributions to the field have been overlooked by the general public. For this reason, Luca Pacioli, also known as Friar Luca dal Borgo, is credited for the "birth" of accounting. His Summa de arithmetica, geometrica, proportioni et proportionalita, a synthesis of the mathematical knowledge of his time, includes the first published description of the method of keeping accounts that Venetian merchants used at that time, known as the double-entry accounting system. Although Pacioli codified rather than invented this system, he is widely regarded as the "Father of Accounting".

The system he published included most of the accounting cycle as we know it today. He described the use of journals and ledgers, and warned that a person should not go to sleep at night until the debits equalled the credits! His ledger had accounts for assets, liabilities, capital, income, and expenses — the account categories that are reported on an organization's balance sheet and income statement, respectively. He demonstrated year-end closing entries and proposed that a trial balance be used to prove a balanced ledger. His treatise also touches on a wide range of related topics from accounting ethics to cost accounting.

The first known book in the English language on accounting was published in London by John Gouge in 1543. It is described as A Profitable Treatyce called the Instrument or Boke to learn to know the good order of the keeping of the famous reconynge, called in Latin, Dare and Habere, and, in English, Debitor and Creditor.

A short book of instructions was also published in 1588 by John Mellis of Southwark, in which he says, "I am but the renuer and reviver of an ancient old copy printed here in London the 14 of August 1543: collected, published, made, and set forth by one Hugh Oldcastle, Scholemaster, who, as appeareth by his treatise, then taught Arithmetics, and this booke in Saint Ollaves parish in Marko Lane." John Mellis refers to the fact that the principle of accounts he explains is "after the forme of Venice". A book described as The Merchants Mirrour, or directions for the perfect ordering and keeping of his accounts formed by way of Debitor and Creditor, after the Italian manner, by Richard Dafforne, accountant, published in 1635, contains many references to early books on the science of accountancy. In this book, headed "Opinion of Book-keeping's Antiquity," the author states, on the authority of another writer, that the form of book-keeping referred to had then been in use in Italy about two hundred years, "but that the same, or one in many parts very like this, was used in the time of Julius Caesar, and in Rome long before."

An early Dutch writer appears to have suggested that double-entry book-keeping was even in existence among the Greeks, pointing to scientific accountancy having been invented in remote times. There were several editions of Richard Dafforne's book - the second edition in 1636, the third in 1656, and another in 1684. The book is a very complete treatise on scientific accountancy, beautifully prepared and containing elaborate explanations.

The numerous editions tend to prove that the science was highly appreciated in the 17th century. From this time on, there has been a continuous supply of literature on the subject, many of the authors styling themselves accountants and teachers of the art, and thus proving that the professional accountant was then known and employed. The requirements for entry in the profession of accounting vary from country to country. Accountants may be licensed by a variety of organisations, such as the British qualified accountancy bodies including Association of Chartered Certified Accountants and Institute of Chartered Accountants, and are recognized by titles such as Chartered Certified Accountant and Chartered Accountant, Certified Public Accountant, Certified Management Accountant, Certified General Accountant, or Certified Practising Accountant .

Some Commonwealth countries often recognise both the certified and chartered accounting bodies. The majority of "public" accountants in New Zealand and Canada are Chartered Accountants; however, Certified General Accountants are also authorized by legislation to practise public accounting and auditing in all Canadian provinces, except Ontario and Quebec, as of 2005. There is, however, no legal requirement for an accountant to be a paid-up member of one of the many Institutes and other bodies which are effectively a form of professional trade union. Unlike the Law Society, which can legally stop a solicitor from practising, accountancy institutes do not have such authority. However, auditors are regulated.

Before the Enron and other accounting scandals, there were five large firms and were called the Big Five. Since Arthur Andersen's assurance practice split with a plurality joining KPMG in the US and Deloitte and Touche outside of the US, Arthur Andersen left from the group. Previous to this there were also groupings referred to as the "Big Six" and the "Big Eight". Enron turned out to be only the first of a series of accounting scandals that enveloped the accounting industry in 2002.

This is likely to have far-reaching consequences for the U.S. accounting industry. Application of International Accounting Standards originating in International Accounting Standards Board headquartered in London and bearing more resemblance to UK than current US practices is often advocated by those who note the relative stability of the UK accounting system. Accounting reform of a far more comprehensive sort is advocated by those who see issues with capitalism or economics, and seek ecological or social accountability.

According to Accountancy Age's 2005 league table, fee income amongst the Top 50 accounting firms in the UK rose from £6.3bn to £7.0bn. This followed two successive years in which fee income had declined, largely a result of the sale by some of the larger firms of their consultancy arms. Fee income in most business areas - audit, tax, corporate finance and consultancy - rose in the 2005 survey, with insolvency and wealth management being the only segments where revenue fell. Price water house Coopers remains the largest firm with fee income totalling £1,780m followed by Deloitte, KPMG and Ernst and Young . The combined revenue of the Big Four accounted for £5.0bn, 72% of the fee income of the Top 50, down from 78-79% in the years up to the 2002 survey and the third year in succession a decline in their share has occurred . Ernst and Young's fee income is the smallest of the largest four firms, but still over three times that of the next largest firm; Grant Thornton. The amount of fee income tapers off amongst the mid-tier firms so that in total there were only 25 firms that each generated more than £15m of revenue in the 2005 survey. For more details regarding British qualified accountancy professionals, please refer to the page of British qualified accountants.

Management Accounting

Management accounting is concerned with the provisions and use of accounting information to managers within organizations, to provide them with the basis in making informed business decisions that would allow them to be better equipped in their management and control functions.

Unlike financial accountancy information, management accounting information is used within an organization and is usually confidential and access to which is only available to a select few. According to CIMA, The Chartered Institute of Management Accountants, Management Accounting is "the process of identification, measurement, accumulation, analysis, preparation, interpretation and communication of information used by management to plan, evaluate and control within an entity and to assure appropriate use of and accountability for its resources. Management accounting also comprises the preparation of financial reports for non management groups such as shareholders, creditors, regulatory agencies and tax authorities".

Aims:

- Formulating strategies;
- Planning and constructing business activities;
- Making decisions;
- Well use of resources;
- Supporting financial reports preparation; and
- Safeguarding assets.

In the late 1980s, accounting practitioners and educators were heavily criticized on the grounds that management accounting practices had changed little over the preceding 60 years, despite radical changes in the business environment. Professional accounting institutes, perhaps fearing that management accountants would increasingly be seen as superfluous in business organizations, subsequently devoted considerable resources to the development of a more innovative skills set for management accountants.

The distinction between 'traditional' and 'innovative' management accounting practices can be illustrated by reference to cost control techniques. Traditionally, management accountants' principal technique was variance analysis, which is a systematic approach to the comparison of the actual and budgeted costs of the raw materials and labour used during a production period.

While some form of variance analysis is still used by most manufacturing firms, it nowadays tends to be used in conjunction with innovative techniques such as life cycle cost analysis and activity-based costing, which are designed with specific aspects of the modern business environment in mind. Lifecycle costing recognizes that managers' ability to influence the cost of manufacturing a product is at its greatest when the product is still at the design stage of its product lifecycle, since small changes to the product design may lead to significant savings in the cost of manufacturing the product. Activity-based costing recognizes that, in modern factories, most manufacturing costs are determined by the amount of 'activities' and that the key to effective cost control is therefore optimizing the efficiency of these activities. Activity-based accounting is also known as Cause and Effect accounting.

Both lifecycle costing and activity-based costing recognize that, in the typical modern factory, the avoidance of disruptive events is of far greater importance than reducing the costs of raw materials. Activity-based costing also de-emphasizes direct labour as a cost driver and concentrates instead on activities that drive costs, such as the provision of a service or the production of a product component.

The most significant recent direction in managerial accounting is throughput accounting, which recognizes the interdependencies of modern production processes and provide managers with a tool that will allow them to measure the contribution per unit of constrained resource for any given product, customer or supplier. A seldom expressed alternative view of management accounting is that it is neither a neutral or benign influence in organizations, rather a mechanism for management control through surveillance. This view locates management accounting specifically in the context of management control theory.

There are several related professional qualifications in the field of accountancy including:

- Management Accountancy Qualifications
  - CIMA
  - MA
  - Institute of Cost and Works Accountants of India
  - AAFM
- Other Professional Accountancy Qualifications
  - Chartered Certified Accountant,
  - Chartered Accountant,
  - Certified Public Accountant,

Accounting Management is the practical application of management techniques to control and report on the financial health of the organization. It involves the analysis, planning, implementation, and control of programmes designed to provide financial data reporting for managerial decision making. This includes the maintenance of bank accounts, developing financial statements, cash flow and financial performance analysis. Accounting management is a mandatory knowledge module of any MBA programme. Accounting is often referred to as billing management. The goal is to gather usage statistics for users. Using the statistics the users can be billed and usage quota can be enforced.

Examples:

- Disk usage
- Link utilisation
- CPU time

For non-billed networks, 'Administration' replaces 'Accounting'. The goals of Administration is to administer the set of authorized users, by establishing users, passwords and permissions; and to administer the operations of the equipment such as by performing software backup and synchronization.

Activity-based Costing

Activity-based costing is a method of allocating costs to products and services. It is generally used as a tool for planning and control.

This is a necessary tool for doing value chain analysis. The concepts of ABC were developed in the manufacturing sector of the U.S. during the 1970s and 80s.

During this time, the Consortium for Advanced Manufacturing-International, now known simply as CAM-I, provided a formative role for studying and formalizing the principles that have become more formally known as Activity-Based Costing. Robin Cooper and Robert Kaplan, proponent of the Balanced Scorecard, brought notice to these concepts in a number of articles published in Harvard Business Review beginning in 1988.

Cooper and Kaplan described ABC as an approach to solve the problems of traditional cost management systems. These traditional costing systems are often unable to determine accurately the actual costs of production and of the costs of related services. Consequently managers were making decisions based on inaccurate data especially where there are multiple products.

Instead of using broad arbitrary percentages to allocate costs, ABC seeks to identify cause and effect relationships to objectively assign costs. Once costs of the activities have been identified, the cost of each activity is attributed to each product to the extent that the product uses the activity. In this way ABC often identifies areas of high overhead costs per unit and so directs attention to finding ways to reduce the costs or to charge more for costly products. Activity-based costing was first clearly defined in 1987 by Robert S. Kaplan and W. Bruns as a stage in their book Accounting and Management. They initially focused on manufacturing industry where increasing technology and productivity improvements have reduced the relative proportion of the direct costs of labour and materials, but have increased relative proportion of indirect costs. For example increased automation has reduced labour, which is a direct cost, but has increased depreciation, which is an indirect cost.

Traditionally cost accountants had arbitrarily added a broad percentage onto the direct costs to allow for the indirect costs. However as the percentages of overhead costs had risen, this technique became increasingly inaccurate because the indirect costs were not caused equally by all the products. For example one product might take more time in one expensive machine than another product, but since the amount of direct labour and materials might be the same, the additional cost for the use of the machine would not be recognised when the same broad 'on-cost' percentage is added to all products. Consequently, when multiple products share common costs, there is a danger of one product subsidising another.

Like manufacturing industries, financial institutions also have diverse products which can cause cross-product subsidies. Since personnel expenses represent the largest single component of non-interest expense in financial institutions, these costs must also be attributed more accurately to products and customers. Activity based costing, even though developed for manufacturing, can therefore be a useful tool for doing this. This extended use of ABC to financial institutions was presented in 1990 in an article appearing in the Journal of Bank Cost and Management Accounting by Richard Sapp, David Crawford and Steven Rebishcke.

Direct labour and materials are relatively easy to trace directly to products, but it is more difficult to directly allocate indirect costs to products. Where products use common resources differently, some sort of weighting is needed in the cost allocation process. The measure of the use of a shared activity by each of the products is known as the cost driver. For example, the cost of the activity of bank tellers can be ascribed to each product by measuring how long each product's transactions takes at the counter and then by measuring the number of each type of transaction. Even in activity-based costing, some overhead costs are difficult to assign to products and customers, for example the chief executive's salary. These costs are termed 'business sustaining' and are not assigned to products and customers because there is no meaningful method. This lump of unallocated overhead costs must nevertheless be met by contributions from each of the products, but it is not as large as the overhead costs before ABC is employed.

Although some may argue that costs untraceable to activities should be "arbitrarily allocated" to products, it is important to realise that the only purpose of ABC is to provide information to management. Therefore, there is no reason to assign any cost in an arbitrary manner. Management accountants can be creative in finding other ways to represent these costs on internal reporting statements.

MANAGING BUDGET

Budget generally refers to a list of all planned expenses and revenues. A budget is an important concept in microeconomics, which uses a budget line to illustrate the trade-offs between two or more goods. A personal budget is among the most important concepts of personal finance. In a personal or family budget all sources of income are identified and expenses are planned with the intent of matching outflows to inflows . There are a wide variety of personal budgeting methods and tools that can be employed to help individuals and families with the budgeting process. Also the level of planned finance available to a person, corporation or government, as set by a certain person.

The budget of a government is a summary or plan of the intended revenues and expenditures of that government. In the United States, the federal budget is prepared by the Office of Management and Budget, and submitted to Congress for consideration. Invariably, Congress makes many and substantial changes. Nearly all American states are required to have balanced budgets, but the federal government is allowed to run deficits. In the UK the budget is prepared by the Chancellor of the Exchequer, the second most important member of the government, and must be passed by Parliament. The Parliament seldom makes changes to the budget. The budget of a company is compiled annually. A finished budget usually requires considerable effort and can be seen as a financial plan for the new financial year.

While traditionally the Finance department compiles the company's budget, modern software allows hundreds or even thousands of people in the various departments to contribute their expected revenues and expenses to the final budget. If the actual numbers delivered through the financial year turn out to be close to the budget, this will demonstrate that the company understands their business and has been successfully driving it in the direction they had planned.

On the other hand, if the actuals diverge wildly from the budget, this sends out an 'out of control' signal and the share Cost-plus pricing is a pricing method commonly used by firms. It is used primarily because it is easy to calculate and requires little information. There are several varieties, but the common thread in all of them is that you first calculate the cost of the product, then include an additional amount to represent profit. Cost-plus pricing is often used on government contracts, and has been criticized as promoting wasteful expenditures.

CALCULATING PRICE USING THE COST-PLUS METHOD

There are several ways of determining cost, and the profit can be added as either a percentage markup or an absolute amount. One example is:

$$P = (AVC + FC\%) \times (1 + MK\%)$$

where:

- P = price
- AVC = average variable cost
- FC% = percentage allocation of fixed costs

- MK% = percentage markup

For example: If variable costs are 30 yen, the allocation to cover fixed costs is 10 yen, and you feel you need a 50% markup then you would charge a price of 60 yen:

$P = (30 + 10) \times (1 + 0.50)$

$P = 40 \times 1.5$

$P = 60$

An alternative way of doing a similar calculation is:

P = (AVC + FC%)/(1 " MK%)

To make things simpler, some firms, particularly retailers, ignore fixed costs and just use the purchase price paid to their suppliers as the cost term. They indirectly incorporate the fixed cost allocation into the markup percentage. To simplify things even further, sometimes a fixed amount is applied rather than a percentage. This fixed amount is usually determined by head-office to make it easy for franchisees and store managers. This is sometimes referred to as turnkey pricing. Another variant of cost plus pricing is activity based pricing.

This involves being more careful in determining costs. Instead of using arbitrary expense categories when allocating overhead, every activity is linked to the resources it uses. Cost will need to be recalculated and the percentage markup will likely need to be adjusted as the product goes through its life cycle. This is sometimes referred to as product life cycle pricing, although it is seldom done deliberately or in a planned and organized manner. Price skimming and penetration pricing are also types of product life cycle pricing but they are demand based pricing methods rather cost based.

Advantages of Cost-plus Pricing:

- Easy to calculate
- Minimal information requirements
- Easy to administer
- Tends to stabilize markets - insulated from demand variations and competitive factors
- Insures seller against unpredictable, or unexpected later costs
- Ethical advantages

Disadvantages:

- Tends to ignore the role of consumers
- Tends to ignore the role of competitors

- Use of historical accounting costs rather than replacement value
- Use of "normal" or "standard" output level to allocate fixed costs
- Inclusion of sunk costs rather than just using incremental costs
- Ignores opportunity costs
- Contractors may not focus on performance because the cost is always covered by the client

In microeconomics, Production is simply the conversion of inputs into outputs. It is an economic process that uses resources to create a commodity that is suitable for exchange. This can include manufacturing, storing, shipping, and packaging. Some economists define production broadly as all economic activity other than consumption.

They see every commercial activity other than the final purchase as some form of production. Production is a process, and as such it occurs through time and space. Because it is a flow concept, production is measured as a "rate of output per period of time".

There are three aspects to production processes:

1. The quantity of the commodity produced,
2. The form of the good produced,
3. The temporal and spatial distribution of the commodity produced.

A production process can be defined as any activity that increases the similarity between the pattern of demand for goods, and the quantity, form, and distribution of these goods available to the market place. A production process is efficient if a given quantity of outputs cannot be produced with any less inputs. It is said to be inefficient when there exists another feasible process that, for any given output, uses less inputs. Some economists use the term X-efficiency to indicate that production processes tend to be inherently inefficient due to satisfying behaviour.

The "rate of efficiency" is simply the amount of outputs divided by the amount of inputs. If a production process uses 50 units of input to produce one unit of output it is more efficient than a process that uses 55 units of input to produce the same level of output. It is said to be 10% more efficient .

The inputs or resources used in the production process are called factors by economists. The myriad of possible inputs are usually grouped into four or five categories.

These factors are:

- Raw materials
- Labour services
- Capital goods
- Land

Sometimes a fifth category is added, entrepreneurial and management skills, a subcategory of labour services. Capital goods are those goods that have previously undergone a production process. They are previously produced means of production. Some textbooks use "technology" as a factor of production.

In the "long run" all of these factors of production can be adjusted by management. The "short run" however, is defined as a period in which at least one of the factors of production is fixed. A fixed factor of production is one whose quantity cannot readily be changed. Examples include major pieces of equipment, suitable factory space, and key managerial personnel. A variable factor of production is one whose usage rate can be changed easily. Examples include electrical power consumption, transportation services, and most raw material inputs. In the short run, a firm's "scale of operations" determines the maximum number of outputs that can be produced. In the long run, there are no scale limitations.

The total product of a variable factor of production identifies what outputs are possible using various levels of the variable input. This can be displayed in either a chart that lists the output level corresponding to various levels of input, or a graph that summarizes the data into a "total product curve". The diagram shows a typical total product curve. In this example, output increases as more inputs are employed up until point A. The maximum output possible with this production process is Qm. If there are other inputs used in the process, they are assumed to be fixed. The average physical product is the total product divided by the number of units of variable input employed. It is the output of each unit of input. If there are 10 employees working on a production process that manufactures 50 units per day, then the average product of variable labour input is 5 units per day. The average product typically varies as more of the input is employed, so this relationship can also be expresses as a chart or as a graph. A typical average physical product curve is shown. It can be obtained by drawing a vector from the origin to various points on the total product curve and plotting the slopes of these vectors.

The marginal physical product of a variable input is the change in total output due to a one unit change in the variable input or alternatively the rate of change in total output due to an infinitesimally small change in the variable input. The discrete marginal product of capital is the additional output resulting from the use of an additional unit of capital. The continuous marginal product of a variable input can be calculated as the derivative of quantity produced with respect to variable input employed. The marginal physical product curve is shown. It can be obtained from the slope of the total product curve.

Because the marginal product drives changes in the average product, we know that when the average physical product is falling, the marginal physical product must be less than the average. Likewise, when the average physical product is rising, it must be due to a marginal physical product greater than the average. For this reason, the marginal physical product curve must intersect the maximum point on the average physical product curve.

MPP keeps increasing till it reaches its maximum. Up until this point every additional unit has been adding more value to the total product than the previous one. From this point onwards, every additional unit adds less to the total product compared to the previous one. But the average product is still increasing till MPP touches APP. At this point, an additional unit is adding the same value as the average product. From this point onwards, MPP starts to reduce and so does APP because every additional unit is adding less to APP than the average product. But the total product is still increasing because every additional unit is still contributing positively. Therefore, during this period, both, the average as well as marginal products, are decreasing, but the total product is still increasing. Finally we reach a point when MPP crosses the x-axis.

At this point every additional unit starts to diminish the product of previous units, possibly by getting into their way. Therefore the total product starts to decrease at this point. This is point A on the total product curve.

Diminishing returns can be divided into three categories:

1. Diminishing Total returns, which implies reduction in total product with every additional unit of input. This occurs after point A in the graph.
2. Diminishing Average returns, which refers to the portion of the APP curve after its intersection with MPP curve.
3. Diminishing Marginal returns, refers to the point where the MPP curve starts to slope down and travels all the way down to the x-axis and beyond. Putting it in a chronological order, at first the marginal returns start to diminish, then the average returns, followed finally by the total returns.

These curves illustrate the principle of diminishing marginal returns to a variable input. This states that as you add more and more of a variable input, you will reach a point beyond which the resulting increase in output starts to diminish. This point is illustrated as the maximum point on the marginal physical product curve. It assumes that other factor inputs are held constant.

An example is the employment of labour in the use of trucks to transport goods. Assuming the number of available trucks is fixed, then the amount of the variable input labour could be varied and the resultant efficiency determined. At least one labourer is necessary. Additional workers per vehicle could be productive in loading, unloading, navigation, or around the clock continuous driving. But at some point the returns to investment in labour will start to diminish and efficiency will decrease. The most efficient distribution of labour per piece of equipment will likely be one driver plus an additional worker for other tasks. Resource allocations and distributive efficiencies in the mix of capital and labour investment will vary per industry and according to available technology. Trains are able to transport much more in the way of goods with fewer "drivers" but at the cost of greater investment in infrastructure.

With the advent of mass production of motorized vehicles, the economic niche occupied by trains has become more specialized and limited to long haul delivery. There is an argument that if the theory is holding everything constant, the production method should not be changed, *i.e.*, division of labour should not be practiced. However, the rise in marginal product means that the workers use other means of production method, such as in loading, unloading, navigation, or around the clock continuous driving. For this reason, some economists think that the "keeping other things constant" should not be used in this theory.

The total, average, and marginal physical product curves mentioned are just one way of showing production relationships. They express the quantity of output relative to the amount of variable input employed while holding fixed inputs constant. Because they depict a short run relationship, they are sometimes called short run production functions. If all inputs are allowed to be varied, then the diagram would express outputs relative to total inputs, and the function would be a long run production function. If the mix of inputs is held constant, then output would be expressed relative to inputs of a fixed composition, and the function would indicate long run economies of scale.

Rather than comparing inputs to outputs, it is also possible to assess the mix of inputs employed in production. An isoquant relates the quantities of one input to the quantities of another input. It indicates all possible combinations of inputs that are capable of producing a given level of output. Rather than looking at the inputs used in production, it is possible to look at the mix of outputs that are possible for any given production process. This is done with a production possibilities frontier. It indicates what combinations of outputs are possible given the available factor endowment and the prevailing production technology. You can use a lot of labour with a minimal amount of capital, or you could invest heavily in capital equipment that requires a minimal amount of labour to operate, or any combination in between. For most goods, there are more than just two inputs.

For example in agriculture, the amount of land, water, and fertilizer can all be varied to produce different amounts of a crop. An isoquant, in the two input case, is a curve that shows all the ways of combining two inputs so as to produce a given level of output. In the three input case it will be a surface. Iso is Latin for equal and quant is short for quantity. Movement along an isoquant depicts a constant rate of output, but a changing input ratio.

A unique isoquant can be constructed for every level of output, and a family of isoquants can be created to represent various output levels. Isoquants further from the origin represent greater amounts of output. Isoquants are usually considered to be everywhere dense, meaning an infinite number of them could be plotted in any two input space. A typical isoquant is illustrated in the diagram to the right. At point A in the diagram Ka units of capital are combined with La units of labour to produce 100 units of output.

It is downward sloping, convex to the origin, and non-intersecting . A complete isoquant is actually a closed curve, but only the "down sloping to the right" portion makes economic sense. The upward sloping parts of isoquants, for example, indicate that level of output could be produced by less of both inputs so this section is of little interest to decision makers. The economic section of the isoquants is defined by a pair of lines called ridge lines.

The "downward to the right" slope of the economic region of an isoquant is due to the possibility of substituting one input for another in the production process while keeping the level of output constant. Isoquants are typically convex to the origin reflecting the fact that the two factors are substitutable for each other at varying rates. This rate of substitutability is called the "marginal rate of technical substitution" or occasionally the "marginal rate of substitution in production". It measures the reduction in one input per unit increase in the other input that is just sufficient to maintain a constant level of production. For example, the marginal rate of substitution of labour for capital gives the amount of capital that can be replaced by one unit of labour while keeping output unchanged.

To move from point A to point B in the diagram, the amount of capital is reduced from Ka to Kb while the amount of labour is increased only from La to Lb. To move from point C to point D, the amount of capital is reduced from Kc to Kd while the amount of labour is increased from La to Lb. The marginal rate of technical substitution of labour for capital is equivalent to the absolute slope of the isoquant at that point. It is equal to 0 where the isoquant becomes horizontal, and equal to infinity where it becomes vertical.

The opposite is true when going in the other direction. In this case we are looking at the marginal rate of technical substitution capital for labour. It can also be shown that the marginal rate of substitution labour for capital, is equal to the marginal physical product of labour divided by the marginal physical product of capital. In the unusual case of two inputs that are perfect substitutes for each other in production, the isoquant would be linear. If, on the other hand, there is only one production process available, factor proportions would be fixed, and these zero-substitutability isoquants would be shown as horizontal or vertical lines.

Fixed Assets Management

Fixed assets management is an accounting process that seeks to track fixed assets for the purposes of financial accounting, preventive maintenance, and theft deterrence. Many organizations face a significant challenge to track the location, quantity, condition, maintenance and depreciation status of their fixed assets. A popular approach to tracking fixed assets utilizes serial numbered Asset Tags, often with bar codes for easy and accurate reading. Periodically, the owner of the assets can take inventory with a mobile barcode reader and then produce a report. Off-the-shelf software packages for fixed asset management are marketed to businesses small and large. Some Enterprise Resource Planning systems are available with fixed assets modules.

Free Cash Flow

Free cash flow measures a firm's net increase in:

- Cash from operations,

- Less the dividends paid to preferred shareholders, and
- Less expenditures necessary to maintain assets.

Increases in non-cash current assets may, or may not be deducted, depending on whether they are considered to be maintaining the status quo, or to be investments for growth.

Problems with Capx

- The expenditures for maintenance of assets is only part of the capx reported on the Statement of Cash Flows. It must be separated from the expenditures for growth purposes. This split is not a requirement under GAAP, and is not audited. Management is free to disclose maintenance capx or not. Therefore this input to the calculation of free cash flow is easy to manipulate. Since it is a very large number, maintenance capx's questionable validity is the basis for some people's dismissal of 'free cash flow'.
- A second problem with the maintenance capx measurement is its intrinsic 'lumpyness'. By their nature, expenditures for capital assets that will last decades are infrequent, but costly when they occur. 'Free cash flow', in turn, will be very different from year to year. No particular year will be a 'norm' that can be expected to be repeated.

Uses of the Metric

- Free cash flow measures the ease with which businesses can grow and pay dividends to shareholders. Even profitable businesses may have negative cash flows. Their requirement for increased financing will result in increased financing costs reducing future income. It is easier to grow with organic cash flows than with additional financing.
- According to the discounted cash flow valuation model, the intrinsic value of a company is the present value of all future free cash flows, plus the cash proceeds from its eventual sale. The presumption is that the cash flows are used to pay dividends to the shareholders. Bear in mind the lumpyness discussed.
- Some investors prefer using free cash flow instead of net income to measure a company's financial performance, because free cash flow is more difficult to manipulate than net income.

The problems with this presumption are itemized at cash flow and return of capital.

- The payout ratio is a metric used to evaluate the sustainability of distributions from REITs, Oil and Gas Royalty Trusts, and Income Trust. The distributions are divided by the free cash flow. Distributions may include any of income, flowed-through capital gains or return of capital.

This metric is used only by shareholders. Debt holders are not concerned with maintaining the operating capital assets, or with growing the business. Nor are they concerned with taxes paid since their payments come first. The appropriate metric for debt holders is EBITDA.

Change Management

There are several phrases regarding organizational change and development that look and sound a lot alike, but have different meanings. As a result of the prominence of the topic, there seems to be increasingly different interpretations of some of these phrases, while others are used interchangeably. Without at least some sense of the differences between these phrases, communications about organizational change and development can be increasingly vague, confusing and frustrating. There are different overall types of organizational change, including planned versus unplanned, organization-wide versus change primarily to one part of the organization, incremental versus transformational, etc.. Knowing which types of change you are doing helps all participants to retain scope and perspective during the many complexities and frequent frustrations during change.

Successful change efforts often include several key roles, including the initiator, champion, change agent, sponsor and leaders. Organization-wide change in corporations should involve the Board of Directors. Whether their members are closely involved in the change or not, they should at least be aware of the change project and monitor if the results are being achieved or not. As the change agent, you might be performing different roles during the project.

Appreciative Inquiry is a recent and powerful breakthrough in organizational change and development. It's based on the philosophy that "problems" are often caused as much by our perception of them as problems as by other influencing factors. The philosophy has spawned a strong movement that, in turn, has generated an increasing number of models, tools and tips, most of which seem to build from the positive perceptions of those involved in the change effort.

There are numerous well-organized approaches from which to manage a change effort. Some of the approaches have been around for many years — we just haven't thought of them as such. For example, many organizations undertake strategic planning. The implementation of strategic planning, when done in a systematic, cyclical and explicit approach, is strategic management. Strategic management is also one model for ensuring the success of a change effort.

There are numerous, major methods and movements to regularly increase the performance of organizations. Each includes regular recurring activities to establish organizational goals, monitor progress towards the goals, and make adjustments to achieve those goals more effectively and efficiently. Any or all of the following approaches will improve organizational performance depending on if they are implemented comprehensively and remain focused on organizational results. Some of the following, *e.g.*, organizational learning and knowledge management, might be interpreted more as movements than organization performance strategies because there are wide interpretations of the concepts, not all of which include focusing on achieving top-level organizational results.

However, if these two concepts are instilled across the organization and focus on organizational results, they contribute strongly to organizational performance. On the other hand, the Balanced Scorecard, which is deliberately designed to be comprehensive and focused on organizational results, will not improve performance if not implemented from a strong design.

Chapter 3

Service Facilities in Hospitality and Tourism Industry

SATISFACTION IN THE HOSPITALITY INDUSTRY

In the year 2000, the tourism sector will be the largest industry in the world. Today it is estimated to provide about 255 million jobs and amounts to 10 per cent of world employment. It has now grown into a modern, mature industry where workers are forming their professional identity. These "hospitality professionals" are primarily concerned with customer satisfaction. But that's not always easy to achieve and many problems can and do arise.

The restructuring of work today has important consequences. Unlike their agricultural or industrial counterparts, workers in the service sector find the fruits of their labour are frequently intangible. In some cases, their emotions are involved. One can easily broaden management guru Peter Drucker's concept of "the knowledge worker" to include "the emotion worker," who must deal with people on a more interpersonal level. In our modem, service-oriented society, there is a need for literature devoted to the special needs of this kind of worker, especially in the area of "spirituality of work"

By its very nature, hospitality work has a spiritual dimension. Of all industries, it is the most intensely interactive, with people serving people and providing comfort, sustenance, conviviality, transport, amusement, enlightenment, employment and much more. Given the complexity of human behaviour, concerns about the work's spiritual dimension can be neither ignored nor hidden. For this reason, perhaps the most challenging of all hospitality industry problems today is not so much job satisfaction as a proper spirituality of work.

In short, the challenge is to help hospitality professionals find genuine meaningfulness in their work so they experience the peace and joy that God has prepared for them. As Pope John Paul II reminds us in his Encyclical entitled Laborem Exercens, "Work is a good thing for man — a good thing for his humanity — because through work man not only transforms nature, adapting it to his own needs, but he also achieves fulfillment as a human being and indeed in a sense becomes 'more a human being.'" This is certainly true in the hospitality industry.

IMPORTANCE OF SERVICE IN MODERN SOCIETY

The growth of services is nothing new. More early as 1900, both America and Britain had more jobs in services than in industry. By 1950, services employed half of all American workers. And in 1993, America had the biggest service sector, accounting for 72 per cent of its Gross Domestic Product . Services are also the fastest growing part of international trade, accounting for 20 per cent of total world trade and 30 per cent of American exports.

Tourism is one of these services. By the year 2000, it is likely to be the world's most important economic activity. According to a report of the World Travel and Tourism Council, there were 255 million jobs in tourism in 1996. This amounts to 10.2 per cent of all world employment. The Special Nature of Work in the Service Sector. Work in the service sector is quite different from that in agriculture or manufacturing. A service has been described as a "deed, act, or performance. Two functional issues are: at whom is the act directed, and is this act tangible or intangible in nature?

These two questions result in Lovelock's four-way classification scheme involving: tangible actions to people's bodies, such as hair cutting and surgery; tangible actions to goods and other physical possessions, such as air freight, lawn mowing and janitorial services; tangible actions directed at people's minds, such as broadcasting and education; and intangible actions directed at people's intangible assets, such as insurance, investment banking and consulting.

This categorization scheme is useful in answering questions like the following, having to do with analysing and marketing services. Does the customer need to be physically present: throughout service delivery? Only to initiate or terminate the service transaction? or not at all? Does the customer need to be mentally present during the service delivery? Can mental presence be maintained across physical distances through mail or electronic communications? In what ways is the target of the service act "modified" by the receipt of the service? And how does the customer benefit from these modifications?

Work in the Hospitality Industry. Especially in the tourism sector—where services are created as they are consumed and the customer is often involved in the production process—there are many different ways to tailor the service to meet the needs of individual customers. Customisation can proceed along at least two dimensions. First of all, you have to consider whether the characteristics of the service and its delivery system lend themselves to customisation. Second, you have to determine how much judgment customer contact personnel can exercise in defining the nature of the service received by individual customers. Some service concepts are quite standardized, while other services offer customers a wide range of options.

There is a class of services that not only involves a high degree of customisation, but also requires customer contact personnel to exercise judgment about the characteristics of the service and how it is delivered to each customer. This type of service is called "prescriptive" and the focus of control shifts from the user to the supplier. Professional services such as law, medicine, accounting, architecture and tour guiding fall within this category. They are all white-collar, "knowledge industries," requiring extensive training to develop the requisite skills and judgment needed for satisfactory service delivery. As a result, much of the literature on the service industry refers to the encounter between the customer and the service contact personnel as "the moment of truth," because it determines the level of customer satisfaction. This is especially true in the hospitality industry.

Alienation in Marxist Understanding of Work. Karl Marx was undoubtedly the harshest and most influential critic of the inequalities that private property institutions and free markets are accused of creating. In his writings, he detailed the suffering and misery capitalism placed upon its workers. The living conditions that capitalism imposed on the lower working classes contrasted sharply with Marx's view of how human beings should live.

According to Marx, human beings should be enabled to realise their human nature by freely developing their potential for self-expression and by satisfying their real human needs. People should develop their productive potential and have control over what they produce.

They know what their real needs are, and are able to form satisfying social relationships. Capitalism "alienated" the lower working classes by neither allowing them to develop their productive potential nor satisfy their real human needs. The service sector is one area where this alienation can be overcome if workers are truly empowered in their work situations.

Spirituality of Work

Today people are less and less sure about what "work" really means. Their expectations of work, especially getting it and enjoying it, are now matters of both deep anxiety and mundane reality. There are several reasons for this. First, there are high unemployment rates in industrialized societies. For many people in modern society, work is no longer something that happens in a fixed place during a fixed unit of time, producing a fixed output and reward. Come points out how societies frequently define human beings in terms of the work they perform. The question "what do you do?" is a central one in many people's lives. Religion teaches that work is its own reward, and that it will lead a person towards the virtuous life, if not salvation. Work is the natural course of action a human follows to find his or her role, niche, position, and the shape of his or her soul. Therefore, steady employment, a life in which one's lot continually improves, sits as the cornerstone of rational and calculable human action. It may well be the cornerstone of physical and mental health as well. How can it not shape the nature of spirituality?

It is in the work and working that a person's consciousness takes shape and life reveals its meaning. For it is in working that a person believes he or she has made sense of life's mystery and has found reasonable ways to avoid vexing metaphysical questions. For the content and structure of a person's consciousness, story and spirit remain his or her work, or lack of it.

Faith and the World of Work

Wright points out that many contemporary Christians experience some discomfort when they seek to relate their faith to the world of work, especially the work of wealth creation in industry, commerce and other services. The workplace is perceived as a Godless and even immoral part of their human condition. As a result, many people feel the need to find consistency between their work and the rest of their life.

Christians should be affirmed in their work as a central part of the human condition for the very reasons that it involves wealth creation and the provision of services. The problem is that written materials do not offer enough concrete guidance regarding a comprehensive theology and spirituality of the modern world of work a few notable exceptions include the core teaching of the series of Papal Encyclicals that have followed Rerum Novarem in 1891, Laborem Exercens in 1981, as well as Centesimus Annus in 1991, all of which contain much profound thinking about human work.

In any case, there is a fundamental question here. Why should one be concerned with the relationship between faith, work, and the world of wealth creation and provision of services? First of all, work is where most people spend a great deal of their time. Second, the creation of wealth and provision of services are the processes whereby all people survive on this earth, since they serve to satisfy their needs and wants. Finally, and most important, there is a unique Christian truth and revelation: the Incarnation.

Christians believe that, in Jesus, God became human at a particular moment of time and lived on this same earth that we inhabit. Jesus was very much involved in the world of work of his day. Many of his stories came from everyday life and the workplace. The world of work and wealth creation is very clearly part of God's creation, and God took part in these very activities. Hence, there is a need to relate them to our Christian beliefs and to face up to any discomfort we perceive and feel in doing so.

Difficulties Relating Faith and Work

According to Wright, there are four main reasons Christians find it difficult to relate their faith to their work in today's industry, commerce and other service sectors:

- The experimental and scientific method has transformed our understanding of the world in which we live. This growth in understanding has been most uncomfortable for the Church. Many have the false impression that advances in the fields of science and business are made at the expense of God and religion.
- The world of work may lie in what is popularly referred to as the "Protestant work ethic." Hard work and the accumulation of wealth were the routes of salvation. The problem here is that there are harsh realities in today's work world, such as indifferent supervision, employee turnover, caste system attitudes and long working weeks. In the hotel industry, these concepts are sometimes considered justified in order to attract better-qualified employees and to remedy the alarming shortage of labour.

- The reconciliation of the contemplative life and the life of every day action has been difficult. There has been a tendency for Christians to regard the active life as in some way inferior to the passive or spiritual one. Teilbard de Chardin looked for a general sanctification of human endeavors in all aspects. He rejected the notion that the active life is inherently inferior to the passive. Hence, Christians engaged in business are in fact contributing as positively to God's work as when they engage in prayer.
- The dominical and Church teaching present difficulties here. Jesus had some very hard things to say about the dangers of material goods and excessive attachments to riches. Nevertheless, nowhere does one find in the Gospels or the teachings of the Church any suggestion that the process of wealth creation and provision of services is in itself reprehensible or to be condemned. The encyclical Centesimus Annus identifies the tension between the role of the individual in the wealth creation and service provision process and the needs of the community. The system itself must not overwhelm the individual. People must in fact recognize the limits of private wealth.

Panmunin concluded that to improve public perceptions and enhance employees' experiences, industry must create a working climate that is challenging, secure, trusting, caring and promising. Unfortunately, employees' eroding working conditions have eroded the traditional Thai spirit of hospitality. Ensuring the return of Thai hospitality will take some doing, in areas like: nurturing a pride in serving, wearing a service uniform, providing the opportunity for learning and advancement, and demonstrating employer appreciation both in words and pay.

The Nature of Spirituality

The Historical Background and Methodology of Spirituality Studies. Before World War II, spirituality, as it refers to a person's life experiences, was an almost exclusively Roman Catholic term. But now it has taken on new meaning with the Second Vatican Council's invitation to a new awareness of, dialogue with and appreciation of other denominations and non-Christian religions. For example, there is now growing interest in the spirituality of various Protestant traditions as well as the traditions of Judaism, Hinduism, Islam and Buddhism. The Second Vatican Council has also called Catholics to a new dialogue with the human sciences—especially in the fields of psychology, sociology and anthropology—in which spirituality refers to the human spirit apart from religion. Some even speak of the spirituality of inter-religious movements, such as secular feminism and atheistic Marxism.

In short, spirituality has become a broad, inclusive term that is no longer confined to, or defined by, religion. It names a human reality difficult to define but whose patterns can be verified in quite different religions and movements. Spirituality now focuses on the human spirit of believers and non-believers in their lives as a whole; that is, on the physical and emotional, the intellectual and social, the political and cultural, and the secular and religious dimensions of their lives. According to Kinerk, the study of spirituality needs: a definition of itself, some tools for analysing a particular spirituality, some guidelines of relating a spirituality to other spiritualities, and some criteria for evaluation.

The features of a workable definition of spirituality should: limit the material to what is expressed, and contain the idea of personal growth. Thus, spirituality is the expression of a dialectical personal growth from the inauthentic to the authentic. There are, in fact, three ingredients in this definition: expression, dialectical personal growth, and movement from inauthentic to authentic. According to Thompson, a person's spirituality is individual and collective, and reflects how a person responds to God's initiative while facing the challenges of everyday life within his or her specific historical and cultural environment.

Just how does God's Spirit work in some one's life? First, it works in the subjective element. Second, it works in the objective dimension of one's real-life experiences and situations—encompassing all creations and all other people you encounter in your life. Put simply, God works in the people you meet and acts through your real life. He is present in human events and their history. His presence gives a necessary meaning to how you relate to other people and the world.

According to Kinerk, the questions or tools for analysing a spirituality must serve two purposes. They must: provide a means of organizing the material of a spirituality so it can be more easily assimilated, and provide for comparison and contrast such that they can be asked more or less equally of any spirituality. Here are two questions that can help focus and organize the material: What are the expressions of the authentic and inauthentic? What is the organizational form that could give the expressions depth and a relationship to one another? All spiritual life is a type of growth, but in many well-developed spiritualities there are specific stages, and the key to detecting these stages lies with the expressions of both the authentic and the inauthentic forms.

Hope Replace Obedience

According to Regan, personal development of healthy human qualities occupies a more central position in one's personal outlook towards spirituality today. Accepting what is authentically human leads people to use their native talents, creative expressions and heightened personal initiatives. On the other hand, anything that dehumanizes a service provider or "receiver" in the hospitality industry is viewed as unchristian. This approach allows more emphasis on an individual's personal response of his or her religious and inner values, both human and Christian. Empowerment, decentralization, co-responsibility and subsidiarity become the new hallmarks of what was once viewed as religious "obedience."

Many post-Second Vatican Council authors now present the Christian life based on a central theme of God's call and a person's response. This "call-response" morality and spirituality replaces the former stress on law and self-perfection. In the basic meaning of grace—God's self-gift—God gives Himself to a person and acts in them, enabling them to respond. Furthermore, New Testament teachings hold that the virtue of charity directed towards God and neighbour takes precedence over all other virtues. The law-centred approach has thus given way to a more love-centred approach: life is seen in its entirety as a loving response to a personal and loving God. A morality of relationships conceived along these lines sees each person in dialogue with God and meeting God in the events, people and prayer experiences of daily living.

Spirituality has important consequences for the overall tone or mood Christian professionals adopt in their lives. These professionals represent an intense cell of vibrant Christian life. They witness to Heavenly values, which imply that they should show what faith in God can mean based on the way they live their lives. Specifically, it means: hope, confidence, optimism in ultimate destinies; faith and charity in everyday concerns. By moving away from an excessively "obedience-centred" approach, they instead experience a Christian life and spirituality centre on faith, love, hope in God and in ultimate realities, manifested in the love and service of humankind. These constitute Gospel values that should characterize a renewed professional life and genuine Christian spirituality.

Kinerk has emphasized that, ultimately, evaluating a Catholic spirituality is the responsibility of the Catholic Church and over the centuries she has generally given a wide latitude to the expressions claiming to be of the Spirit As long as a spirituality refrained from making its charisma normative for all Christians, maintained a balanced view of theology and human nature, and did not habitually defy the directions of the hierarchy, the Church has been at least tolerant, if not actively supportive.

What Makes a Good Spirituality? There are three indicators of a good spirituality: good theology, good sense and good results. Good spirituality must flow out of the Christian community's understanding of the Gospel and hence must exhibit good theology. Spirituality is a human movement, and so good spirituality should reflect a keen sensitivity to the human condition—good sense. Finally, a good spirituality will produce good results because it will be the work of the Holy Spirit. To develop models of spirituality it is necessary to select criteria for differentiation. This selection is always arbitrary, however. It simply establishes the parameters by which the models are distinguished. Here the criteria will be "attitudes" towards two potential environments for expressions: the world and history. We can determine the models by asking the question: Does a spirituality view the world and/or history as a positive locus for expressions of the authentic? If a spirituality is not positive towards both, we call it apopathic; if it is positive towards both, we call it apostolic; if it is positive towards the world but not towards history, we call it city-of-God; and if it is positive towards history but not towards the world, we call it prophetic.

Most spiritualities are mixtures of all four, with perhaps one or more predominating. However, it is clear that a spirituality for hospitality professionals must be apostolic. Regan has pointed out that it is no longer possible to hold a monolithic conception of spirituality due to the pluralism in modern Church life and theology today. With the obedience-centred approach, the traditional stress on a person's spiritual life focused on the rules, authority and the virtue of obedience. This is similar to the law-centred approach of moral theology. A person's individual acts received more emphasis than his or her overall stance or attitude. Obedience to law in all exactness comes through in traditional moral theology as the centre of Christian life.

With today's personal response-to-inner values approach, there's a greater emphasis placed on personal responsibility and individuality. In this approach to the spiritual life, a person is viewed as entering a profession or a community to develop oneself fully in the service of Christ and neighbour, to put one's full talents at the disposal of people, and to take part in and share responsibility for the Church and for the community itself. Rather than obedience, selfless charity becomes the primary Christian virtue. Life itself is seen as a response of love to God and in the neighbour in accordance with Jesus' teaching. This approach seems particularly appropriate for hospitality professionals, whose training now emphasizes their empowerment to make decisions by themselves.

Spirituality of Work

Cassin points out that in the Christian scheme, work has always been understood as a human sharing in the creative activity of God. This means believing in the inherent dignity of work itself and the ultimate worth of any of the products of work. According to another, different Christian view, work has been seen as a penalty, a consequence of original sin or the Fall, rather than something intrinsic to God's creative purpose. This pessimistic view is certainly present in the thought of many influential figures in the history of theology, especially in the Western Church.

However, our Catholic and Protestant tradition does, thankfully, allow for a more positive theology of work. For example, there are the two creation accounts in the Book of Genesis; Paul's exhortation on the new creation in the Letter to the Romans; the unification prayer and work found in the Benedictine Rule; the impetus given to lay spirituality by Protestant and Catholic reforms; the Papal Encyclicals, especially Laborem Exercens by Pope John Paul II; and, attempts in the middle decades of the 20th century to affirm human dignity in the face of industrial blight and oppression.

In spite of all this, it is not easy to affirm the dignity of work and the worker when the characteristic form of work in an industrial society is symbolized by the assembly line. Repetitively carrying out a mechanical task gives faint image of the worker as a sharer in God's creative activity. It was much easier to promote the Christian vision of labour in a pre-industrial society when the dominant form of work was a craft, with the worker involved in the entire production process. The same is true of work in the service sector, including the hospitality industry.

New work structures, therefore, pose challenges, but also offer opportunities. To be efficient, the new workplace requires employees to take pride in their work and each other, and promoting such feelings can provide multiple benefits for any manager. It fosters loyalty towards the firm and one's fellow workers. At the same time, the experience of building solidarity vindicates a traditional Christian understanding of the dignity of the human person. For Wright, the starting point for a

Christian perspective on the world of work is Teilbard's divinization of human activity. The Incarnation substantially strengthens that perception, showing that the tension and paradox in the human condition are part of our working lives. According to the analysis of Svoboda, the book of Genesis tell us three important things about work.

First, God works. Second, God works not because He has to, but because He wants to work. His work is not for His own sake but for others' sake, mankind's sake and our sake. God chooses to work because He chooses to share something of Himself with someone else. Therefore, work is seen as being intimately associated with the act of self-giving — a self-giving for the benefit of others.

Third, God seems to enjoy His work. God takes delight in the work process, pronouncing creation, the product of His labours, as "good" at the end of each day. In other words, work is good — even God works. Work is an act of self-giving directed towards the good of others. Work consists primarily of cultivating and care, in bringing forth new life. Work should basically be a joyful activity, even though it often entails fatigue and pain. Don't forget, though, that rest and leisure are good, too, and are, in their own way, integral to the work process.

Spirituality of Work for Hospitality Professionals

There are many qualities of life rooted in the example of Jesus, with three basic qualities specifically reflecting Jesus' life of hospitable service to others: responsiveness, competence and respect. Underlying Jesus' desire to serve those in needs were sensitivity, adaptability and willingness that are today basic building blocks for an apostolic spirituality of hospitality. Sensitivity to the situation at hand is essential if a hospitality professional's response is to be effective. Adaptability to the situation as it changes is also essential if their response is to be appropriate. Willingness to be involved is essential if their response is to be consistent ultimately, the driving force behind this responsiveness is compassion, which is not the same as pity. The true core of compassion is the urgency to act. Compassion never merely observes; it initiates and interacts. In Jesus' work, compassion is second only to love.

On the other hand, when personal benefit becomes the primary goal of service in the hospitality industry, this compassion gives way to conceit. Competence shapes the overall effectiveness of our response. However sensitive, adaptable and willing that response maybe, its lasting effect must reflect competence. Service industries require a level of competence quite different from that in agricultural or manufacturing work. The hospitality industry revolves around two separate realities: material variables and personal variables. Material variables differ among the various areas of the hospitality industry, but they generally include some common elements. First, there is a body of living knowledge, with new information replacing old on a regular basis. Second, there are natural or acquired skills that enable hospitality professionals to use their knowledge. Third, there are the willingness, capacity and commitment to acquire new and refined skills to match developments within the field of knowledge now called hospitality, leisure or tourism studies. Finally, there are resources necessary for hospitality professionals to use skills with knowledge. Personal variables for hospitality professionals include the personalities, preferences and predicaments of those they serve.

Respect is characterized by a hospitality professional's recognition of each person's uniqueness. It is their affirmation of the dignity of each person, a dignity based on their creation as God's image and likeness, as well as their efforts to listen, communicate and interact through ways and means consistent with that uniqueness and dignity. Work in the hospitality industry brings professionals to encounters and interactions with many people. Respect reminds them that, regardless of what they have to do in the work of hospitality, the value of a human being can never be compromised. The driving force behind respect is love. Christian spirituality should acknowledge the goodness of all that is human. Emotions, sexuality, temperament, personality and the prayer life should all enter into the Christian response of the whole person. Development and fulfillment of these truly human aspects should be incorporated into any authentic approach to the Christian spirituality of work in the hospitality industry.

JOB SATISFACTION IN THE HOSPITALITY INDUSTRIES

The "rational" parts of any organization put a high value on efficiency. All jobs and tasks should be designed to achieve the organization's goals as efficiently as possible. Jobs are specialized along two dimensions: horizontally and vertically . Job specialization is most obvious at the operating levels of organizations. However, highly specialized work can injure the well-being of workers and thus poses an important problem of justice for employers . Such injustice can actually lead to decreased productivity.

On the other hand, there is a significant link between worker productivity and programmes that improve the quality of the work life of workers by giving greater involvement in, and control over, a variety of work tasks. Velasquez points out that there are two determinants of job satisfaction:

1. Experienced Meaningfulness. The individual must perceive his or her work as worthwhile or important by some system of values he or she accepts.
2. Knowledge of Results. The worker must be able to determine, on some regular basis, whether or not the outcomes of his or her work are satisfactory.

To influence these determinants, jobs must be expanded along five dimensions:

1. Skill Variety. The degree to which a job requires the worker to perform activities that challenge his or her skills and abilities.
2. Task Identity. The degree to which the job requires completing a whole and identifiable piece of work — doing a job from beginning to end with a visible outcome.
3. Task Significance. The degree to which a job has a substantial and perceivable impact on the lives of other people, whether in the immediate organization or the world at large.
4. Autonomy. The degree to which the job gives the worker freedom, independence and discretion in scheduling work and determining how he or she will carry it out.
5. Feedback. The degree to which a worker, in carrying out the work activities required by the job, gets information about the effectiveness of his or her efforts.

Traditionally, employees have relied on their supervisors for task guidance and good feelings—especially consideration and being treated like adults in order to perform their jobs both well and happily. Schneider and Bowen point out that when employees do not get this from their supervisors, they may turn to customers as "substitutes for leadership". Customers may be given a say in designing the organization that produces the goods and services. With services, it's often possible—and desirable—for customers to actually participate in production.

But the problem is that customers are not subject to the same kinds of fears, commitments and structures as employees, so they are very difficult to manage. To best capitalize on customer competencies, management must be able to:

1. Explicitly determine exactly what role/job they want their customer to perform.

2. Ensure that customers have what it takes to perform their jobs well through role clarity, ability and motivation.
3. Regularly appraise customer performance.

Service customers also often play the roles of directors, guides and even "order-givers" for employees. Customers play a dual leadership role by providing employees with guidance and providing them with positive feelings. There are two reasons. First, the employees' supervisors tend not to provide the guidance and good feelings they should. Second, customers of service firms feel they have a right to give orders. Employees like the positive feelings they receive from customers but do not like customers telling them what to do. The lesson here is fairly simple but too often overlooked: Feedback is a critical part of job enrichment. Service firms need to think creatively about how to respond to these opposite reactions to customers' leadership behaviours.

Customers can be trained to be a source of good feelings for employees and, at the same time, socialized to limit task direction over employees. Although management may have great "legitimate influence" over its employees, service work puts employees closer to their customers and, therefore, more involved with the kinds of rewards they receive and the distribution of those rewards. When a hospitality enterprise meets the various needs of employees through rewards—dispersed equitably and fairly—customers will experience superior service quality as well.

COMBINING JOB SATISFACTION WITH SPIRITUALITY FOR HOSPITALITY PROFESSIONALS

Mainardi has pointed out that hospitality professionals are dependent on contact with, and reception of, the public. Therefore, they presuppose some degree of availability towards the client, a considerable margin of initiative and a generally strong sense of personal responsibility. In fact, employees in the tourist transaction play an intermediary role between the industry's structure and its clientele.

This role is particularly decisive in achieving the results desired by both sides. AM these situations are undoubtedly favourable to bearing witness to the spirit and practice of the Gospel before others. The hospitality professional's conduct is not only circumscribed by the material manifestations of the tourist industry.

It must also be determined by psychological and ethical factors aimed at completely satisfying the tourist's wishes. Tourists want to be treated differently—better—than they are normally treated in their daily routines . Furthermore, there is substantial evidence that customers like to interact directly with people in the tourism trade, not machines. This is also unavoidable, since providing tourist services without human assistance remains inconceivable. This contact with the hurried or solitary traveller enables tourist professionals to reveal their own personalities—both as expert and human being—responding to each client's unique wishes via their own mental attitude, manner, initiative and creativity.

The human person is truly the central and fundamental point of the tourism industry, with the economic aspect clearly secondary. Simon used the concept of satisfying behaviour to accommodate the balancing act of achieving multiple objectives in human behaviour. Normative economics fails to include some of the central problems of conflict and dynamics. Simon attacks the hypothesis that firms strive to maximize profits for three key reasons: The theory leaves ambiguous whether it is short-run or long-run profit that is to be maximized; The entrepreneur may obtain all kinds of "psychic income" from the firm apart from monetary rewards; and the entrepreneur may simply want to earn a satisfactory return, not looking to maximize gains.

Simon points out that "economic man" is a satisfying animal whose problem-solving is based on his or her search to meet certain aspiration levels, rather than a "maximizing animal" whose problem-solving involves finding the best alternatives in terms of specified criteria This is certainly true in the case of the hospitality professional who seeks job satisfaction rather than merely looking to maximize salary. The true mark of hospitality professionalism is excellence on the technical level and fellowship towards the client on the moral level.

Such a global commitment involves a wide range of material services and mental attitudes in welcoming, guiding and assisting the tourist It also opens up more far-reaching horizons to practice Christian witness in so many privileged circumstances—in the form of personal contacts, conversations, exchanges of view, good conduct, etc. Nevertheless, this world also brings a lot of "baggage" with it for most people in the tourist and similar industries. Such difficulties include stress, high anxiety, burn out, low social status, feeling like a "hired host," low pay, tensions between career and one's personal and family life, as well as high turnover and mobility.

In professional activity, a concrete and unmistakable sign of integrity is to observe professional ethics. In other words, professionals should conduct their business honestly—giving clients the right amount of service and goods proportionate to their requested price. Whether you're talking about a travel agency or a tour company, a hotel or a restaurant, personal service must focus on the needs of the beneficiary of hospitality—*i.e.*, the client Specifically, the 10 dimensions of service quality are: reliability, responsiveness, competence, access, courtesy, communication, credibility, security, understanding/knowing the customer, and tangibles that include the physical evidence of the service.

Generally speaking, hospitality clients are not equipped with the controls and consumer protections many other customers enjoy when they purchase industrial products. With the exception of large-scale fraud, it is, in fact, very difficult for clients to contest the quality of tourist goods or services purchased. In the majority of cases, the tourist client is thus put in an inferior position. That's why it's all too easy for hospitality professionals to "swindle" and behave in unjust and dishonest ways. This is a recurrent risk faced even by the well-intentioned, and one that can only be dispelled if the will to bear witness is cultivated systematically in the depths of the individual conscience.

Regard towards the client's "person" can—and should—be demonstrated by imbuing him or her with a sense of psychological and physical well-being, and by being willing to serve. Customers should also benefit from: material protection of their person and possessions, the constant good functioning of the tourism facilities, professional correctness and an effort by service providers to achieve maximum standards of hygiene . Modern managerial conduct should also aim to overcome the "coldness" and lack of intimacy typical of bureaucratic organizations. What's more, the influence exerted by hospitality managers and their staff may play a significant role in "educating" clients in the use of tourism, whether aimed at recreation or any creative endeavor. In the words of Paul VI, we should strive to "humanize and spiritualize tourism."

The spirituality of work for hospitality professionals needs to be considered in relation to the general concept of job satisfaction. Using Simon's concept of satisfying behaviour, hospitality work needs to be seen simultaneously in all its dimensions: economic, human, professional, moral, cultural and spiritual. Because of the interpersonal nature of their work, hospitality workers need to consider the guests they serve. In other words, hospitality is a single phenomenon that simultaneously involves three components—employers, employees and guests—in different and interacting ways.

Welcoming strangers as our brothers and sisters, understanding that they need us, and always regarding them as worthy of our help are concepts that should fascinate and encourage those in the hospitality field. This approach to service lightens the cares and overcomes the thousand difficulties that can intervene when you're coming into constant contact with strangers. It also adds greatly to job satisfaction. Unfortunately, strangers can often be hostile to the host's principles of contact, even when they're at their best. In these cases, the inspiration of the Gospel will help overcome any embarrassing situation and even educate the guest.

The hospitality professional's response to the Gospel call enhances, uplifts and augments the act of being hospitable and of receiving tourists as guests. It is no longer a job, but a vocation from God. Furthermore, the search for spiritual peace and authenticity comes in the reciprocal interplay of influences, intentions and actions between the hospitality professional and the guest. It emphasizes the privileged position given to those who are professionally engaged in providing hospitality. The Christian hospitality professionals are called to perform their duties scrupulously and promptly in each circumstance and in each relation. In this way, others may derive satisfaction from them, and receive the beneficial influences wished for by the Christian call to be a loving person. All work understood in this fashion is worthy of the reward promised by Christ at the final judgment, when the just will receive their eternal job satisfaction based on how they served those in need.

ORDER IN THE HOTEL SETTING

Although the vast majority of what might be considered "deviant" activity is handled informally, most of the sociological literature dealing with the regulation of deviance has a formal control agency emphasis. Thus, while Emerson and Messinger explicitly discuss the "micro-politics of trouble," only a small number of materials, focus on the informal regulation of deviance.

This paper examines the work world of hotel security people, particularly as this pertains to the "informal regulation" of deviance. It sheds light on routine operations of "control agencies," as well as depicting the management of order by those whose authority is less well defined than that of police officers and court officials. Following statements on the setting and dimensions central to "keeping order in the hotel setting," the emphasis shifts to "doing security work" as this pertains to: learning about trouble; keeping the premises clear of undesirables; responding to trouble in the bar; handling trouble in the rooms; dealing with theft; and deciding to call the police.

In examining these elements, the focus is largely on "activities" and differs from themes developed in the literature on security work and private police. The existing literature concentrates on the control and prevention of crime. Highly prescriptive, it focuses on equipment, policing styles, organizational policies, and the like.

THE SETTING

The data for this paper was gathered from interviews with 28 security officers from 7 chain and 3 independent hotels in two Eastern Canadian cities. This material was supplemented by related discussions with desk staff and management in these and other hotels as well as through Styllianoss' employment as a desk clerk over a five year plus period. Typically only the larger hotels employ security officers. In smaller hotels, troublesome incidents are handled by the desk clerk or other staff.

The hotels studied are well known for providing hospitality, a wide range of facilities, and safe family accommodations. All the chain hotels contain at least one bar featuring live entertainment, as well as dining rooms, coffee shops, swimming pools, banquet rooms, and such. Further, while some are interconnected with major shopping malls, all cater to the convention trade. The independent hotels, as a group, have fewer facilities, and are less likely to cater to large conventions. The lobby areas are large, providing plush, pleasant lounging facilities. In addition to security officers, all employ bellhops to assist guests with their luggage and other circumstances.

While some contacts with hotel security people were established in an attempt to place in context an earlier and larger study of the hotel community, the security people were generally approached at their work places, as strangers. Our familiarity with hotel routines facilitated acceptance, but in contrast to situations in which one is previously accepted as an insider, we have not been able to gain access to this milieu as fully as we would like.

Of the officers interviewed, five have had some formal post-secondary school education, but most have either completed or are a few grades short of completing high school. Although some had no prior experience related to hotel security work, others have had backgrounds in the police, the military, or other security work. For some, the job was viewed as "the major career;" for some, it was a second position; and for others, it was a job of indefinite future or one to be kept until "something better turns up," possibly in the area of law enforcement. In short, while the hotels seem more selective in their hiring practices than employers in some other areas of security work, the people doing hotel security work are apt to reflect a wide range of experiences and backgrounds.

In discussing hotel security work, it is useful to distinguish workers along two dimensions. First, while most of the hotels we studied employed their own security staff exclusively, some also supplemented their ranks with personnel leased to them by security firms. Although only one of the hotels examined relied exclusively on outside security people, this practice has certain legal and economic advantages and may be more widespread elsewhere. Typically, however, when outsiders are brought in, they are assigned the more minor and less problematic areas of hotel security. Secondly, within hotels, distinctions are often made between "uniformed" and "plainclothes" security, with the latter usually reflecting higher levels of responsibility in hotels in which both are employed. The following extracts denote concerns associated with employing "inside" as opposed to "leased" security people:

The hotels, when they're advertising for help, they want someone with experience, so they'll get ex-policemen, ex-firemen, ex-private investigators, people with security work in other areas. They don't want to wait while people are learning the job. You have to have some knowledge of your basic laws, and the laws pertaining to the liquor control board. And you have to know, with your hookers or drunks, for example, what you can charge them with, like creating a disturbance. A lot of these things are gained by your prior experience and knowledge. You're there to prevent mainly, but if there is a problem, you're there to solve it. Security companies, they'll take people off the street. They tell them where to go and where to patrol, maybe what to look for and such. The security company may give them some instructions, but these people just wouldn't have that much in the way of experience.

You wouldn't consider these people for any sort of management position in hotel security. There you would want someone who's got some police background, something like that, or a long time experience in security work. The hotel will sometimes hire a security company, but usually, they like to be able to control this area themselves, where they can pick the kind of people they want, in experience and other skills. The hotel is not so responsible for the actions of rented security, but they figure their own people are more responsible to the hotel. They need someone who will know what to do when the trouble arises, and that is where you're needed, and when you have to make the right decisions. You might only get one chance. Also, if you have your own security there, they get to know all the staff, and they get to know all the nooks and crannies of the hotel. You get to know the guests, who are staying regularly, and so on, where with a security company, there's too much changeover of personnel. So the hotel would prefer to have their own people. In the hotel business, there are just certain things to learn before you can do an effective job in the hotel. It's different than doing a patrol in a factory.

They hire us out to the hotel. The hotel has its own security that are not in uniform. They do the undercover patrolling, the real security work around here. I do some too, but mostly little things, like report on damage, like broken locks, let tradesmen in the rooms, transfer sets of keys, check up on employee punch cards, check up on false alarms, things like that during my shift. There are a lot of public relations involved in that too, because I'm the first person they come to when something goes wrong.

Central Concerns

The particular policies defining staff duties in hotels will vary somewhat, as will the moral orientations of the supervisors, and the nature of the clientele and "intruders" encountered, but from the security officer's perspective, keeping order is characterized by two major elements. The first and most apparent responsibility is that of "protecting hotel guests, staff, and property from theft or other abuse." Secondly, the security officer is expected to operate in a "public relations capacity;" to help make the guests' stays pleasant and to maintain a respectable image of the hotel. While much more important than might first seem, this second concern has profound implications for the management of trouble. It places limitations on the ways in which security officers may respond to troublesome persons, suggesting that deviance be handled informally and as unobtrusively as possible. Security officers vary somewhat in their perceptions of the relative importance of these two concerns of protection and public relations, but they are fundamental to hotel security work:

The security guard is to see to the well being of the guests and to see that the rules of the hotel are obeyed and carried out, to make sure everything goes on without incident. . . . Basically, its public relations, I see myself as public relations more than anything else. The effectiveness, or how good a security guard am I, all depends on how I can relate to people and come across to people in a positive sort of way. If you can give them the impression that things are under control and everything is smooth, where the people are relaxed and having a nicer time here because of this, then you're a tremendous asset to that hotel. . . . That's our philosophy here, to make the public relations thing very important in doing your job.

While some work on the police suggests that the police also operate more in a public relations capacity than might be commonly supposed, security guards see sharp differences in their relative concerns about "enforcing the law" and their legal power to detain and arrest offenders:

Security work is not police work, we're not really involved in the apprehension of criminals. What we do is maintain order in the hotel, protecting the hotel property, and just keeping things quiet. We also don't have the same powers as the police do in terms of dealing with troublesome people. We don't have the authority to get very physical with the people. You have to be very careful with the people because if you get too rough with them, they could take you to court with assault charges. Now, maybe they wouldn't hold up in court, but just the same, it would create problems for you because you just don't have the same rights as policemen do.

We're not out to arrest anybody or put them behind bars. Our job is to protect the hotel property and to make sure nothing happens to the patrons, especially where the hotel could be held accountable for that. But putting people behind bars, or catching criminals, that's police business and not really our job. So, we'll be patrolling the floors occasionally and checking the doors as we make our rounds, walking slowly down the hall, trying to make sure that everything looks right. So, if we see or hear anything unusual, then we'll act on that, but otherwise, most of our business will come from complaints that people call in. Also, we look for other kinds of things, like a wet carpet, where maybe somebody's left the water running in the bathroom, or we pick up some smoke coming out of the doors, or there's some unusual noise, or things of that nature.

As defined in section 449 of the Canadian Criminal Code, security officers have the legal authority to arrest anyone whom they find committing an indictable offense and/or any criminal offense on or in relation to property over which they have authority. This "citizen's arrest" requires that a peace officer be contacted immediately. Sections 25, 26 and 27 of the Code allow security officers to use force in handling law breakers, but they may be subject to providing that this force was "reasonable and necessary" under the circumstances:

We don't have any more legal rights than anyone else. However, we do have the power to make a citizen's arrest, and to use a reasonable amount of force in dealing with people who might be endangering the safety of the other guests or the hotel property. That's pretty well guided by the situation at the time, but you're supposed to try to reason things out with the person who's causing the trouble. You don't want it to get to that point, but if it does, you would like to have witnesses around to testify that the person was causing trouble, where the people wouldn't be on the side of the troublemaker. But you still have to watch yourself in terms of people, because they will sometimes get confused over what happens in those situations. Also we have had cases where the security has gotten into a lot of trouble, sometimes losing their job, where the guest or someone causing the trouble has pressed charges. And we get some wealthy people, or maybe someone who's a lawyer.

If you're going to detain someone for the police, you want to make sure that you have got the evidence on the person. You have to have absolute assurance that it is something that you can detain them on. You use force, only when necessary, and myself, I've never had to use what you would call a violent force of any kind against someone. With this job, there's very little need for violence. It's better to take your time and work things out reasonably with the people causing the trouble.

Although the Criminal Code provides for arrest and the use of force, it should also be noted that in some hotels, lower ranking officers are expressly cautioned against making arrests, using force, or instituting any searches involving guests. In these instances, any matter of "significance" is to be resolved by reporting to the supervisor.

Perceiving hotel security to be disadvantaged relative to the authority of peace officers and more responsible for public relations, security people place considerable emphasis on abilities to handle incidents with a minimum of physical force. Given management's concerns with the hotel's image and their liability in civil litigation, security guards not able or willing to control troublesome situations nonviolently are apt to find their security careers in major hotels rather short-lived:

The hotel can be held responsible for your actions, so if there is an incident, the management is concerned about how you do things. This is why they like to hire people with experience; they're going to make better decisions, to handle problems in ways not causing any legal hassles for the hotel. We're protected by the hotel, but if we make a miscue, we are going to get hell about it. We're representing the hotel, and we're providing protection for the guests and the staff, but still they're concerned about how you do your job. So say you're dealing with someone who is yelling and cussing you out, you can't just go in there and start punching. You have to try to handle it in other ways. You've got to keep your cool in those situations.

You have to watch yourself in terms of getting into fights. Like, this one friend of mine, he used to almost enjoy getting into fights and when I've seen it, he's pretty well the first person to get in there, throwing punches and what not. This one time he got taken to court, got charged with assault. The hotel defended him, though I guess, in part, they were defending themselves as well. But they supported his lawyer and so forth. Then when the case was over, we won the case, but he was fired, and he hasn't been able to get a job as a security man since. That's sort of a bad mark against him, a lot of hotels, don't want to get involved with someone who might be creating problems for them. At the same time, it's not difficult to get into fights because you're there trying to settle things, and afterwards it might look a little silly, but at the time you're doing everything you can to take care of things. So you can get into trouble just trying to do your job.

An emphasis on the diplomatic resolution of trouble should not be taken, however, as an indication that force or force potential is not valued in this setting. Thus, in addition to their social skills, people being hired and retained as security officers are also assessed relative to their ability to "command respect" and "handle situations that seem to be getting physically out of control:"

A very important thing about being a security officer is being able to handle the situation physically if that's what it takes. It's not that you want to fight with people, or punch them out. It's just that you have to be able to command respect from the situation and take control.

Size is important. Say with me, a larger person asking someone to move along or trying to break up some argument will command more authority than a small person. . . . Also, if you're older, more middle-aged as opposed to being twenty or so, that'll help too, because some of the people wouldn't be so likely to listen to a younger person when he's telling them to straighten out. Somebody who can handle things all around, that's what they look for.

Doing Security Work

Beginning with an examination of the ways in which security people learn about trouble in the hotel setting, we then consider the ways in which they manage trouble in the lobbies, bars, hallways and rooms. In these settings, the concerns are providing protection and doing public relations work; also there is some overlap of actors and incidents. However, each of these "locations" is apt to be characterized by somewhat "different kinds of trouble" and involves "different categories and combinations of actors." In examining these particular settings, one obtains greater insight into the complexities and work routines experienced by security officers.

Learning About Trouble

The kinds of trouble, it's so unpredictable. You know that something is going to happen, but otherwise, it does no good to guess. Like you might get a lot of theft one week and nothing the next. There's no set pattern for trouble. Or you might go for a few weeks and have no problems with the hookers, and then run into a number of them. The same thing with the drunks, and the complaints about noise. It's different than an office job in that way, more unpredictable.

Consistent with the experiences of the city police, much of the trouble known to the hotel security reflects reports from other sources. Thus, in addition to routine patrol discoveries, security people are also informed of trouble by guests and other staff people. It should also be noted, that not all trouble encountered has a "criminal quality" to it and that things are not always what they appear to be. Consequently, while one may learn about trouble in a variety of ways, one does not know the form in which it is apt to be next encountered or to what extent "innocent appearing activities represent trouble" and those "appearing troublesome may be nonthreatening:"

Some of the trouble you learn about through routine surveillance, like people smoking up, where the smell filters out of the room, or things or people looking out of place. . . . My previous police work is a help there too, because you notice things that someone else might miss. The staff, they're some help, but they don't tell you all that much about what is going on. Usually, they just call you if it's something that they figure they can't handle themselves. Then they might call you to help take care of that. Some of the bellhops are pretty good, they'll sometimes alert you to some things. The maids are probably the one's who could help you the most, but they aren't very helpful. A lot of them are foreigners, so they don't understand some things, and they don't seem to really care about the hotel property. A lot of times though, the staff can handle problems themselves, instead of calling you in on a lot of small things. We don't really have enough security people and if you have to stop to do a lot of little things for them, then there's going to be other things we can't attend to.

Usually, if there's a complaint, the guest calls the desk and they put him through to security and then the supervisor or whoever is working the desk will get in touch with you. . . . You get all kinds of things, like people getting stuck in the elevators, parents losing their child who takes off in the corridors or someplace, along with reports of suspicious looking people wandering around. Then you'll get complaints about hookers, where they approached some upstanding citizen, or you'll get complaints about the drunks or the other people pestering or offending the guests. All kinds of things. The vagrants, you'll sometimes find them trying to spend the night in the washroom or some of the storage areas.

In a manner further paralleling city police, one finds security officers reporting more fully on the manner in which they handle incidents coming to their attention through the office than those they discover on their own. Procedures vary by hotel, and within any hotel one will find some variation in the extent to which individual officers are concerned with reporting. It is apparent, however, that assessments of security reflect supervisor impressions of officers' effectiveness in learning about and handling trouble. Recognizing that their careers can be dramatically affected by these assessments, one finds security officers endeavoring to "portray competence:"

You can also get into problems if too many things start happening while you're on shift. The management here, they're very paranoid about theft. When something gets ripped off, they go with the attitude that everyone was in on it, that it was prearranged. You pretty well have to demonstrate that you were somewhere else at the time. That you had no knowledge of it. If a lot of thefts occur on your shift, then they become very suspicious of you and they will definitely check up on you and maybe dismiss you for being incompetent or something like that, even if they can't really prove anything. But they will check up on you, to make sure you're not in on the take. With the head of security, you don't let them know what's actually going on. Like sometimes you'll tell them that you had to deal with some trouble, like some noisy guests or a drunk, but that you handled it with no problem. This is something that most guards do, to leave a favourable impression on the supervisor. You really try to please that guy, the boss. If he thinks you are doing a good job, you're doing okay.

Keeping the Lobby Clear

As quasi-public places, the lobby areas of hotels can represent difficult places in which to keep order. Thus, in addition to the possible confusions which may result from guests checking in and out of the hotel with baggage and other belongings, security officers frequently have unwelcome entrants such as drunks and vagrants, hookers and hustlers, and other "loiterers:" Here we have a very large lobby area and a shopping area of the lobby is leading to the hotel.

So you have all kinds of people coming and going and you really don't know who's a registered guest and who isn't. It just means that if you're the security in the area, then you really dont' have a good idea of what is going on. Also the lobby is so big that you can't see what's happening from one end to the other end and you can easily miss things. Being in the downtown area, we get a lot of riff-raff coming in and that's a problem, because a lot of these people will know that there's a convention or something going on. So you maybe have hookers trying to do business out of the place, or people panhandling, or drunks coming in and maybe sitting down, catching a little sleep or whatever.

You'll even get some of these street musicians coming in and trying to set up, trying to pick up a little collection for themselves. You also have some of the younger kids coming in, trying to steal baggage and purses and that sort of thing. It's the kind of place where it's easy to lose somebody because the place is large, and it's often crowded and you might spot somebody and then you turn around and you don't see them anymore. It's easy for them to sort of get lost in the crowd. You'll also have some people who'll be hanging out in the lobby and they maybe just want to be around people all day. It's a place where they will come and sometimes hang out and so these are the different kinds of things you have to watch for. If you're not staying there and you're not spending money there, then you really don't have any business being there.

So we try to clear the other people out, but as I say, it's big and you have that sort of problem. Hotel location will to some extent affect the categories of "undesirables" security people encounter, and hotel size and architecture will have some effect on the ability of security people to learn of their presence. In general, however, security officers attempt to be firm, expedient, and polite in removing unwanted persons from the premises:

Drunks, mooches, people who are bumming money, with them it's just policy that as soon as you seem them coming in the door, you just turn them away. You don't offer them any explanation, you just tell them, "Sorry, you can't come in here." And if you catch them as they're coming in the revolving door, you might just push them back in the door and get them out that way, right around the circle. You try to take care of them as quickly as possible. That way you don't really have any scenes out there, in the lobby, where people might be registering. After a while you get to know who these people are, so it's quite easy to spot them.

And they kind of size you up, in terms of how far they can push you, so as soon as I seem them, I'll just try to get them out, maybe take them by the arm, "I'm sorry, there's nothing here for you." And here, because of the area we're in, we get quite a few coming by, but I've only had one incident with a drunk, where I've had to get physical, so this seems to work. But you have to watch them, because once they get comfortable here, they start to get a little more confident and more difficult to get rid of. And they might get sick there or mess the place up, where the place gets to stinking or something, so you don't want that. We don't have a lot of trouble with the kids or the drunks here. There's only one major entrance to the lobby, and the lobby's not all that large, so we can quickly spot people as they come in. So that cuts down on people sneaking into the hotel. So that's an advantage. Also, most people who come in that way, we take immediate action, no hesitation. That way, you don't really give them any chance to develop something into a scene. Usually, I just go over and grab them firmly by the arm. Not to where you're pushing them or anything, but escort them out the door, telling them not to bother coming back. . . . You have to be aggressive with them, but not abusive, where you start hitting people. That can create problems for you. When you're throwing out drunks, there's more to it than you might think, because you want to be firm, but not to the point where he's getting upset and wanting to fight with you. Sometimes you'll see some of the guards hitting the drunks, but that's bad for the hotel's image.

Insofar as people appearing to be more respectable are more apt to be thought to have legitimate business at the hotel, most persons ushered out of the hotel are those appearing like vagrants, vandals, hustlers, and the like. In these instances, hotel security people are less concerned about possible reprisals arising from abrupt treatment of the "intruders." In addition to maintaining images of respectability, and providing guest protection, security people tend to be concerned that potential "loiterers" not remove or destroy hotel property:

You might come across some vandalism while on patrol, but usually, it'll be something you just see the results of. Then you report it, and they'll get it fixed up, or cleaned up, depending on what it is. Like usually, there's no one around to prosecute for the damages. There, the big thing is prevention. Watching out for the young punks and such, and keeping them off the premises before they have a chance to mess things up.

Dealing with the Working Girls

Some women thought to be involved in prostitution may be dealt with as "common riff-raff" in the lobby but the other "working girls" present security people with somewhat unique problems. Not only are they often less discernable than other undesirables, but they are apt to be found in a variety of hotel locations and with varying degrees of "legitimacy." Security people generally try to discourage hookers from using the hotel, but they seem most effective in doing so when the women solicit more extensively in the lobby and when they make more extensive use of the rooms:

You definitely do not want any hookers working out of the place, especially the ones that are very obvious. But then you get the higher class hookers, like there's three or four of them, everybody in the hotel knows them. They're only in the hotel once or twice a week, and then they only take out one date and they don't return to the hotel that night, so they're not much of a problem. We can tolerate something like that, but the other thing, you just can't have that. It's in every hotel, some more than others, and the large hotels will have some element of it, with the travelling businessmen. It's just a matter of keeping it under control.

If the guy rents the room, he's entitled to bring his guests with him and so you can't refuse them that way. And as far as I'm concerned, there's no reason to do anything as long as they are not causing any problems. What we're looking for, more, is where the girls are in the lobby, soliciting people that way. Bothering and maybe offending some people that way.

Suspecting that a woman is "working," most security guards attempt to be polite in asking her to leave. When such "gentle" measures fail, security guards are apt to become more aggressive. However, given the gender of these "undesirables," security people are especially reluctant to use physical force in dealing with them, even when they become particularly troublesome:

Some of them, you can explain it to them a hundred times, "Don't come back!", "Don't come back, or we'll call the police!", but they just keep coming back. That creates an awkward position as far as I'm concerned and I get pretty upset with them. There's a group of three or four that just keep coming back. You try to handle these things yourself, because you don't want to have to call the police over something like that. But these girls are aware of this and they kind of take advantage of the situation, so I'll have to work out something there, and maybe I'll just have to resort to calling the police. But with the others, they're more cooperative and they'll leave on their own account, they really don't want any trouble. And, if you had to have any hookers, they would be the kind you would like to have around. They wouldn't give as many problems as the others. Some of them are very rude and belligerent. You also learn who the hookers are, when you're just starting out, from the other security people. They'll point them out to you. And after a while, you can sort of sense who's a hooker and who isn't. Just by kind of watching them and seeing who they're with, the other girls, things like that. Then once you figure out what they're doing, you just go up to them and tell them that they have to leave.

A few women discreetly working within a hotel can be overlooked, but even here, security people tend to be concerned about other activities they associate with prostitution. A place beginning to acquire a reputation as a "hooker hotel" may suggest other kinds of trouble: The hookers are one thing you cannot let out of control because what you might find is that one girl might come and start doing some business, maybe inconspicuously, and then she tells her friends, and then you have more of them coming around. Also the people who hang around hookers, like the pimps and the pushers, once they find out about the place, well they're going to start coming around and sort of making a hangout here. Before you know it, you've got all these undesirables in the hotel.

Brewing in the Bar

In contrast to some of the rougher bars, those located in hotels employing security officers are generally among the more peaceful. While this may partially reflect the general level of respectability associated with larger hotels, it may also denote the efforts of security guards to keep "undesirables" off the premises before they enter hotel bars. Although not frequent sources of trouble for the security people, bar calls represent some of their more unpredictable and risky assignments: There's no bouncers at the bar here, and usually the male staff, the bartender or the waiters will take care of things themselves. But if someone gets especially belligerent or things get more widespread, we'll get called in. We don't have that many fights here, but we do get them now and then. Usually, when we get there, things will be going full tilt, so I get very apprehensive whenever I do get a call from the bar, because you know that the first line of defence, which would be the waiter or waitress, has broken down, and you expect a more major problem. It's not always the staff and the patrons, but sometimes, the patrons will start things themselves and then you may get called to break up something they've already started, and then, if there's other person there, you really don't know what to expect. But if things get really rough, then some of the other staff might try to help you out.

It'll depend on how the bar staff handles things too, so if they're a little more cool or can relate to people better, they won't need to call you as often. They can take care of a lot of situations themselves. But sometimes, the waitresses or the girls working the desk, they won't say anything to the people, they'll just call security and say they're having trouble. So you come running in, ready to jump into action, and it turns out to be some minor thing they could have easily taken care of themselves.

As with guests renting rooms, bar patrons subsequently having problems navigating in the lobbies or creating other disturbances tend to be treated more considerately than those initially defined as "undesirables." However, the most tolerance for bar patrons is accorded to "regulars" and people registered in the hotel. Their disruptive behaviour remains the object of control, but they are apt to be treated in a more courteous manner.

Handling Trouble in the Room

Much like calls from the bar, those pertaining to trouble in the room have an ambiguous and ominous nature. And, given the privacy afforded occupants behind the doors, they can be even more disconcerting. Consequently, as with police answering "domestics" 25 security people responding to calls concerning "noise" and "disturbances" tend to view these with some apprehension:

If anything scares me about security work, it's the room calls. You have no idea what to expect. Its unknown, the other side of the door and you can't really see what you're going to face. When that door opens, you've got to be ready for anything!

One of the bellboys said he heard screaming coming from one of the rooms. I was on patrol then so I told him to call the police and I rushed to the room. I heard a woman's scream, so I charged in with the pass key. When I got in there, there was a woman screaming, but there was no one else in the room. She was screaming about a hornet being in the room. She looked like she was going to die or something. She was too scared to even get out of the room. I was upset at the time, getting all worked up over nothing and having to explain this to the police.

Trouble in the rooms involves the guests in some respect, but the knowledge that trouble is taking place in these locations is of limited value in predicting its form. Thus, while noise, drug use, theft, and vandalism are among the more common sources of trouble, guests may also call security in matters pertaining to physical violence, accidents, sicknesses, and misplaced items.

Being Noisy

One of the most common complaints received in the hotel setting pertains to the noise "other guests" are making. While noise, in itself, may seem somewhat inconsequential, it is important to recognize that having paid for a room guests may become "righteously indignant" over what they perceive as a violation of their trust. Thus, while hotel security may be unaware of, or unconcerned about, existing noise levels, an irrate call to the desk makes them suddenly attentive to the significance of noise. However, insofar as the disturbance may emanate from a variety of causes the simple information that the guests in room 422 are making too much noise is of little assistance in preparing the officer for his duty: Usually when we have a complaint, we ask the people to keep the noise down. Usually we find people are pretty cooperative in that regard, but you never know how things are going to turn out. The other day we got this call in the next room that these people are yelling, screaming, fighting and everything. The room was in a mess and the mirror was broken and the table was turned over.

The woman was bleeding rather badly and so I went over and I tried to sort of get the man over to one side and try to calm him down. This woman took exception to that and she started coming after me. So now she's like punching me in the back and yelling, "Leave my husband alone!". "Don't hurt him!", and this sort of thing. These domestic scenes they're really awkward to deal with.

Not all noise in the vicinity of guest rooms takes place within the rooms. Some of it "spills over" into the adjacent hallways: Another thing you have to worry about, that you get calls about, is people having parties in the hallway. This is especially a problem here, since we get a lot of tourists and conventioneers coming in, in groups, and they will have parties as much as they can. But their rooms are often too small for all that they want to do, so sometimes you get them running from one room to another and partying in the hallways. Then you get the other people who are not in on the party, but are on the same floor.

They'll complain about the noise. Also you get some people who'll be drunk, going around knocking on people's doors and bothering them. Like, maybe they've heard that there's a good looking girl staying in that room or something, so they'll get a bit out of hand that way. So then you get called up to take care of that. But a lot of times, people will call up for very little reason, and you find that you get a lot of false alarms. Some people are scared of every little noise that happens. They figure that someone is trying to break in and rob them or something like that.

Drug Use

Many of the noise-related problems security agents encounter involve drinking and/or drug use. However, to the extent drug use is illegal, it presents a special problem for security people. It is also in this area that one encounters some of the most varied responses to guests. While some security guards do not consider the use of drugs a problem, others express grave concern about it, perceiving it as a serious threat to the hotel's well-being.

Those considering the use of drugs to be nonproblematic assume that the absence of guest complaints makes security intervention unnecessary. However, other hotel securities maintain that drug use is directly related to violent behaviour, and is damaging to the hotel's reputation. Thus, when encountering drug use, security guards' responses range from non-intervention to calling the police for forceful removal.

As with other disturbances, it is also apparent that the treatment offenders eventually receive often reflects their willingness to recognize the legitimacy of the security officers' requests for cooperation. This parallels police officers' concerns for respect. It also suggests that although deference may not be particularly effective in avoiding negative sanctions, a lack of "appropriate respect" may be viewed as adequate justification for more fully invoking one's legal powers:

I don't really care if someone is doing dope myself. I have the odd take myself, so how can I tell someone else not to do it. As long as it doesn't bother anyone and nobody complains, then I let it pass. Most of the problems with the drug users are from people who might be taking the drugs and getting too loud. Or else, we have people doing joints in the hall. Some of the other patrons get upset about that and they won't come back. So we try and watch for that as much as we can.

If you don't, you'll be attracting the wrong kind of people, people you really don't want, so we'll try to watch for that. Like if somebody is using it in their own room, well we're not so concerned about that, like we're not there to arrest anybody, but if it's too obvious and people are complaining, or if you're walking down the hall and you notice the smell coming from a room, well, you have to ask the people to stop it. If they don't, then you have to get them out of there. And you have always this thing where you can call the police if you have to. If they get snotty with you, you just call the police and have them arrested.

Damaging Rooms

Patrolling the hallways and the lobby area may discourage persons from disfiguring or destroying some hotel property, but vandalism is especially difficult to prevent when the offenders are registered guests "messing up" their own rooms. As property damage is sometimes encountered in connection with investigations into noise, drinking, or drug complaints, security people tend to be more alert to and concerned with the possibilities of vandalism in these situations:

Sometimes we have a bit of a problem with some younger people. They'll maybe get high on drugs and maybe smash things or fall over the furniture or break lamps, this kind of thing, or making a lot of noise. That can create problems for us as well. We've had particular problems from, let's say, people in rock bands. Some of them just really mess the place up. There's not much you can do about vandalism in the room. That is the desk clerk's responsibility mostly, you know, not letting in any of these young punks.

If there's a lot of noise and there is a complaint, then we might catch someone in the act, but that's the only way to stop it. Like I said the desk clerk is the one who can prevent a lot of this. When you see some of these people in the room, they look like the type that would wreck the room. The desk clerk had no business even renting to these people. That's where you can prevent the vandalism in the rooms as far as I'm concerned.

Dealing with Theft

In addition to theft involving "loiterers" and other "undesirables", security people also find themselves concerned with guests, employees, and burglars. Although security agents cannot pinpoint the source of each loss, these represent their major categories of suspects.

The Guests

Theft of hotel property by guests is a common occurrence, but one that gains significance mainly in terms of the collective value of the items taken. Thus, while guests often "defray" the costs of their stay by collecting small items, more ambitious thefts tend to be infrequent. Further, given the privacy guests are afforded and a strong reluctance on the part of security people to risk offending guests by searching their luggage or otherwise confronting them, security officers tend to overlook suspected theft:

You have to be very careful how you approach them and how you search them. . . . It would be good for the hotel to make spot checks on guests as they're leaving, and I think that way you'd be able to recover quite a bit of the hotel's property, but you really can't do that because it would be a violation of the privacy of the people, and the guests would not like that! And most of the people who come to the Fairly, they are going to be spending a fair bit of money and some of them might be staying for a week or two, and they're at the bar and in the restaurant. They might be spending 700 or $1,000 over that time, so you have to be careful with people because you really don't want to lose their business.

You want to make sure that you have the goods on them before you go checking through their bags when they're leaving. Especially if they have spent a fair amount of money in the hotel, and even then, if you come up with a towel or two, they'll say. "Well look, I've spent so much money here. I thought I might have a little souvenir of the place." So there, you want to get someone who's trying to walk away with a great deal, not a couple of little items, where it's more of an embarrassment than anything else.

A less frequent, but not inconsequential, form of guest theft involves people "skipping out on room rental charges." This is viewed very seriously by hotel personnel, but unless security people catch someone in the act of absconding without paying his bills, or are called to deal with someone who refuses to pay his bill, this matter is likely to be the responsibility of the credit department.

Staff Involvements

Despite the total cost of theft involving guests, theft involving employees is of greater concern to security officers. Employee theft is seen as a serious, extensive, and continuous problem: You aren't all that concerned about theft by the guests, because sure, they can steal small things like ashtrays, glasses, towels, but the staff, they know their way around the place a lot better, all the exits, so it's a little easier for them to walk off with something from the hotel, and they may have some idea of your routines as well.

This place is so big and there's so many employees and there are so many things that aren't nailed down, that it seems that just about everybody is taking something. We have a lot of things, tables, chairs, television sets. Dishes, laundry, a lot of things could be taken. In fact, this one guy was a bartender here. We found out through a friend, who knew one of his friends that all the furniture in the bartender's place was from the hotel. He had completely furnished his apartment with hotel material. That included everything, like desks and tables, a kitchen table, chesterfield, t.v., bedsheets, cutlery, dishes, everything. You find that employee theft, it's a very common thing. It's something that you really can't stop. All you can try to do is slow it down as much as you can and try to prevent the big thefts from happening.

In addition to "straight forward" thefts of dishes, sheets, bottles of liquor, beef roasts, and the like, employees may also steal by "mismanaging" guests' orders, either by pocketing money received for orders or by working out exchanges with other employees:

We'll have people, let's say room service people who become good friends with the cooks, whatever. They'll get their meals free, and they might be taking things home for the family as well. Like, if there's maybe a room order, then what the cook might do is throw a few extra things, or maybe another plate for the room service people, so that they then can get their meal over a couple of different orders. Sometimes the customer will wonder why they didn't get a very big portion, and sometimes it'll be that someone has made another meal out of some of his dinner. While somewhat concerned about these other forms of theft, security people concentrate their efforts on the more visible types of employee theft. Hotels will occasionally bring in undercover people in an attempt to detect theft among staff, but tend to rely most heavily on routine surveillance, spot checks, management reports, and tips from other staff people:

We have the right to periodically check their bags as they're leaving, to see if they're walking off with anything. They have a greater opportunity than anyone else to steal from the place, so when you're checking bags, they're the ones you really look out for. . . . A lot of them think that it's okay to take things from the hotel, that it's not a serious thing, so every now and then, when you find someone stealing, you try to make an example of that person, to deter others from stealing things from the hotel.

Another way of deterring the staff from stealing is to go and make sure that you are highly visible to them. With the guests, you don't want to be too obvious with your security, except when you have your suspicions with somebody, where you might directly confront people to discourage from doing something in your hotel. With the staff you do get some resistance from them when you're around more often, looking over their shoulders, or questioning them. especially with the staff that have been there longer because they might had something going for years, and they don't want you interfering with that.

You get to know the employees and you learn or you just kind of sense who's up to no good, again that's the police background coming into play. You also hear through the grapevine who's stealing and taking this and that. Like if you see a guy who's a cook's helper and he's coming in with new clothes and rings, you wonder, "How is he getting these goods at his salary?" Then you watch him, check upon him, and make sure he isn't making it on the side at the hotel's expense. Even those security officers most willing to overlook employee theft are concerned that they not jeopardize their own position as a result: All I want from them, is that if you're doing something, just don't flash it in front of me. If it's kept quiet, and it's not going on in front of me, I'll just kind of let it pass. But if I do catch somebody, then I've got my job to do and I'll report it. You have to show that you are there to do a job and that you can do the job.

Once the security officer reports an instance of employee theft to his superiors, the subsequent future of the employee is largely out of his hands. If the evidence is stronger, or if the hotel suspects that the person implicated may be linked to a larger or persistent loss, the employee may be dismissed, and prosecuted. If it seems less serious, the matter may simply go on record or the employee may be warned, as the hotel waits until the next "suspicious incident" involving the employee emerges. The occasion may also be used as a means to question the employee about other thefts, and it may also be used as a basis for requesting a search of the employee's premises. Unless the theft is fairly extensive, however, or the employee becomes more belligerent towards the hotel officials, the most serious result is likely to be dismissal. Basically, the hotels are concerned about minimizing their losses by retrieving stolen goods and/or deterring subsequent theft. They are not eager to prosecute offenders, viewing this as an event which does little for the reputation of the hotel, and which offers a poor return for any time-cost units involved.

Even when the evidence is strong, and the theft significant, "justified" dismissals may be open to negotiation, with hotel unions playing an especially noteworthy role in these "reconciliations:"

If it's a case of theft, the nonunion people are more likely to be in trouble than the union members. The security guards will often watch a new person more closely than someone who's been there longer, because they know it will be harder to get rid of someone that's part of the union, and you don't get union protection until you've been there some time . . . . Like this one chef, we found him stealing a case of dishes. They were worth quite a little bit of money. But the union fought the case, claiming that he had mental duress, family problems, and he had a lot of expenses at that time. And, they argued that he had a spotless record before that, that he was prompt and a good worker, and the other workers stuck up for him on that. The guy was reinstated.

Concerns with employee theft create special problems for security people. Security people are "staff", and have an affinity with the other staff in terms of the expectations of serving guests and management. However, as "in-house policemen" they experience considerable distancing:

Sometimes you are really in a bind. You have to keep watch over other employees, but if you do, then the other employees think you is a rat. I guess it goes right back to school, you know, about not being a snitch. Nobody likes a snitch. But you let things go by, then management says you're letting the staff walk all over you.

While security people sense the hostility directed towards them by other hotel staff, and recognize that other employees may attempt to manipulate them, it would be erroneous to assume that all interpersonal relationships between hotel security and other staff are characterized by distance and hostility. Encounters with the guests and the necessity of acting as a "team" helps create a sense of affinity amongst both sets of employees. Thus, relationships between hotel security and other employees vary between close friendship and pronounced animosity, but generally reflect the circumstances specific to that situation.

Hotel Burglars

Hotel security people have little actual contact with hotel burglars. Thus, while some guards report particular incidents involving hotel burglars and most indicate attempts to discourage "suspicious people" from hanging around the hallways directly leading to the guests' rooms, this represents one of the less frequent forms of theft security people encounter:

I know for a fact that I have prevented professional thieves from working in this hotel. . . . This one fellow, I knew he was a thief. He had an attach case and he was looking over everyone in the lobby, and he'd be especially interested in someone who looked well-off. And he'd go over and talk to them, probably to find out where they were staying. Later on, I saw this man on the 11th and 6th floors. When I saw him trying a door on the sixth floor, I went over and said. "Having problems? Let me try your key for you." He said, "I think I forgot my keys inside the room. Could you open it for me?" I said, "Let me see some identification, sir, and I'll check it at the desk, just to make sure you're registered here." "That's alright," he said, "I'll wait for my wife to come." Then I said, "Be more careful, I'm watching you, and I know what you're up to!" A few minutes later, he left the hotel.

With the hotel burglars, the hotel association will sometimes circulate pictures and other information on people believed to be working in your area. But still, you look for suspicious people and there you especially look for burglary tools that they might use to break into somebody's room.

Thus, unless the theft appears more systematic or one room has been extensively "cleaned", given instances of theft are apt to be attributed to the guests and/or staff. Reflecting varying degrees of skill and experience, burglars may employ a variety of techniques, such as cutting master keys, picking locks, using celluloid cards to slip locks, working with hotel employees, and trying unlocked doors: Hotel burglars are more difficult to catch. They'll come dressed like businessmen and you just can't tell them apart. One crew beat the hotel while I was on. That was the only contact I've had with them. They jammed the locks on a few doors and stole some wallets. They didn't wake up anybody.

I patrolled that area while they were there, but they must have been inside at the time. I found out about it when a guest complained that someone had just been in his room that was around 5:30 a.m. We never saw them. They got clean away! But they just took wallets that were the extent of it. Usually, we tell the guests that if they have any valuables, to leave them in the safe at the desk. Otherwise, we're not responsible for anything that might be stolen. We had one case where the maid was leaving the doors on some of the rooms unlocked, and this fellow who was working with her would go into the rooms and get what he wanted. We caught him because he had so many bags that he really couldn't handle them and he came out the front lobby. I asked him if he was checking out, and he kind of stumbled and couldn't tell which room he was in. Eventually he admitted what he was up to and informed on the woman on the housekeeping staff.

To a very large extent, hotel security people endeavor to handle trouble without calling the police. In part, this reflects their concern with the hotel's image, wherein they anticipate that more frequent calls to the police will result in a lowered assessment of the hotel on the part of the guests, the police department, the liquor control board, and so forth. Additionally, having to call for outside assistance may also suggest that the security a person the hotel employs are incompetent and/or do not respect the serious nature of police work:

They're really an important part of my job, because when the chips are down, you can count on them being there to help out. You try not to call them unless you have to. Otherwise, they won't take you seriously when you really need them. Also, if you have to call the police, it might mean that you weren't capable or smart enough to handle the situation yourself. That's one of the things I don't like about the staff. They're perfectly capable of handling a lot of their situations themselves, and I figure the same thing applies to us calling the police. They respect you more if you can handle things better yourself, and only call them when something has gotten fairly serious.

Security people do not call the police for all types of trouble. However, their reservations based on the hotel image, on security competence, and on the seriousness of police work are likely to diminish sharply when an incident threatens to become physically dangerous or legally vulnerable: You don't want to have to call the police any more than you have to. Like if you get to the point of calling the police to clear out drunks and deal with other minor problems, after a while they won't be too eager to come down and you might really need them. If the situation warrants it, where there are weapons involved, or if it looks like things will get violent, then you can't hesitate because a few seconds there can make all the difference. We'll call the police if it involves any further legal action, or for insurance purposes when it's been a larger theft or vandalism. Also, if a guest wants to make a theft official, we'll call the police for them. Then it's more or less between them and the police.

Occupying a position somewhat between that of the police officer and the average citizen, the work world of the hotel security officer provides some valuable insights into the maintenance of social order. While police officers define their roles more in service terms that some might assume, hotel security officers have less legal authority than do the police, and are more apt to have their jobs defined in "public relations" terms. While it is also the case that security officers are less responsible for "upholding the law," they are, nevertheless, responsible for "maintaining order" in the hotel setting. Like the police, security guards have no particular interest in the details of people's lives. However, they are concerned that the activities of those coming under the hotel's "umbrella" not interfere with their responsibilities for keeping order in their jurisdictions, as these are interpreted and conveyed to them by their supervisors.

Faced with the dual responsibilities of providing protection and promoting a favourable hotel image, security officers find themselves placing a heavy emphasis on "public relations" work in the management of trouble. Not all those with whom they deal are seen as having equally legitimate claims to hotel facilities, but security officers are highly dependent on their abilities to indicate and evoke respect in their dealings with others. Their jobs very much represent a continual exercise in "deference and demeanor", as they endeavor to achieve cooperation from those whom they encounter, and yet acknowledge the rights of these others to assert themselves. Thus, while expected to deter, discover, and handle trouble effectively, and with a minimum of subsequent disturbance or complaints, hotel security people are also expected to avoid becoming openly indignant even when encountering resistance and disrespect. In depicting how security guards learn of, and manage, a wide variety of troublesome situations involving many guests, staff, and "intruders," evidence is provided that "deviance" is perspective, problematic, and negotiable, in its resolution as well as in its definition.

It is also apparent that a great deal of the deviance encountered in this "quasi-official" context is handled informally, suggesting that we pay more attention to the informal regulation of deviance. One might profitably examine the activities of other "quasi-control agents," such as teachers, social workers, and attendants in nursing homes, in somewhat similar terms, endeavoring to see how they go about doing "control work" central to their jobs. In the process, we seem likely to learn more about "law and order" as an ongoing and negotiable activity.

It is hoped that this paper also illustrates the value of studying occupations in reference to "activities." While one can learn about occupations by considering organizational structures, the backgrounds of the role occupants, worker attitudes towards their jobs, and the like, it seems especially instructive to focus on "the activities in which people in particular occupations are engaged, and how they go about working things out with the other people their activities involve.

Chapter 4

Importance of Consumer Behaviour

The study of consumers helps firms and organizations improve their marketing strategies by understanding issues such as how.

- The psychology of how consumers think, feel, reason, and select between different alternatives;
- The psychology of how the consumer is influenced by his or her environment;
- The behaviour of consumers while shopping or making other marketing decisions;
- Limitations in consumer knowledge or information processing abilities influence decisions and marketing outcome;
- How consumer motivation and decision strategies differ between products that differ in their level of importance or interest that they entail for the consumer; and
- How marketers can adapt and improve their marketing campaigns and marketing strategies to more effectively reach the consumer.

One "official" definition of consumer behaviour is "The study of individuals, groups, or organizations and the processes they use to select, secure, use, and dispose of products, services, experiences, or ideas to satisfy needs and the impacts that these processes have on the consumer and society."

Although it is not necessary to memorize this definition, it brings up some useful points:

- Behaviour occurs either for the individual, or in the context of a group or an organization.

- Consumer behaviour involves the use and disposal of products as well as the study of how they are purchased. Product use is often of great interest to the marketer, because this may influence how a product is best positioned or how we can encourage increased consumption. Since many environmental problems result from product disposal this is also an area of interest.
- Consumer behaviour involves services and ideas as well as tangible products.
- The impact of consumer behaviour on society is also of relevance. For example, aggressive marketing of high fat foods, or aggressive marketing of easy credit, may have serious repercussions for the national health and economy.

There are four main applications of consumer behaviour:

- The most obvious is for *marketing strategy—i.e.*, for making better marketing campaigns. For example, by understanding that consumers are more receptive to food advertising when they are hungry, we learn to schedule snack advertisements late in the afternoon. By understanding that new products are usually initially adopted by a few consumers and only spread later, and then only gradually, to the rest of the population, we learn that
  - Companies that introduce new products must be well financed so that they can stay afloat until their products become a commercial success and
  - It is important to please initial customers, since they will in turn influence many subsequent customers' brand choices.
- A second application is *public policy*. In the 1980s, Accutane, a near miracle cure for acne, was introduced. Unfortunately, Accutane resulted in severe birth defects if taken by pregnant women. Although physicians were instructed to warn their female patients of this, a number still became pregnant while taking the drug. To get consumers' attention, the Federal Drug Administration took the step of requiring that very graphic pictures of deformed babies be shown on the medicine containers.
- *Social marketing* involves getting ideas across to consumers rather than selling something. Marty Fishbein went on sabbatical to work for the Centres for Disease Control trying

to reduce the incidence of transmission of diseases through illegal drug use. The best solution, obviously, would be if we could get illegal drug users to stop. This, however, was deemed to be infeasible. It was also determined that the practice of sharing needles was too ingrained in the drug culture to be stopped. As a result, using knowledge of consumer attitudes, Dr. Fishbein created a campaign that encouraged the cleaning of needles in bleach before sharing them, a goal that was believed to be more realistic.

- As a final benefit, studying consumer behaviour should make us better consumers. Common sense suggests, for example, that if you buy a 64 liquid ounce bottle of laundry detergent, you should pay less per ounce than if you bought two 32 ounce bottles. In practice, however, you often pay a size *premium* by buying the larger quantity. In other words, in this case, knowing this fact will sensitize you to the need to check the unit cost labels to determine if you are *really* getting a bargain.

There are several units in the market that can be analysed. Our main thrust in this course is the *consumer*. However, as suggested, also need to analyse our own firm's strengths and weaknesses and those of *competing firms*. Suppose, for example, that we make a product aimed at older consumers, a growing segment. A competing firm that targets babies, a shrinking market, is likely to consider repositioning towards our market. To assess a competing firm's potential threat, we need to examine its assets against pressures it faces from the market. Finally, we need to assess conditions. For example, although we may have developed a product that offers great appeal for consumers, a recession may cut demand dramatically.

CONSUMER RESEARCH METHODS

Market research is often needed to ensure that we produce what customers really want and not what we *think* they want. Primary vs. secondary research methods. There are two main approaches to marketing. *Secondary* research involves using information that others have already put together. For example, if you are thinking about starting a business making clothes for tall people. *Primary* research, in contrast, is research that you design and conduct yourself. For example, you may need to find out whether consumers would prefer that your soft drinks be sweater.

Research will often help us *reduce risks* associated with a new product, but it *cannot take the risk away entirely*. It is also important to ascertain whether the research has been complete. For example, Coca Cola did a great deal of research prior to releasing the New Coke, and consumers seemed to prefer the taste. However, consumers were *not* prepared to have this drink replace traditional Coke. Sources of influence on the consumer. The consumer faces numerous sources of influence.

Often, we take cultural influences for granted, but they are significant. An American will usually not bargain with a store owner. This, however, is a common practice in much of the World. Physical factors also influence our behaviour. We are more likely to buy a soft drink when we are thirsty, for example, and food manufacturers have found that it is more effective to advertise their products on the radio in the late afternoon when people are getting hungry.

A person's self-image will also tend to influence what he or she will buy-an upwardly mobile manager may buy a flashy car to project an image of success. Social factors also influence what the consumers buy-often, consumers seek to imitate others whom they admire, and may buy the same brands. The social environment can include both the mainstream culture and a subculture. Thus, sneaker manufacturers are eager to have their products worn by admired athletes. Finally, consumer behaviour is influenced by learning-you try a hamburger and learn that it satisfies your hunger and tastes good, and the next time you are hungry, you may consider another hamburger.

CONSUMER CHOICE AND DECISION-MAKING: PROBLEM

One model of consumer decision making involves several steps. The first one is problem recognition-you realise that something is not as it should be. Perhaps, for example, your car is getting more difficult to start and is not accelerating well. The second step is information search-what are some alternative ways of solving the problem?

You might buy a new car, buy a used car, take your car in for repair, ride the bus, ride a taxi, or ride a skateboard to work. The third step involves evaluation of alternatives. A skateboard is inexpensive, but may be ill-suited for long distances and for rainy days.

Finally, we have the purchase stage, and sometimes a post-purchase stage. In reality, people may go back and forth between the stages. For example, a person may resume alternative identification during while evaluating already known alternatives. Consumer involvement will tend to vary dramatically depending on the type of product. In general, consumer involvement will be higher for products that are very expensive or are highly significant in the consumer's life in some other way.

It is important to consider the consumer's motivation for buying products. To achieve this goal, we can use the Means-End chain, wherein we consider a logical progression of consequences of product use that eventually lead to desired end benefit. Thus, for example, a consumer may see that a car has a large engine, leading to fast acceleration, leading to a feeling of performance, leading to a feeling of power, which ultimately improves the consumer's self-esteem. A handgun may aim bullets with precision, which enables the user to kill an intruder, which means that the intruder will not be able to harm the consumer's family, which achieves the desired end-state of security.

In advertising, it is important to portray the desired end-states. Focusing on the large motor will do less good than portraying a successful person driving the car.

INFORMATION SEARCH AND DECISION-MAKING

Consumers engage in both internal and external information search. Internal search involves the consumer identifying alternatives from his or her memory. For certain low involvement products, it is very important that marketing programmes achieve "top of mind" awareness.

For example, few people will search the Yellow Pages for fast food restaurants; thus, the consumer must be able to retrieve one's restaurant from memory before it will be considered. For high involvement products, consumers are more likely to use an external search.

Before buying a car, for example, the consumer may ask friends' opinions, read reviews in Consumer Reports, consult several web sites, and visit several dealership. Thus, firms that make products that are selected predominantly through external search must invest in having information available to the consumer in need-*e.g.*, through brochures, web sites, or news coverage.

A compensatory decision involves the consumer "trading off" good and bad attributes of a product. For example, a car may have a low price and good gas mileage but slow acceleration. If the price is sufficiently inexpensive and gas efficient, the consumer may then select it over a car with better acceleration that costs more and uses more gas.

Occasionally, a decision will involve a non-compensatory strategy. For example, a parent may reject all soft drinks that contain artificial sweeteners. Here, other good features such as taste and low calories cannot overcome this one "non-negotiable" attribute. The amount of effort a consumer puts into searching depends on a number of factors such as the market, product characteristics, consumer characteristics, and situational characteristics.

Two interesting issues in decisions are:

- *Variety seeking* where consumers seek to try new brands not because these brands are expected to be "better" in any way, but rather because the consumer wants a "change of pace," and
- *"Impulse" purchases*—unplanned buys. This represents a somewhat "fuzzy" group. For example, a shopper may plan to buy vegetables but only decide in the store to actually buy broccoli and corn. Alternatively, a person may buy an item which is currently on sale, or one that he or she remembers that is needed only once inside the store.

A number of factors involve consumer choices. In some cases, consumers will be more *motivated.* For example, one may be more careful choosing a gift for an in-law than when buying the same thing for one self. Some consumers are also more motivated to *comparison shop* for the best prices, while others are more *convenience* oriented. *Personality* impacts decisions. Some like variety more than others, and some are more receptive to stimulation and excitement in trying new stores. *Perception* influences decisions.

Some people, for example, can taste the difference between generic and name brand foods while many cannot. *Selective* perception occurs when a person is paying attention only to information of interest. For example, when looking for a new car, the consumer may pay more attention to car ads than when this is not in the horizon. Some consumers are put off by perceived *risk.*

Thus, many marketers offer a money back guarantee. Consumers will tend to change their behaviour through *learning—e.g.*, they will avoid restaurants they have found to be crowded and will settle on brands that best meet their tastes. Consumers differ in the *values* they hold. As suggested, consider the issue of lifestyle under segmentation.

ORGANIZATIONAL BUYERS

A large portion of the market for goods and services is attributable to *organizational*, as opposed to individual, buyers. In general, organizational buyers, who make buying decisions for their companies for a living, tend to be somewhat more sophisticated than ordinary consumers. However, these organizational buyers are also often more risk averse. There is a risk in going with a new, possibly better supplier whose product is unproven and may turn out to be problematic. Often the fear of running this risk is greater than the potential rewards for getting a better deal. In the old days, it used to be said that "You can't get fired for buying IBM." This attitude is beginning to soften a bit today as firms face increasing pressures to cut costs.

Organizational buyers come in several forms. *Resellers* involve either wholesalers or retailers that buy from one organization and resell to some other entity. For example, large grocery chains sometimes buy products directly from the manufacturer and resell them to end-consumers. Wholesalers may sell to retailers who in turn sell to consumers. *Producers* also buy products from sub-manufacturers to create a finished product.

For example, rather than manufacturing the parts themselves, computer manufacturers often buy hard drives, motherboards, cases, monitors, keyboards, and other components from manufacturers and put them together to create a finished product. *Governments* buy a great deal of things. For example, the military needs an incredible amount of supplies to feed and equip troops. Finally, large *institutions* buy products in huge quantities. For example, UCR probably buys thousands of reams of paper every month.

Organizational buying usually involves more people than individual buying.

Often, many people are involved in making decisions as to:

- Whether to buy,
- What to buy,
- At what quantity, and
- From whom.

An engineer may make a specification as to what is needed, which may be approved by a manager, with the final purchase being made by a purchase specialist who spends all his or her time finding the best deal on the goods that the organization needs.

Often, such long purchase processes can cause long delays. In the government, rules are often especially stringent—*e.g.*, vendors of fruit cake have to meet fourteen pages of specifications put out by the General Services Administration. In many cases, government buyers are also heavily bound to go with the lowest price. Even if it is obvious that a higher priced vendor will offer a superior product, it may be difficult to accept that bid.

CUSTOMER VALUE AND SATISFACTION

CUSTOMER VALUE

As it is used in the business world, customer value is the amount of benefit that a customer will get from a service or product relative to its cost. Some business people explain customer value as "realisation" compared to "sacrifice." Realisation is a formal term for what customers get out of their purchases. Sacrifice is what they pay for the product or service.

Businesses of all sizes use customer value as part of a greater analysis to determine how well they are supplying their customer base. Detailed research might include what customers generally do with the products they receive, or how they use services to increase the value of assets like real estate. Businesses also look at the prices of their products in order to price them competitively.

Businesses that identify the value of their wares to customers might go a step further and consider other similar ideas. In order to generate more thought about customer value, and to reach out to a customer base, a business might promote a customer value proposition. The customer value proposition is basically a promise of benefits from a vendor to customers. We see examples of customer value propositions all the time in advertising. Companies pinpoint the benefits that they believe a customer will realise, and display them in advertising to attract more customers. The question is whether these propositions are made in good faith, or whether they may not be entirely true. When business leaders and others are talking about customer value, it is important that everyone at the table understands that customer value does not relate to the value of customers, but to the value that customers receive from the business. Those who are talking about how valuable customers are to a business might use terms like customer retention, or refer to the customer base as "valued customers," or VIPs. Since customer service is also a critical element for many businesses, it's possible that these two ideas might sometimes get confused.

Along with the basic idea of customer value, other terms help further define that value precisely. Relative performance identifies how the product or service gives customer value relative to what competitors offer. Access cost is something that business analysts add into the mix as an estimated cost of the effort involved in purchase. Value propositions often include these levels of detail to help leaders look at how well a business is serving its intended audience.

SATISFACTION

Customer satisfaction, a business term, is a measure of how products and services supplied by a company meet or surpass customer expectation. It is seen as a key performance indicator within business and is part of the four of a Balanced Scorecard. In a competitive marketplace where businesses compete for customers, customer satisfaction is seen as a key differentiator and increasingly has become a key element of business strategy. There is a substantial body of empirical literature that establishes the benefits of customer satisfaction for firms.

Measuring Customer Satisfaction

Organizations need to retain existing customers while targeting non-customers;. Measuring customer satisfaction provides an indication of how successful the organization is at providing products and/or services to the marketplace. Customer satisfaction is an abstract concept and the actual manifestation of the state of satisfaction will vary from person to person and product/service to product/service. The state of satisfaction depends on a number of both psychological and physical variables which correlate with satisfaction behaviours such as return and recommend rate. The level of satisfaction can also vary depending on other factors the customer, such as other products against which the customer can compare the organization's products.

Work done by Parasuraman, Zeitham and Berry between 1985 and 1988 delivered SERVQUAL which provides the basis for the measurement of customer satisfaction with a service by using the gap between the customer's expectation of performance and their perceived experience of performance. This provides the researcher with a satisfaction "gap" which is semi-quantitative in nature. Cronin and Taylor extended the disconfirmation theory by combining the "gap" described by Parasuraman, Zeithaml and Berry as two different measures into a single measurement of performance relative to expectation.

The usual measures of customer satisfaction involve a survey with a set of statements using a Likert Technique or scale. The customer is asked to evaluate each statement in terms of their perception and expectation of performance of the service being measured.

Improving Customer Satisfaction

Published standards exist to help organizations develop their current levels of customer satisfaction. The International Customer Service Institute has released The International Customer Service Standard. TICSS enables organizations to focus their attention on delivering excellence in the management of customer service, whilst at the same time providing recognition of success through a 3rd Party registration plan. TICSS focuses an organization's attention on delivering increased customer satisfaction by helping the organization through a Service Quality Model.

TICSS Service Quality Model uses the 5 P's - Policy, Processes, People, Premises, Product/Services, as well as performance measurement. The implementation of a customer service standard should lead to higher levels of customer satisfaction, which in turn influences customer retention and customer loyalty.

CONSUMERISM

Consumerism is a social and economic order that is based on the systematic creation and fostering of a desire to purchase goods or services in ever greater amounts. The term is often associated with criticisms of consumption starting with Thorstein Veblen or, more recently by a movement called Enoughism. Veblen's subject of examination, the newly emergent middle class arising at the turn of the twentieth century, comes to full fruition by the end of the twentieth century through the process of globalization.

In economics, consumerism refers to economic policies placing emphasis on consumption. In an abstract sense, it is the belief that the free choice of consumers should dictate the economic structure of a society.

FACTORS INFLUENCING CONSUMER BEHAVIOUR

Consumer purchases are influenced strongly by or there are four factors.

- ❖ Cultural Factor
- ❖ Social Factor
- ❖ Personal Factor
- ❖ Psychological Factor.

CULTURAL FACTOR

Cultural factor divided into three sub factors:

1. Culture
2. Sub Culture
3. Social Class

- ❖ *Culture*:
  - The set of basic values perceptions, wants, and behaviours

learned by a member of society from family and other important institutions. Culture is the most basic cause of a person's wants and behaviour. Every group or society has a culture, and cultural influences on buying behaviour may vary greatly from country to country.

❖ *Sub Culture*:
   - A group of people with shared value systems based on common life experiences and situations.
   - Each culture contains smaller sub cultures a group of people with shared value system based on common life experiences and situations. Sub culture includes nationalities, religions, racial group and geographic regions. Many sub culture make up important market segments and marketers often design products.

❖ *Social Class*:
   - Almost every society has some form of social structure, social classes are society's relatively permanent and ordered divisions whose members share similar values, interests and behaviour.

SOCIAL FACTORS

A consumer's behaviour also is influenced by social factors, such as the:

1. Groups
2. Family
3. Roles and status

❖ *Groups*:
   - Two or more people who interact to accomplish individual or mutual goals.
   - A person's behavious is influenced by many small groups. Groups that have a direct influence and to which a person belongs are called membership groups.
   - Some are primary groups includes family, friends, neighbours and coworkers. Some are secondary groups, which are more formal and have less regular interaction. These includes organizations like religious groups, professional association and trade unions.

❖ *Family*:
- Family members can strongly influence buyer behaviour. The family is the most important consumer buying organization

society and it has been researched extensively. Marketers are interested in the roles, and influence of the husband, wife and children on the purchase of different products and services.

- *Roles and Status*:
  - A person belongs to many groups, family, clubs, organizations.
  - The person's position in each group can be defined in terms of both role and status.
  - For example. M&"X" plays the role of father, in his family he plays the role of husband, in his company, he plays the role of manager, etc. A Role consists of the activities people are expected to perform just as to the persons around them.

PERSONAL FACTORS

- *It includes*:
  - (i) Age and life cycle stage
  - (ii) Occupation
  - (iii) Economic situation
  - (iv) Life Style
  - (v) Personality and self concept.
  - *Age and Life cycle Stage*:
    a. People changes the goods and services they buy over their lifetimes. Tastes in food, clothes, furniture, and recreation are often age related. Buying is also shaped by the stage of the family life cycle.
  - *Occupation*:
    a. A person's occupation affects the goods and services bought. Blue collar workers tend to buy more rugged work clothes, whereas white-collar workers buy more business suits. A Co. can even specialize in making products needed by a given occupational group. Thus, computer software companies will design different products for brand managers, accountants, engineers, lawyers, and doctors.
  - *Economic situation:*
    a. A person's economic situation will affect product choice
  - *Life Style:*
    a. Life Style is a person's Pattern of living, understanding

these forces involves measuring consumer's major AIO dimensions.

b. *i.e.* activities interest and opinions

– *Personality and Self concept*:

a. Each person's distinct personality influence his or her buying behaviour. Personality refers to the unique psychological characteristics that lead to relatively consistent and lasting responses to one's own environment.

PSYCHOLOGICAL FACTORS

❖ It includes these Factors.

(i) Motivation
(ii) Perception
(iii) Learning
(iv) Beliefs and attitudes

❖ *Motivation*:

– Motive a need that is sufficiently pressing to direct the person to seek satisfaction of the need

❖ *Perception*:

– The process by which people select, Organize, and interpret information to form a meaningful picture of the world.

❖ *Learning*:

– Changes in an individuals behaviour arising from experience.

❖ *Beliefs and attitudes:*

– Belief is a descriptive thought that a person holds about something

– Attitude, a Person's consistently favourable or unfavourable evaluations, feelings, and tendencies towards an object or idea

CONSUMER BUYING BEHAVIOUR

Consumer Buying Behaviour the decision processes and acts of final household consumers associated with evaluating, buying, consuming, and discarding products for personal consumption. Consider the purchase an automobile. You generally will not consider different options until some event triggers a need, such as a problem needing potentially expensive repair. Once this need has put you "on the market", you begin to ask your friends for recommendations regarding dealership and car models. After visiting several dealership, you test drive several models and finally decide on a particular model.

After picking up your new car, you have doubts on the way home, wondering if you can afford the monthly payments, but then begin to wonder if instead you should have purchased a more expensive but potentially more reliable model. Over the next five years, the car has several unexpected breakdowns that lead you to want to purchase a different brand, but you have been very happy with the services of the local dealership and decide to again purchase your next car there.

In this particular case, the following generic model of consumer decision making appears to hold:

- Need recognition
- Information search
- Evaluation of alternatives
- Purchase decision
- Postpurchase behaviour

Now consider the purchase of a quart of orange juice. This product when you do your grocery shopping once per week. You have a favourite brand of orange juice and usually do your grocery shopping at the same store. When you buy orange juice, you always go to the same place in the store to pick it up, and never notice what other brands are on the shelf or what are the prices of other brands. How is it that the generic model works differently in this second scenario? Why does it work differently? Why would we generally need the ministrations of a sales person in the sale of a car, but we generally do not need the help of a salesperson in the purchase of orange juice? How can the marketer of orange juice get a consumer like you to exert more effort into information search or to consider alternative products? How is it that the marketer of your brand got you to ignore alternative competing brands? What is the involvement of salespeople in *sales promotions* that might be associated with products such as orange juice? Consumer behaviour researchers are not so interested in studying the validity of the generic model, but are more interested in various factors that influence how such a model might work.

GROUP INFLUENCES ON CONSUMER BEHAVIOUR

Culture

Culture the set of basic values, beliefs, norms, and associated behaviours that are learned by a member of society Note that culture is something that is *learned* and that it has a relatively long lasting effect on the behaviours of an individual. As an example of cultural influences, consider how the salesperson in an appliance store in the U.S. must react to different couples who are considering the purchase of a refrigerator. In some subcultures, the husband will play a dominant role in the purchase decision; in others, the wife will play a more dominant role.

Social Class

Social Class a group of individuals with similar social rank, based on such factors as *occupation*, *education*, and *wealth*

Reference Groups

Reference groups, often temporary, that affect a person's values, attitude, or behaviours:

- *E.g.*, your behaviours around colleagues at work or friends at school are probably different from your behaviours around your parents, no matter your age or stage in the family life cycle. If you were a used car salesperson, how might you respond differently to a nineteen year old prospect accompanied by her boyfriend from one accompanied by two girlfriends?
- Opinion leader a person within a reference group who exerts influence on others because of special skills, knowledge, personality, etc.
  - You might ask the webmaster at work for an opinion about a particular software application. Software manufacturers often give away free beta copies of software to potential opinion leaders with the hope that they will in turn influence many others to purchase the product.

Family

Family a group of people related by blood, marraige, or other socially approved relationship

INTERNAL INFLUENCES ON CONSUMER BEHAVIOUR

Personality

Personality a person's distinguishing psychological characteristics that lead to relatively consistent and lasting responses to stimuli in the environment

We are each unique as individuals, and we each respond differently as consumers. For example, some people are "optimizers" who will keep shopping until they are certain that they have found the best price for a particular item, while other people are "satisficers" who will stop shopping when they believe that they have found something that is "good enough." If you are a salesperson in a retail shoe store, how might you work differently with these two personalities?

Lifestyle and Psychographics

- Lifestyle is a pattern of living expressed through a person's activities, interests, and opinions
- Psychographics is a technique for measuring personality and lifestyles to developing lifestyle classifications

Motivation: Multiple Motives

Consumers usually have multiple motives for particular behaviours. These can be a combination of:

- Manifest known to the person and freely admitted
- Latent unknown to the person or the person is very reluctant to admit

Note: different motives can lead to the same behaviour; observing behaviour is not sufficient to determine motives.

Involvement

Involvement has to do with an individual's:

- *Intensity of interest* in a product and the
- *Importance* of the product for that person

The purchase of a car is much more risky than the purchase of a quart of orange juice, and therefore presents a higher involvement situation. This modifies the way that the generic model works. As involvement increases, consumers have greater motivation to comprehend and elaborate on information salient to the purchase. A life insurance agent, for example, would typically be more interested in contacting a young couple who just had a baby than an eighteen year old college student - even though the new parents might be struggling to make ends meet while the student is living more comfortably. Although the annual investment into a policy is much lower if started at a younger age, most young college students are not open to thinking about long term estate planning. A young couple with a new child, however, is much more open to thinking about issues associated with planning for the child's future education, saving to buy a house, or even saving to take an extended vacation upon retirement.

TYPES OF CONSUMER PROBLEM-SOLVING PROCESSES

Routenized

- Used when buying frequently purchased, low cost items
- Used when little search/decision effort is needed
- *E.g.*, buying a quart of orange juice once per week

Limited Problem Solving

- Used when products are occasionally purchased
- Used when information is needed about an unfamiliar product in a familiar product category

Extended Problem Solving

- Used when product is unfamiliar, expensive, or infrequently purchased
- *E.g.*, buying a new car once every five years

POST-PURCHASE CONSUMER BEHAVIOUR

Satisfaction

After the sale, the buyer will likely feel either satisfied or dissatisfied. If the buyer beleives that s/he received more in the exchange than what was paid, s/he might feel satisfied. If s/he believes that s/he received less in the exchange than what was paid, then s/he might feel dissatisfied. Dissatisfied buyers are not likely to return as customers and are not likely to send friends, relatives, and acquaintences. They are also more likely to be unhappy or even abusive when the product requires post-sale servicing, as when an automobile needs warranty maintenance.

The idea can be modeled as Homans' basic exchange equation:

Profit = Rewards–Costs

Unfortunately, even a buyer who "got a good deal" with respect to price and other terms of the sale might feel dissatisfied under the perception that the salesperson made out even better.

This idea is called equity theory, where we are concerned with:

Outcomes of A Inputs of A

vs.

Outcomes of B Inputs of B

Consider value is listed at $16,000. You are probably delighted with the purchase until you accidentally meet the prior owner who had received a trade-in of $10,000 on the car just a few days before. That the dealer appears to have received substantially greater benefit than you could lead to extreme dissatisfaction, even though you received good value for the money spent.

An issue related to this is attribution theory. Attribution theory, people tend to assign cause to the behaviour of others. Mary's life insurance agent advises her to purchase a whole life policy, while her accountant advises her, "buy term insurance and invest the difference."

The reason, explains the accountant, "is that insurance agents receive substantially higher commission payments on sales of whole life policies." If Mary believes that the insurance agent is recommending a product merely because he receives a higher commission, she will likely be displeased with the relationship and will not take his recommendation. If the agent is able to show Mary that the recommended product is the best solution for her situation, then she will likely attribute his recommendation to having her best interests in mind and will not be concerned about how it is that he is compensated for his services.

Cognitive Dissonance

Cognitive dissonance has to do with the doubt that a person has about the wisdom of a recent purchase. It is very common for people to experience some anxiety after the purchase of a product that is very expensive or that will require a long term commitment. Jane and Fred, for example, signed a one year lease on an apartment, committing themselves to payments of $1500 per month.

A week later, they are wondering if they should have instead leased a smaller $900 apartment in a more rough part of town; they are not sure if they really can afford this much of a monthly obligation. Dick and Sally, on the other hand, ultimately rented the $900 apartment, and now are wondering if the savings in rent will be offset by noisy and sometimes unsafe conditions in this neighbourhood. Perhaps neither couple would be experiencing this anxiety if their landlords had given them just the smallest of assurances that they had made a good decision. After a close on products that are expensive or that require a long term commitment, the salesperson should provide the prospect with some reasons to be happy with the decision. Allow the car buyer to reinforce her own positive feelings by calling her a week after the purchase to ask how things are going. Call the new life insurance policy holder after two months to see if there are any questions; a lack of questions can only help the buyer to convince himself that he did the right thing.

BUYING DECISION PROCESS

Whenever folks make a buying decision, that decision represents the culmination of a process. It may take place almost instantaneously or stretch out over a long period of time–but it's a process, not an event. No matter how long the process takes, the buying decision always begins when folks become aware of a need. Once they have identified that need, they begin to search for and explore possible avenues for meeting it. While gathering information, they refine and evaluate all the buying criteria that will affect the decision to purchase and narrow the field of choice to the "best few" alternatives. Once they reach a decision and choose, they take action by making a purchase. The final step in the process involves a reevaluation of the decision and its results.

To summarize, the steps of the buying decision process are:

- Identify
- Search
- Evaluate
- Decide
- Purchase
- Reevaluate

NATURE OF THE BUY

The way folks make buying decisions depends on the complexity of the problem they are trying to solve and the complexity of each step in the decision process. This will affect how you manage the sale.

If their needs and the decision-making process are simple, all you need to do is make your visitors aware of you, build confidence, differentiate yourself, demonstrate value and guide them through a very simple shopping and buying process. This is why lower-end, branded products sell so well. If the needs and the decision-making process are highly complex, then you need to make people aware of you, build relationships, educate them show sensitivity to the different decision-makers, influencers and groups, and resolve conflicting needs, so you can custom-tailor your solutions and make the buying process as painless and positive as possible. Think of purchasing a multi-million dollar piece of equipment that needs five departments to sign off to close the deal.

It also helps if you understand and incorporate how folks think about buying what you offer. Are they going to compare similar models in different brands? Are they looking for the range offered by one manufacturer? Do they think of the purchase in terms of a hierarchy of benefits, with some more important than others? Is the best way to showcase your product or service to compare it with someone else's stuff?

PROPENSITY TO BUY

You get four types of traffic, and each group is primed with a different level of motivation and preparedness - the classic "propensity to buy." First, you've got the to-die-for perfect visitors; they are the ones who know exactly what they want and come to you looking for features, brands, and model numbers. Then you've got the visitors who sort of know what they want. These are folks who have identified a strongly felt need, but they're still in the process of narrowing down their search criteria.

Then there are the window shoppers, folks who aren't sure they want anything, but might buy if they saw something that interested them. They have no strongly felt need in mind, but one could be suggested to them. The fourth group aren't really prospects. They're lost or there by mistake. Be happy when they go away. You don’t know where your visitors are in the process when they land on your site, so you’ve got to plan for each possibility. You’ve got to help the folks who know exactly what they want get to it quickly; make them jump through too many hoops and they’re gone. You’ve got to help the ones still mulling it over by offering pertinent information where and when they are most likely to need it, as well as persuading them you’re the logical business choice. You’ve got to be most engaging and appealing for the window shopper. It also helps to consider that not all your visitors are prepared or even inclined to make a decision when they first visit your site–sometimes a successful conversion is the result of multiple visits. So you’d like to give folks a reason to come back.

BUYING IS AN EMOTIONAL DECISION

It really is the piece that pulls it all together. Folks rationalize the decision to buy based on facts, but they make the decision to buy based on feelings. The single biggest motivator in buying is emotional response. And that takes place on two levels. In part, it’s the emotional response that comes when folks imagine themselves enjoying the benefits of what you offer. Put them in the driver's seat, and they are that much closer to being able to see themselves making the decision to buy. "Ditch the features?" Absolutely not. You should make your features available and present them as corollaries to benefits. After all, some of your visitors, particularly analytic types who will pointedly look for this stuff, feel more comfortable emotionally with facts and specifications. And that brings me to the other aspect of emotional response. Folks buy when they feel comfortable, when they feel they can trust you, when the process feels natural and reassuring, and when they come to believe that buying will make them feel good. Ignore this, and most of your visitors will bail out. Tap into it, and watch your conversion rate climb. Because, at then end of the day, it's not facts that convince customers to go with your company. It's emotion.

PACKAGE BUYING WITH SELLING

The persuasive architecture of your entire site must recognize every step of the buying decision process. Each step feeds and leads to the others. Although the process ultimately is linear, there can be feedback loops within the process as folks reevaluate information. So, it's not unusual to address multiple steps on a single page.

To successfully get your visitors to take action you must be able to see the world from their "buying" point of view. So learn how to address and package the buying process within your selling process. It will make a world of difference!

CONSUMER ADOPTION PROCESS

Adoption is an individual's decision to become a regular user of a product. Sequence of events beginning with consumer awareness of a new product leading to trial usage and culminating in full and regular use of the new product. Over time the adoption process resembles a bell curve formed by innovators, early adopters, the majority of consumers, late adopters, and laggards. An innovation is any good, service, or idea that is perceived by someone as new. The idea may have a long history, but it is an innovation to the person who sees it as new. Innovations take time to spread through the social system. Rogers defines the innovation diffusion process as "the spread of a new idea from its source of invention or creation to its ultimate users or adopters." The consumer-adoption process focuses on the mental process through which an individual passes from first hearing about an innovation to final adoption.

Adopters of new products have been observed to move through five stages:

1. *Awareness*: The consumer becomes aware of the innovation but lacks information about it.
2. *Interest*: The consumer is stimulated to seek information about the innovation.
3. *Evaluation*: The consumer considers whether to try the innovation.
4. *Trial*: The consumer tries the innovation to improve his or her estimate of its value.
5. *Adoption*: The consumer decides to make full and regular use of the innovation.

The new-product marketer should facilitate movement through these stages. A portable electric dishwasher manufacturer might discover that many consumers are stuck in the interest stage; they do not buy because of their uncertainty and the large investment cost.

But these same consumers would be willing to use an electric dishwasher on a trial basis for a small monthly fee. The manufacturer should consider offering a trial-use plan with option to buy.

FACTORS INFLUENCING THE ADOPTION PROCESS

People differ in their approach towards change. Some differ in adopting new fashion, some in adopting new appliances, some doctors are hesitant to apply new medicines and still some farmers do not apply new implements. This is called adoption culture. After the early adoption, they increase the use and then others follow. Others are late adopters by nature.

Let us categorize these customers into three units:

- *One who are early adopters*: They are very quick in their response. These people are venture some and willing to try new ideas. In fact they are innovators in life and early adopters.
- *Secondly Early Majority*: They are very careful people and take time to adopt things. They tend to collect information about the change or the product, study carefully and then adopt on the basis of their merits.
- *The third ones are late majority and traditionalists*: They are the ones who adopt late and then use the product.

As marketing managers, we must study the demographics, the psychographics and media characteristics of the product and also keep the theme of advertising message on these lines. We must find the innovators of the product and also opinion leaders and keeping in view the financial stature of the consumers and their category.

Then there are certain areas where product change is imminent and quicker while some areas change or innovation in the product is least desired or welcomed

CONSUMER MARKET

The consumer market is composed of individuals who buy a specific good or service. Rarely does one product interest the entire population. This statement applies even to staples, such as sugar, flour, and salt. A small percentage of households do not eat these products, so even if a company did target the entire population, not everyone would be a potential consumer.

The same statistical truth applies to cultural products. However, because of the extremely fragmented nature of the cultural sector, some distinctions are in order. For example, looking at this sector as a whole, it can be said that nearly 100% of the population consumes one type of cultural product or another. Indeed, in its broadest sense, the cultural sector encompasses everything from the performing arts to heritage, compact disks, movies, book and magazine publishing, and radio and television, with each of these disciplines appropriating a more or less important share of global demand. In Canada, for example, statistics show that 37.0% of families attend a performing arts event at least once a year: movies 62.2%, museums and art galleries 32.9%. In the United States the figures for cultural consumption are: classical music 15.6%, opera 4.7%, musicals 24.5%, plays 15.8%, ballet 5.8%, art museums 34.5%, and historical parks 46.9%. In Australia the figures are: musical theatre 19.3%, classical music 7.7%, festivals 21.9%, concerts 23%, and museums 27.8%. Of course, within each of these sectors, consumers cluster just as to specific poles of interest.

This leads to sharper market segmentation. The consumer makes a discriminating choice among various cultural products to acquire or consume the type of product desired. The distribution of consumers just as to various market segments differs in both time and space. Markets undergo and reflect the influence of opinion leaders, trends, tastes, and societal characteristics. Markets also vary from country to country just as to different social structures. Over the past 40 years, various surveys focusing on the socio-demographic profile of consumers of cultural products have been carried out in nearly every European country as well as in Canada, the United States, Australia, and Japan. It is fascinating to note that, regardless of whether the surveys were conducted in the 1970s, 1980s, or 1990s, they all obtained the same attendance rates and the same socio-demographic profiles.

Differences in the measuring tools used can sometimes make it difficult to compare countries; nonetheless, these studies have consistently and systematically revealed strong polarization of audiences between high art and popular culture across all countries over the past four decades. They show, for example, that cultural products catering to high art attract educated consumers, whereas those catering to popular culture draw on all segments of the population, in accordance with the relative weight of each.

The proportion of university graduates making up Canadian audiences, for example, ranges between 50% and 70% for high art, compared with 10% to 25% for popular culture. By way of comparison, the overall percentage of university graduates in Canada is 25%. Similar results have been found in other countries, most notably in France but also in Russia, where university graduates make up 50% of performing arts audiences but only 7% of the general population. Other socio-demographic variables are also linked to attendance, including average income and type of occupation. It should be pointed out once again that this profile is based on averages. Less-educated individuals with lower income may be great consumers of culture, as is the case for students and those specialized or working in the cultural milieu.

Indeed, it is well known that, as a rule many people active in the arts are highly educated yet so ill paid that they struggle to stay the poverty line. On the other hand, there are people with both very high salaries and very high educational levels who are not interested in the arts and gladly keep their distance. Four factors are known to influence an individual's penchant for complex cultural products: family values that encourage or discourage high art; the educational milieu and the value it places on high art; the fact of having attended performances or visited museums as a child; and amateur art practice. A more detailed analysis of the typical cultural consumer's traits reveals other nuances based on the different disciplines. For example, dance audiences are relatively younger and even more female in composition than those of the other performing arts; similarly, more women than men read novels, although a larger proportion of men read daily newspapers. In the film sector, there are two very different segments of avid cinemagoers; one of these segments is dominated by a young clientele, while the other is made up of educated people. The majority of consumers in the film sector belong to one or the other of these two segments.

BUSINESS BUYING BEHAVIOUR

The business market is comprised of organizations that, in some form, are involved in the manufacturer, distribution or support of products or services sold or otherwise provided to other organizations. The amount of purchasing undertaken in the business market easily dwarfs the total spending by consumers. Because the business market is so large it draws the interest of millions of companies worldwide that market exclusively to business customers.

For these marketers understanding how businesses make purchase decisions is critical to their organizations' marketing efforts. In some ways understanding the business market is not as complicated as understanding the consumer market. For example, in certain business markets purchase decisions hinge on the outcome of a bidding process between competitors offering similar products and services.

In these cases the decision to buy is often whittled down to one concern–who has the lowest price. Thus, unlike consumer markets, where building a recognizable brand is very important, for many purchase situations in the business market this is not the case. However, in many other ways business buying is much more complicated. For instance, the demand by businesses for products and services is affected by consumer purchases and because so many organizations may have a part in creating consumer purchases, a small swing in consumer demand can create big changes in business purchasing. Automobile purchases are a good example. If consumer demand for cars increases many companies connected with the automobile industry will also see demand for their products and services increase.

Under these conditions companies will ratchet up their operations to ensure demand is met, which invariably will lead to new purchases by a large number of companies. In fact, it is conceivable that an increase of just one or two per cent for consumer demand can increase business demand for products and services by five or more per cent. Unfortunately, the opposite is true if demand declines. Trying to predict these swings requires businesses to not only understand their immediate customers but also the end user, which as suggested, discuss, may be well down the supply chain from where the business operates.

Principles of Marketing Tutorials discusses the unique characteristics of the business market. As suggested, see that marketers must appeal to business customers in ways that are distinct from how they would approach consumers. While marketers selling to other businesses operate with most of the same marketing tools used by marketers of consumer products, how they employ these tools to reach their marketing objectives may be quite different.

SUPPLY CHAIN MARKET

The supply chain consists of mostly for-profit companies engaged in activities involving product creation and delivery. Essentially the chain represents major steps needed to manufacture a product that will eventually be sold as a final product. Each member of the supply chain purchases products and services enabling them to carry out its business objectives. When making purchase decisions supply chain members may be motivated by such factors as: product cost, return on investment, assurance of consistent supply, reciprocity with supplying firm, and much more. Examples of purchasing occurring in the supply chain include: manufacturing and plant equipment, information technology, office supplies, professional business services, etc. We arbitrarily identify five main categories of supply chain members primarily based on the stage at which they contribute to the manufacturing process. However, it is conceivable that these categories can be further divided in order to flush out more specific activities.

BUSINESS USER MARKETS

Besides selling final products and services to supply chain companies, several additional user markets also make purchases either for their own consumption or they buy with the intention of redistributing to others. In these purchase situations the buyer generally does not radically change the product from its form when it was purchased from a Product Manufacturer. While technically these markets are also part of the supply chain, members of the business user market do not, in most cases, engage or directly assist in production activities.

BUSINESS VS CONSUMER MARKETS

For marketers, the selling environment of business markets present uniquely different circumstances when compared to selling to consumers.

At the beginning of this tutorial we saw two ways in which consumer and business markets differ:

- Business markets are more likely to be price driven than brand driven, and
- Demand in business markets tends to be more volatile than consumer markets.

However, the two markets are dissimilar in other ways requiring marketers to take a different approach when selling to business customers than to consumers.

These differences include:

- How Decisions Are Made
- Existence of Experienced Purchasers
- Time Needed to Make Buying Decision
- Size of Purchases
- Number of Buyers
- Type of Promotional Effort Needed to Reach Buyer

BUYING DIFFERENCES

Buying Centre Decisions

In the consumer market a very large percentage of purchase decisions are made by a single person. As we discussed in the Consumer Buying Behaviour tutorial, there are situations in which multiple people may be involved in a consumer purchase decision, such as a child influencing a parent to choose a certain brand of cereal or a husband and wife deciding together to buy a house, but most of the time purchases are individual decisions.

The business market is significantly different. While single person purchasing is not unusual, especially within a small company, a significant percentage of business buying, especially within larger organizations, requires the input of many. In the marketing literature those associated with the purchase decision are known to be part of a Buying Centre, which consists of individuals within an organization that perform one or more of the following roles:

- *Buyer*: Responsible for dealing with suppliers and placing orders
- *Decider*: Has the power to make the final purchase decision
- *Influencer*: Has the ability to affect what is ordered such as setting order specifications
- *User*: Those who will actually use the product when it is received
- *Initiator*: Any Buying Centre member who is the first to determine that a need exists
- *Gatekeeper*: Anyone who controls access to other Buying Centre members

For marketers confronting a Buying Centre it is important to first identify who plays what role. Once identified the marketer must address the needs of each member, which may differ significantly. For instance, the Decider, who may be the company president wants to make sure the purchase will not negatively affect the company's bottom line while the Buyer wants to be assured the product will be delivered on time. Thus, the way each Buying Centre member is approached and marketed to requires careful planning in order to address the unique needs of each member.

Experienced Purchasers

As noted in the discussion of the Buying Centre, organizations often employ purchasing agents or professional buyers whose job is to negotiate the best deals for their company. Unlike consumers, who often lack information when making purchase decisions, professional buyers are generally as knowledgeable about the product and the industry as the marketer who is selling to them.

Decision Making Time

Depending on the product, business purchase decisions can drag on for an extensive period. Unlike consumer markets where impulse purchasing is rampant, the number of people involved in business purchase decisions results in decisions taking weeks, months or even years.

Size of Purchases

For products that are regularly used and frequently purchased, businesses will often buy a larger volume at one time compared to consumer purchases. Because of this business purchasers often demand price breaks for higher order levels.

Type of Promotions

Companies who primarily target consumers often use mass advertising methods to reach an often widely dispersed market. For business-to-business marketers the size of individual orders, along with a smaller number of buyers, makes person-to-person contact by sales representatives a more effective means of promotion.

TYPES OF BUSINESS PURCHASE DECISIONS

While it would appear business customers face the same four purchase situations faced by consumers, the nature of the business market has led many marketing academics to group business purchase situations into only three categories. The reason is that the idea of a minor order may not hold as well in the business market, where buyers tend to place larger orders and where suppliers' marketing efforts are directed towards the most profitable buyers.

- *Straight Re-Purchase*: These purchase situations involve routine ordering. In most cases buyers simply reorder the same products or services that were previously purchased. In fact, many larger companies have programmed re-purchases into an automated ordering system that initiates electronic orders when inventory falls a certain pre-determined level. For the supplier benefiting from the re-purchase this situation is ideal since the purchaser is not looking to evaluate other products. For competitors who are not getting the order it may require extensive marketing efforts to persuade the buyer to consider other product or service options.
- *Modified Re-Purchase*: These purchases occur when products or services previously considered a straight re-purchase are for some reason now under a re-evaluation process. There are many reasons why a product is moved to the status of a modified re-purchase. Some of these reasons include: end of purchase contract period, change in who is involved in making the purchase, supplier is removed from an approved suppliers list, mandate from top level of organization to re-evaluate all purchasing, or strong marketing effort by competitors. In this circumstance the incumbent supplier faces the same challenges they may have faced when they initially convinced the buyer to make the purchase. For competitors the door is now open and they must work hard to make sure their message is heard by those in charge of the purchase decision.
- *New Task Purchase*: As the name suggests, these purchases are ones the buyer has never or rarely made before. In some ways new task purchases can be considered as either minor or major depending on the total cost or overall importance of the purchase. In either case the buyer will spend considerably more time evaluating alternatives. For example, if faced with a major new task purchase, which often involves complex items, such as computer systems, buildings, robotic assembly lines, etc., the purchase cycle from first recognizing the need to placement of the order may be months or even years.

Chapter 5

Customer Knowledge Management

Among other reasons firms have a low return on their information technology investments is that they only poorly understand what the technology makes possible. The objectives and role of information in customer-focused management must be understood. Customer-intelligent firms use their customer knowledge to drive all of the firm's activities and decisions.

When firms have so much opportunity to interact with their customers, why is it that they treat their customers like strangers? The reason is not lack of information on their customers, but a lack in a firm's managing of that information. Firms may have the ability to capture that information, but may not process and utilize the knowledge to manage relationships with their customers. Information technology has only placed this realisation in sharp focus. On the other hand, the power of information technology has also raised the ugly specter of abuse of privacy when firms have access to a vast amount of customer information.

Network Solutions, the first company that registered addresses on the. com,. org, and. net domains for the Internet, now a unit of VeriSign, raised eyebrows when it planned to sell names, street addresses, and other information gathered from businesses and individuals who signed up for an Internet address. There are several examples of Internet companies that have been reined in for their use of customer information. DoubleClick Inc., decided against combining Web-tracking data with off-line databases. Toysmart was not allowed to sell its customer database when it shut down.

Hagel and Rayport suggest that customers will become savvy about their personal information and be reluctant to divulge it unless they receive some value for it. They predict that customers will win the battle over their information and firms they call "infomediaries" will "become custodians, agents and brokers of customer information, marketing it to businesses on consumers' behalf while protecting their privacy at the same time." Nevertheless, customer information is crucial for a customer focus because of the need to make and execute customer-focused decisions in all aspects of the business. Firms will continue to require customer information to do business. Information technology will continue to challenge a firm's judgment in obtaining and using customer information.

Traditionally, research on the customer has been at the aggregate level, most utilized during the new product development process, to test new product ideas, in test marketing, and to test new campaign concepts in the realm of advertising. Marketing research has been standard practice preceding the launch of new products or advertising campaigns. Most firms conduct regular market research activities to direct segmentation decisions such as targeting and to determine how to reach segments. This stage does not limit itself to data from market research studies, nor is it about how to conduct market research studies. Instead, this stage is about the consolidation and utilization of information on the customer to align all the activities of the firm to meeting customer needs. The key issues discussed in this stage are central to designing and implementing effective customer knowledge management: the sources and avenues from which customer information is available to the firm; in what form is it available; how this data can and should be analysed and interpreted; and how the information should be utilized.

BENEFITS OF CUSTOMER KNOWLEDGE MANAGEMENT

Scholars have implored managers to "spend a day in the life of your customer" and to "get inside the lives of your customers, " so as to obtain a deeper understanding of customers. The quality of the knowledge on the customer is much greater because of direct observation. Obtaining that knowledge is only the first step. The basic skill of listening involves competence in sensing, evaluating *and* responding. A study of 500 new car buyers found customer perceptions of these three dimensions of listening to be strongly linked to trust in the salesperson. There are also benefits within the firm when the practice of listening to customers is emphasized by senior managers. Senior managers at First Chicago discovered that in emphasizing listening to the customer they found a cultural change within the organization. Customer knowledge gained from firsthand customer contact is very persuasive. Smart CEOs at firms like IBM, Cisco, and EMC intuitively realise this, and their senior managers contact their major customers on a regular basis. These firms also act on that information to improve relationships with those important customers.

The benefits of customer knowledge management have concentrated at the individual level. For example, Dreyfus, like other mutual fund firms, keeps track of client activity, claiming that they can predict when a client is going to shift money out of their mutual funds. Clients receive a call from a Dreyfus representative, who wants to know how the client feels about the investment and if his or her goals are being met. If Dreyfus is able to track clients at all stages of the consumption process, then the firm has a better chance of retaining the customer. A number of CRM- and ERP-type software programmes allow companies to track processes in the life of a specific sales order from order entry all the way to delivery to customer. Of course, FedEx introducing package tracking is a well-known example from years ago. There are a number of benefits of information technology for firms of any size.

Siebel software allows Honeywell to spot problems and opportunities by tracking and analysing all customer interactions; and at Marriott, Siebel empowers sales reps to respond more quickly to customer needs by integrating customer information from different departments. Lexmark International used Microstrategy software to help build what they call a data warehousing solution that accomplished a reduction in product delivery time by 70 per cent, a threefold improvement in being able to deliver a customer's order on the desired date, and a 60 per cent reduction in the information costs. Package delivery firm UPS's selfservice tracking system, built by IBM, saved the company $450,000 a day in customer service expenses; and, the Clarify call centre software helped payroll-processing firm ADP improve customer retention rate by 5 per cent and increase revenues by $100 million in 1999 simply by providing its customer service reps with customer information on its 8000 clients. There are numerous such examples of technology-based customer information management systems having a profound impact on a firm's productivity and in customer retention. Both outcomes are the basis for achieving and sustaining profits.

The marketing research practice has undergone a major transformation in recent years. A primary function of marketing research activities is to collect and analyse customer information. Technology has enabled all phases of the marketing research process ranging from sampling and data collection to analysis and reporting. With newer technologies and faster cycle times, firms conduct research at all stages of the product life cycle and not just at the product development stage or the test marketing stage.

This is at the aggregate level, whereas there is another change in research on the customer at the individual level, where technology is enabling customers to interact with the firm in a multitude of different ways not previously possible. These interactions can now occur during all stages of consumption. At every interaction with the customer, a firm has the opportunity to acquire valuable customer information, as well as to process and utilize the information for creating and delivering superior customer value. Once the data is available, the challenge is to provide the user of the information and decision maker with targeted information. Enter rulesbased approaches, which are simply programmes that make sense of data using preconceived models. Sadly, the majority of CRM and ERP packages fail the firm not for lack of data, but simply because the firm does not have the appropriate understanding and appreciation of the fundamentals of customer-focused management. The rules for decision-making should be founded on customer-focused management principles.

The better the understanding of the customer and the utilization of that knowledge, the more customer focused the rules are. The best technology is only as good as what you tell it to do. CRM and ERP packages are really knowledge management software, tools to manage knowledge of the customer and enable the processes within the firm that are working to meet specific customer needs. To be more effective with these tools, firms need to gather the information, analyse and process it to obtain a good understanding of the customer, and utilize it at every opportunity in the value-creation and delivery process. Therefore, for a thorough understanding on how to manage customer information, it is important to understand the principles of knowledge management, in general.

What is knowledge management? To answer this question, we have first to deal with a more fundamental question: what is the difference between data, information, and knowledge? Are these terms just synonyms that are interchangeable? No, they are not! The simplest way to understand the differences among these terms is to picture a continuum. As we add value to data, it becomes information; and as we add value to information, information becomes knowledge.

When we interpret data in a context, we convert that data into information that has some meaning. When we categorize and elaborate on that information with explanations, then we have added more value and the information can now be considered knowledge. Thus, *knowledge management* is the management of data and information so that a firm can optimally capture, process, and utilize its knowledge for effective decision-making and operation. *Customer knowledge management* is the management of the acquisition, processing, and utilization of customer information for effective customer-focused decision making. Knowledge management practice has been studied in the context of how organizations learn. Before we discuss the methods of managing customer knowledge, it would be useful to understand knowledge management and, specifically, information processing from the perspective of organizational learning.

Organizational learning can be broadly depicted as a three-stage process:

1. Information acquisition or generation
2. Information transmission or dissemination
3. Information analysis or interpretation

Studies have demonstrated that a customer-focused firm has a formal and systematic method for gathering, interpreting and using customer information. To be customer-focused, therefore, firms need to be committed to the importance and value of customer information and to the use of customer information in guiding the creation and delivery of customer value. Thus, recognizing information's value to the firm and realising when and where it is accessible is a prerequisite for knowledge management.

Richard Schulze, CEO of Bestbuy, the runaway success in electronics retailing, says: The best way to find out whether a store is running smoothly is by asking the cashier. "The cashier really understands where the problems lie. They're the last people to see the customer. "To consider all of the sources of customer information we also need to first identify the natural state of the information.

Customer information is available as tacit and as explicit knowledge. The explicit knowledge is present in the databases of the firm or as documented information. Customer information files in databases are usually quantitative data. More and more firms are also using qualitative data when the technology is used to accommodate that type of data. Otherwise, most of this rich information remains as hidden knowledge. This information that is not recorded is the tacit knowledge that is usually resident with the employees and managers of the firm. For example, records of customer service interactions capture the actual transaction, complaint, or feedback from the customer. At the same time, employees, based on their prior experience, will unconsciously record and bring to bear their judgments of the situation, which are not necessarily documented. The knowledge that employees have that is not recorded anywhere is deemed the tacit knowledge of the firm.

While at the individual level information is available from customer information files in the firm's databases, other types of information at the aggregate level may be gathered during the course of product development activities and other specific projects and reside in research reports. There is information on the customer at several locations within the firm, from sales to customer service, to name the most obvious areas. As we know besides this explicit knowledge, there is a wealth of information at both the aggregate and the individual levels. Wherever the firm has interfaced with the customer, the "touch-points, " there is information on the customer. It immediately becomes apparent that several product and service delivery contact points within the firm have access to customer information, but not all are part of the customer information management system.

CRM software packages enable the firm to capture all of the information gathered at each touch-point into a central database and make it available at any touch point. To determine all of the opportunities for gathering information on the customer, firms can develop a blueprint of the order delivery or customer service processes depicting all of the touch-points from the consumption cycle when the customer interacts with the firm. Knowledge gained on the customer from each and every customer interaction when recorded and made available can be valuable in improving the customer focus of any of the firm's decisions or actions.

Customer Information Files are typically transaction-related and purchase-related individual-level customer data found in sales records, customer interaction records, and customer service incident records. What is perhaps not in these files, which needs to be considered as a necessary component of individual customer profiles where available, is information related to the activities of pre-consumption, consumption, and post-consumption.

Research Reports have segment-level aggregate data that are found in product development reports, advertising research reports, sales and marketing reports, and customer service reports. What needs to be seen is whether research on market segments is an ongoing pursuit of the firm—to indicate that the firm is proactively assessing customer value being delivered by the firm.

Knowledge held by employees and managers: Tacit knowledge of the customers—is by definition not completely identified and its utility not realised. If there is no formal process to regularly capture and utilize this information, a wealth of knowledge resident in the firm is being ignored.

Upstream and downstream sources: When suppliers and intermediaries are regularly included in discussions of value-creation and delivery decisions, there is an opportunity to discover information on market trends, technology, ideas for product improvement, and so on that are useful at the aggregate level. At the individual level, where there are intermediaries, if it is possible, it would be highly valuable to obtain individual customer level information.

Now let us look at opportunities that may be missed by firms that are not proactive in looking for customer information. For example, how many firms capture and utilize data on referrals? If it is appropriately captured and analysed, firms can use this information to proactively stimulate referrals. Firms can identify customers who could be bringing in new customers. Firms can determine what incentives would be effective in stimulating referrals. From the referring and referred customers, firms can learn what messages are being conveyed about the firm and which messages are most effective in stimulating product trial from new customers. Firms can learn what types of customers are most liable to switch from their current patronage based on word of mouth. Firms can track and follow the patronage behaviour of these new customers and nurture their loyalty and referral behaviour. Firms can also find out from these new customers valuable information on the competition as well. Similarly, what about prospective customer queries? How well is this information captured and utilized? What would such information contain? They are a good source of what customers look for in a product, a reflection of their choice criteria. How many firms systematically record information on complaints and praises? This type of information would be very helpful in understanding how the firm is faring on creating and delivering customer value. It could highlight fail points in the value-creating processes and provide input into frontline evaluation and motivation activities.

Many firms have loyalty programmes to reward the frequent user. What sort of frequent-user data do these firms maintain? How many firms really use the frequent-purchase data? Some firms who know their customers well recognize the importance of sorting out the most profitable customers from their customer base and treating them differently. Some customers are indeed more equal than others! Most firms use frequent-purchaser data for targeting specials and promotions. However, this data can also provide invaluable information on customer value and customer profile information to align the firm's value-creation and delivery processes.

Traditionally, firms have gathered routine customer information only at purchase and when a customer returns a product for a refund or mechanisms. Feedback forms and customer surveys are administered on a regular basis in some firms. However, most often the information gathered from these efforts is worthless because of faulty designs and worse, sometimes even result in misdirected decisions because of flawed survey methodology.

More often than not, the surveys are neither reliable nor valid. While reliability and validity as statistical measures of the psychometric stability of a scale are important for a scientific, unbiased study, management can improve the utility of customer surveys with a rather simple analysis. Examine the design, administration, and use of any survey along the dimensions of structure, content, and process. Structural features such as length and the time it would take the respondent to fill out the survey, the layout of the various questions in the survey, and the response format for the questions affect the effectiveness of the survey. Content decisions, such as the categories of information sought from the respondent and information identifying the type of respondent filling out the survey, affect the utility of the survey, which will only be as good as the effectiveness of its administration and its usability. Thus, the process of survey delivery, customer response delivery mechanisms, and the customisation of the reports to the decision maker and user of the information in their value-creating and delivery roles is critical to the success of the customer feedback exercise.

There are other sources of customer information that the firm has access to and may not fully utilize. The systematic way of determining what these sources might be is to list all the possible touch-points where customers interact with the firm and placing them in sequence in the three phases of consumption. In the pre-consumption phase, customers may interact with salespeople or customer service or other frontline personnel. Recognizing what these touch-points are and what kinds of information is shared between the firm and the customer is an important step. Firms must decide what data needs to be captured at the touch-points and how it is to be used in guiding decisions and activities.

How many firms systematically utilize frontline operations personnel for gathering customer information? Frontline operations personnel are in an ideal position to gather customer information. They can be trained on when, what, and how to observe or elicit information from customers.

They need to be motivated and recognized for their ability to obtain, process, and disseminate such information. Similarly, there are also the intermediaries or resellers of the firm's products and services that represent the firm in different ways. These intermediaries might perform functions of delivery and distribution, promotion, or customer service on behalf of the firm. Walmart recognized and wielded the power it held with such customer information in negotiating terms with powerful packaged goods manufacturers, including Procter and Gamble. In the consumption phase, customers may call for assistance in using the product or on some aspect of how the solution works. This information needs to be captured and incorporated into customer education activities such as product directions-for-use instructions, or used in product development and improvement efforts. There is also a wealth of information within the firm available from customer complaints and suggestions. Service failures and recovery situations provide valuable information on customers and their experiences with the firm and its solutions. If these are recorded and maintained on a systematic basis, they can be "mined" for patterns that yield insights not otherwise available. For example, recurrent complaints about customer service response time might suggest that the customer service process needs redesigning.

Often when the data is not available on which to base a decision, the firm has to collect that information. For example, say the firm has received several complaints about customer service access and wants to determine what changes need to be made to the customer service operation. In this case, the firm may want to conduct some research in order to determine the customer needs and preferences with regard to customer service. For each decision that directly relates to a customer, the firm has first to determine what kind of information is needed to make the most effective customer-focused decision. Some of this information is available in existing databases, while some may have to be gathered. To gather information, the firm needs to set up a method of determining what information needs to be gathered, how it can be obtained, and in what form it will be available.

When the information is not available from the day-to-day activities of the firm, then research needs to be conducted on the customer on a project-by-project basis. There are a number of choices and decisions to be made regarding the methods available in researching the customer. For example, to determine what changes are needed to improve customer satisfaction, there are formal and informal customer satisfaction measures. There are qualitative and quantitative methods to obtain the information. For unique project-based decisions, there are several data collection methods. Among the quantitative methods typically used are paper and pencil surveys administered over the telephone or by mail. On the other hand, qualitative methods typically utilize structured and unstructured interviews, focus groups, or observation methods. A number of innovative qualitative approaches are being introduced. For example, Kimberly Clark for its diaper market, Intuit with its personal finance software, and Patagonia for its outdoor gear have used the method of "story-telling" by getting customers to tell real-life stories expressing how they use the product and feel about it.

Customer case research is another method that conducts chronological case studies of actual purchases to discover previously unknown purchase drivers by systematically capturing all events leading up to the purchase decision. These approaches can uncover customer experiences and thought processes that may not be accessible through a pencil-and-paper survey approach. Any research project should take a systematic approach for maximum benefit and to reduce errors and biases and follow the following approach.

- *Framing the research*—Management needs for the decision or objective
- *Examining existing and available information*—For hypotheses, specific research questions and to guide research design
- Specifying the research questions
- *Determining the research design*—Questionnaire construction, sampling frame, data collection method, and plan of analysis
- Administering the research and collecting and analysing the data
- Reporting the results and findings

First, the research objective frames the management decision to be made. Information already available is used to guide the research design. The research is then designed by making decisions on what information is needed and how and where to collect the information. The research design includes determining the questions to solicit the information, the method for administering these questions, the sample of subjects, and a plan of analysis. Qualitative research designs are appropriate when there is a need to generate ideas on what to focus on, or to get in-depth information on specific issues. Qualitative research, such as focus-group methods, can complement quantitative research, such as surveys.

Quantitative research designs are useful when a broader cross-section of the customers needs to be polled about a broad range of issues.

Sampling techniques are used when it is not possible or necessary to contact all the sources of information. Statistical techniques allow for generalizing inferences and conclusions on the entire population of interest based on data from a representative sample of that population.

The research instrument or questions and response format are constructed and pretested on a small subset of the population for validity and reliability before obtaining responses from the final sample. The responses are tabulated and statistical procedures applied to the data for analysis. The findings generated are then made available to guide the decision maker. The appropriate format of tables and the report are predetermined in the plan of analysis, so that the data is collected and analysed according to the needs of the user of that information.

Especially in service firms and in the service component of manufacturing firms, where there is a significant opportunity to interact with the customer and to customise value, firms have used customer information in a number of ways. Observe any service encounter and you will see tacit or explicit customer knowledge being used. When the data from these interactions are systematically documented and analysed, patterns in customer data can detect the dynamics in consumption behaviour.

When aggregated, customer data provides an opportunity to analyse customer segments for anything from price sensitivity to demand patterns to why, when, and how customers behave in the various activities within each of the consumption stages. Firms can divide their customer base into segments based on profitability. When customer purchase information is mapped onto capacity utilization data, for example, a deeper analysis of the firm's value-creation and delivery processes can help determine which of the firm's marketing and operations practices contribute to its profitability. Which frequent customer promotion programmes are most/least effective? Where are the low and peak demand periods? A yield analysis of the utilization levels at the various price levels would help determine the most effective pricing decisions.

Each customer has a value to the firm, and that information is also valuable to the firm to determine the right customer. The lifetime value of the customer to the firm is a function of what they bring to the firm as revenues over the lifetime of the customer. By the same token, it is also important to know what it costs the firm to serve that customer. Loyal customers with a favourable disposition towards the service provider are also likely to engage in favourable word-of-mouth behaviour.

They are valuable in trying new products being offered by the firm. They are also less costly to serve because they are familiar with the firm and are socialized into the procedures of the firm that they encounter in their consumption. As customers' loyalty with the firm grows over time, the firm also has a better knowledge of the customer and is more efficient and effective in serving that customer.

Firms that have the data on their customers are able to engage their best resources for their best customers. For example, firms have used information on a customer's profitability to the firm to determine the level of service appropriate for each customer. A *Business Week* special report titled "Why Service Stinks" cites several examples of firms pampering their premium customers. Charles Schwab's premium customer waits no longer than 15 seconds for a phone call to be answered, while others could wait as long as 10 minutes. Centura Bank's most profitable customers—rated 5 on a scale of 1 to 5—get an annual call from the CEO; customer retention in this group improved by 50 per cent in five years. Even utility companies, believed to be less sophisticated in their marketing than the consumer packaged goods firms, have a higher proportion of service representatives per customer for their higher-revenue customer groups. In each example, unless the firm knew what each customer was worth to the firm, it would not be able to proportionally allocate its resources to the "right" customers.

A grid guided by the three consumption stages can be a useful framework for determining what decisions need to be based on what customer information. All the functions and processes that affect the creation and delivery of customer value in each of the stages need to be aligned with customer information.

Technology has revolutionized customer information management. Information technologies allow firms to gather, store, and interpret demographic and behavioural data so that each subsequent interaction with the customer is customised, based on historical data gathered from each customer interaction. Digitized purchase transactions in commerce have enabled numerous opportunities to track customer interactions.

Chip technology has progressed so rapidly that soon there could be a computer chip in just about any product that would enable mind boggling links to improve customer value and the customer-firm relationship. For example, take the Internet and e-commerce. Most Web sites will ask simple unobtrusive questions of customers when they browse the site. This information identifies the customer and tracks the customer's activities or "click streams" on the Web site. Subsequently, software can use this information to personalize the Web site and the experience for the customer.

A number of firms have emerged that provide customer information management software. Such software can customise Web pages for each customer depending on the customer's profile, which is created based on the customer's previous interactions with the firm and the Web site. Vignette's software allows Web sites to dynamically generate pages that are custom-made for each customer. Silknet's virtual sales assistant guides customers through a series of questions about their need situations and then makes product recommendations. Marriott has an enterprise-wide software that integrates information on customers from different departments so that its sales reps can anticipate and respond more quickly to customer needs. Similarly, H&R Block uses software from Clarify to combine and coordinate customer records from its tax offices, discount brokerages, its customer service centre, and its Web site so that customer interaction personnel in each department have access to all of the information on the customer.

There are a variety of methods for analysing data. Data mining techniques attempt to discern patterns in the data where one set of characteristics affects another set in a certain way. SAS Enterprise Dataminer software helps detect patterns in databases and construct models to predict customer response to the firm's actions. Software from iMarket looks at customers' most recent or most frequent purchase decisions and the monetary value of these purchases for the firm and helps decision makers select a subset of customers for targeting specific promotions or new product introductions.

Epiphany and Digimine are examples of firms that use a set of their own proprietary algorithms to analyse customer data for their clients. Early clients of Epiphany included Charles Schwab and Hewlett Packard, and for Digimine include Nordstrom. Edify has software that will link customer feedback such as survey responses to individual customer profiles for anlaysis. There is also software such as Nudist available for the analysis of qualitative data.

When firms are able to sort through their customer databases and group customers by the relevant characteristics with such datamining software, the power of segmentation and targeting is fully realised with such datamining software. In general, data is useless for decision making unless it is organized for interpretation. When organized appropriately, data can be contextualized so as to be transformed into information. Displaying and disseminating information is critical to the firm's success. Without proper reporting procedures, decision makers do not benefit from the information that the firm has. For example, ESRI has a programme called Arcview that allows the user to spatially display numerical data. The user can view the data in his or her preferred format to match individual cognitive styles. As Peter Drucker notes, no two executives organize the same information in the same way. Therefore, software that allows the users to display information in their own preferred formats is valuable in customer information management.

The task of the customer information management system is to generate intelligence on the customer so that firm can be more customer-focused in its serving the customer. Intelligence generation capability has been shown to be positively correlated to superior customer value. In a study that involved hour-long in-depth interviews and surveys of sixty-six of the largest one thousand electronic firms by scholars interested in the characteristics of the market-oriented firm, firms are urged to treat learning about the customer as an investment.

Ultimately, customer information is useless unless it is available to the user. Scholars researching the value of information have called this the "value in use" metric. The more the information is used, the more value it has! Customer information management, therefore, involves determining how the information needs to be made available, to whom, when, and in what form.

The focus here is on who needs the information. In the spirit of customer focus, the information system serves an internal customer—the decision maker. What will the user need the information for? What specific information is needed for the firm's decisions and activities? Is the user of the information able to enhance customer value with the information? At what level of aggregation is the information used: policy level and customer level, segment level, and individual level? Such decisions need to be made so as to prioritize the customer information according to its impact on customer value. In making judgments about committing resources to managing and leveraging customer information, the firm should consider the worth of the information in terms of how it would help the firm provide superior customer value at a reasonable profit. Customer information must drive any business process and activity.

These run the gamut of decisions regarding creating and delivering customer solutions, product improvements, attracting and retaining customers, customer service, recovering from product failures, hiring and motivating employees, and ensuring a customer-oriented climate and culture.

Chapter 6

Segmentation and Targeting

Segmentation, targeting, and positioning together comprise a three stage process.

We first:

- Determine which kinds of customers exist, then
- Select which ones we are best off trying to serve and, finally,
- Implement our segmentation by optimizing our products/ services for that segment and communicating that we have made the choice to distinguish ourselves that way.

Segmentation involves finding out what kinds of consumers with different needs exist. In the auto market, for example, some consumers demand speed and performance, while others are much more concerned about roominess and safety. In general, it holds true that "You can't be all things to all people," and experience has demonstrated that firms that specialize in meeting the needs of one group of consumers over another tend to be more profitable.

Generically, there are three approaches to marketing. In the *undifferentiated* strategy, all consumers are treated as the same, with firms not making any specific efforts to satisfy particular groups.

This may work when the product is a standard one where one competitor really can't offer much that another one can't. Usually, this is the case only for commodities. In the *concentrated* strategy, one firm chooses to focus on one of several segments that exist while leaving other segments to competitors. For example, Southwest Airlines focuses on price sensitive consumers who will forego meals and assigned seating for low prices.

In contrast, most airlines follow the *differentiated* strategy: They offer high priced tickets to those who are inflexible in that they cannot tell in advance when they need to fly and find it impractical to stay over a Saturday. These travellers—usually business travellers—pay high fares but can only fill the planes up partially. The same airlines then sell some of the remaining seats to more price sensitive customers who can buy two weeks in advance and stay over.

Note that segmentation calls for some tough choices. There may be a large number of variables that can be used to differentiate consumers of a given product category; yet, in practice, it becomes impossibly cumbersome to work with more than a few at a time. Thus, we need to determine which variables will be *most* useful in distinguishing different groups of consumers.

We might thus decide, for example, that the variables that are most relevant in separating different kinds of soft drink consumers are: light consumers.

- Preference for taste vs. low calories,
- Preference for Cola vs. non-cola taste,
- Price sensitivity—willingness to pay for brand names;
- Heavy vs.

We now put these variables together to arrive at various combinations.

Several different kinds of variables can be used for segmentation:

- *Demographic* variables essentially refer to personal statistics such as income, gender, education, location, ethnicity, and family size. Campbell's soup, for instance, has found that Western U.S. consumers on the average prefer spicier soups—thus, you get a different product in the same cans at the East and West coasts. Facing flat sales of guns in the traditional male dominated market, a manufacturer came out with the Lady Remmington, a more compact, handier gun more attractive to women. Taking this a step farther, it is also possible to segment on *lifestyle and values*."
- Some consumers want to be seen as similar to others, while a different segment wants to stand apart from the crowd.
- Another basis for segmentation is *behaviour*. Some consumers are "brand loyal"—*i.e.*, they tend to stick with their preferred

brands even when a competing one is on sale. Some consumers are "heavy" users while others are "light" users. For example, research conducted by the wine industry shows that some 80% of the product is consumed by 20% of the consumers—presumably a rather intoxicated group.

- One can also segment on *benefits sought*, essentially bypassing demographic explanatory variables. Some consumers, for example, like scented soap, while others prefer the "clean" feeling of unscented soap. Some consumers use toothpaste primarily to promote oral health, while another segment is more interested in breath freshening.

In the next step, we decide to target one or more segments. Our choice should generally depend on several factors. First, how well are existing segments served by *other* manufacturers? It will be more difficult to appeal to a segment that is already well served than to one whose needs are not currently being served well. Secondly, how large is the segment, and how can we expect it to grow?. Thirdly, do we have strengths as a company that will help us appeal particularly to one group of consumers?

Firms may already have an established reputation. While McDonald's has a great reputation for fast, consistent quality, family friendly food, it would be difficult to convince consumers that McDonald's now offers gourmet food. Thus, McD's would probably be better off targeting families in search of consistent quality food in nice, clean restaurants. Positioning involves *implementing* our targeting. For example, Apple Computer has chosen to position itself as a maker of user-friendly computers. Thus, Apple has done a lot through its advertising to promote itself, through its unintimidating icons, as a computer for "non-geeks." The Visual C software programming language, in contrast, is aimed a "techies."

That most successful firms fall into one of three categories:

- Operationally excellent firms, which maintain a strong competitive advantage by maintaining exceptional efficiency, thus enabling the firm to provide reliable service to the customer at a significantly lower cost than those of less well organized and well run competitors. The emphasis here is mostly on low cost, subject to reliable performance, and less value is put on customising the offering for the specific customer. Wal-Mart is an example of this discipline. Elaborate logistical designs allow goods to be moved at the lowest cost, with extensive systems predicting when specific quantities of supplies will be needed.

- Customer intimate firms, which excel in serving the specific needs of the individual customer well. There is less emphasis on efficiency, which is sacrificed for providing more precisely what is wanted by the customer. Reliability is also stressed. Nordstrom's and IBM are examples of this discipline.
- Technologically excellent firms, which produce the most advanced products currently available with the latest technology, constantly maintaining leadership in innovation. These firms, because they work with costly technology that need constant refinement, cannot be as efficient as the operationally excellent firms and often cannot adapt their products as well to the needs of the individual customer. Intel is an example of this discipline.

Treacy and Wiersema suggest that in addition to excelling on one of the three value dimensions, firms must meet acceptable levels on the other two. Wal-Mart, for example, does maintain some level of customer service. Nordstrom's and Intel both must meet some standards of cost effectiveness. The emphasis, beyond meeting the minimum required level in the two other dimensions, is on the dimension of strength. *Repositioning* involves an attempt to change consumer perceptions of a brand, usually because the existing position that the brand holds has become less attractive.

Sears, for example, attempted to reposition itself from a place that offered great sales but unattractive prices the rest of the time to a store that consistently offered "everyday low prices." Repositioning in practice is very difficult to accomplish. A great deal of money is often needed for advertising and other promotional efforts, and in many cases, the repositioning fails.

To effectively attempt repositioning, it is important to understand how one's brand and those of competitors are perceived. One approach to identifying consumer product perceptions is *multidimensional scaling*. Here, we identify how products are perceived on two or more "dimensions," allowing us to plot brands against each other.

It may then be possible to attempt to "move" one's brand in a more desirable direction by selectively promoting certain points. There are two main approaches to multi-dimensional scaling. In the *a priori* approach, market researchers identify dimensions of interest and then ask consumers about their perceptions on each dimension for each brand.

This is useful when:

- The market researcher knows which dimensions are of interest and
- The customer's perception on each dimension is relatively clear.

In the *similarity rating* approach, respondents are not asked about their perceptions of brands on any specific dimensions. Instead, subjects are asked to rate the extent of *similarity* of different pairs of products Using a computer algorithms, the computer then identifies positions of each brand on a map of a given number of dimensions. The computer does not reveal what each dimension means—that must be left to human interpretation based on what the variations in each dimension appears to reveal. This second method is more useful when no specific product dimensions have been identified as being of particular interest or when it is not clear what the variables of difference are for the product category.

MARKET SEGMENTATION

Segmentation is the term given to the grouping of customers with similar needs by a number of different variables. Once this has been done, segments can be targeted by a number of targeting strategies. The stage that then follows is known as positioning which is the place that products or services occupy in the marketplace in relation to the competition, as perceived by the target market.

MARKET-SEGMENTATION CONCEPT

The underlying principle of market segmentation is that individual customers have different product and service needs. Mass marketing, the marketing of a single product to everyone, is rarely a viable strategy, just as it is to customise products to an individual.

MARKET SEGMENTATION PROCESS

The segmentation process is generally regarded as consisting of three stages; segmentation, targeting, and positioning.

SEGMENTATION VARIABLES

The first stage of the segmentation process involves the selection of suitable variables for grouping customers. These are also referred to as base variables or the segmentation basis. There is rarely one best way of segmenting a market and more than one variable can be used. There are a number of segmentation variables that can be used for consumer and business-to-business markets.

SEGMENTATION ANALYSIS

Research plays an important role in segmentation as segmentation analysis requires a range of data form a wide variety of sources on markets, customers' attitudes, motives and behaviour as well as competitor information.

TARGETING

Targeting is the next step in the sequential process and involves a business making choices about segment on which resources are to be focused. There are three major targeting strategies: undifferentiated, concentrated, and differentiated. During this process the business must balance its resources and capabilities against the attractiveness of different segments.

POSITIONING

Positioning follows on logically from the segmentation and targeting stages. Customer perceptions are central to the product position especially in relation to the competition's offering. The product or service has to satisfy key customer requirements and this has to be clearly communicated to customers. A tool that helps marketers understand customer perceptions of their brand is perceptual mapping and a simple 7- step approach can be used to develop a clear positioning strategy. However, a number of positioning problems can arise.

GETTING THE MOST OUT OF MARKET SEGMENTATION

Market segmentation, targeting and positioning are not always easy to apply and problems can arise for a number of reasons. There are a number of steps that can be taken to avoid these problems and, in addition, there are a set of segmentation criteria that can help.

FUTURE OF MARKET SEGMENTATION

The two key factors that will affect segmentation in the future are competitive and technological forces. In addition, there is a rising trend towards one-to-one marketing.

OBJECTIVES OF MARKET SEGMENTATION

Market segmentation is the first of three important steps in developing marketing strategy. Segmentation groups customers with similar needs and responses; targeting determines which segments to serve; positioning is about how the product should compete with others in the market. The objectives of market segmentation are to more accurately meet the needs of selected customers in a more profitable way. Precisely how this can be achieved will vary by company capability. For example, a single product company may be able to boost sales and cut advertising costs if they can target consumers with a high likelihood of product purchase. On the other hand, a company with several brands in a category will benefit by positioning each brand within the portfolio against a distinct set of consumer needs–ideally each brand should be sufficiently distinct so that there is little cannibalisation.

SEGMENTATION BASES

There is a large array of possible segmentation bases.

Demographics

Consumers can be grouped on the basis of characteristics such as age or household composition. This is easy to do and it is easy to reach such segments with media. But age and other demographics are only loosely related to behaviour.

Socioeconomic Characteristics

Similarly, characteristics such as income, occupation and education can be used to derive segments that are easy to reach. Such segments are indicators of behaviour such as lifestyle, price sensitivity, and brand preference.

Product Usage

Potential to use the firm's product is a behaviourally based segmentation basis. Potential could be determined by administering questions about disposition to use in a survey and respondents grouped accordingly. The problem is then how to reach the most attractive segments. This is done either by using a large-scale single source survey that asks consumers about product disposition and media usage or by relating product disposition to demographics. Both approaches are usually imperfect as behaviour is rarely strongly correlated with demographics or media usage.

Psychographics

Personality, attitudes, opinions, and life styles are often used a segmentation bases. These characteristics have some relationship to behaviour and provide insight into how to communicate with chosen segments. Reaching the chosen segments is then the issue, as discussed under product usage.

Generation

Generation, or cohort, refers to people born in the same period of time. For example, the Baby Boomer generation can be defined as those people born between 1946 and 1955. Such cohorts share much in common. Not only are they of a similar age, but they experienced similar economic, cultural, and political influences in formative years. Thus generation is probably a better segmentation basis than age and just as easy to reach.

Benefits Sought

Some people are price sensitive, others seek quality or service. Some people are brand loyal, while others frequently switch brands. It is possible to group consumers on the basis of these factors. Note that price/quality sensitivity can vary by category. Some people are very concerned about the quality of the food they eat but will buy cheap laundry detergent. Others will feed themselves any rubbish but are fastidious about cleanliness. This is a very powerful basis for segmentation but it is not easy to buy media on this basis. These segments can be reached by the message but this is not necessarily cost effective.

Geography

There are two reasons why people who live in the same area may share similar characteristics. First, some areas have more expensive properties than others and so people with similar socioeconomic characteristics may cluster together. Second, they have similar transport and shopping options. It is easy to reach particular areas by using local newspapers, cinema, outdoor, and selective direct mail but mass media is less effective.

Geodemographic

There are several commercial geodemographic segmentation plans available, that combine demographics and geography as a segmentation basis. This approach aims to identify groups of small geographic areas that have similar demographic profiles. These tend to suffer from the fallacy of averages. Some areas may be genuinely relatively homogenous but many are not and this can be very misleading.

HOW MARKET SEGMENTATION CAN INCREASE PROFIT

Increasing profits is the major objective of companies. We can write the profit for a product down as a formula:

Profit = Volume*(Price–Variable Cost) – Marketing Costs–Fixed Costs

There are several ways in which effective segmentation can boost profits:

- By better meeting customer needs, through better positioning to chosen segments, we may be able to increase market share and hence volume.
- By better meeting needs, we may also be able to increase price without sacrificing much volume.
- By only targeting the most profitable segments, we may be able to reduce marketing costs.

METHODS OF MARKET SEGMENTATION

There is a large array of analytical techniques applicable to market segmentation..

Cluster Analysis

Cluster analysis is a set of techniques for discovering structure, or groups of individuals, within a set of data comprising measures on each individual. The measures could be, for example, an attitudinal battery. There is no dependent variable–all variables are treated equally.

Conjoint Analysis

This technique aims to decompose preference into component parts, such as brand, quality, and price. This technique views products as bundles of attributes and uses an experimental design to vary attribute levels to create product descriptions. Survey respondents then rank the products and the analysis works out how much each attribute contributes to preference. It is a good technique for benefit segmentation.

CHAID/Regression Trees

This was called Automatic Interaction Detection for a long time and now also goes under various names used by software vendors, including Regression Tree, Answer Tree, Classification Tree and CART. It is a technique frequently employed in Data Mining and it is a useful exploratory analysis technique prior to regression analysis. It can quickly analyse a large set of candidate explanatory variables to determine the most influential variables on a dependent variable. The basic idea is to hierarchically segment the population on the database based on a dependent variable such as bought/did not buy a product.

The explanatory variables are categorical too, such as:

- Demographic variables;
- Attitudes;
- Previous behaviour.

Discriminant Analysis

This technique is used to quantify the relationship between segment membership and explanatory variables such as income and attitudes. It is often used after CHAID identifies candidate explanatory variables, to formally quantify and test the significance of relationships.

DEVELOPING A TARGET MARKET STRATEGY

Developing a target market strategy has three phases:

1. Analysing consumer demand
2. Targeting the market(s)
   - Undifferentiated
   - Concentrated
   - Multisegmented
3. Developing the marketing strategy

SELECTING TARGET MARKETS

Need to aggregate consumers with similar needs. Demand patterns: Do all potential customers have similar needs/desires or are there clusters?

Types of demand patterns are:

- Homogeneous Demand-uniform, everyone demands the product for the same reason(s). Very rare in the US, staple foods...
- Clustered Demand-consumer demand classified in 2 or more identifiable clusters.

IE Automobiles:

- Luxury
- Cheap
- Sporty
- Spacious

- Diffused Demand-Product differentiation more costly and more difficult to communicate IE Cosmetic market, need to offer hundreds of shades of lipstick. Firms try to modify consumer demand to develop clusters of at least a moderate size. Or uses one MM.

TARGETING

After the process of segmentation the next step is for the organisation to decide how it is going to target these particular group(s). There are three targeting options an organisation can adopt.

UNDIFFERENTIATED MARKETING

Sometimes referred to as mass marketing the firm may decide to aim its resources at the entire market with one particular product. Coca Colas original marketing strategy was based on this form. One product aimed at the mass market in the hope that a sufficient amount of buyers would be attracted., although there are now changes in their product line to cater for growing dietary and caffeine free needs of consumers.

DIFFERENTIATED MARKETING STRATEGY

Where the firm decides to target several segments and develops distinct products/services with separate marketing mix strategies aimed at the varying groups. An example of this would be airline companies offering first, business or economy class tickets, with separate marketing programmes to attract the different groups.

CONCENTRATED MARKETING

Where the organisation concentrates its marketing effort on one particular segment. The firm will develop a product that caters for the needs of that particular group. For example Rolls Royce cars aim its vehicles at the premium segment, same as Harrods within the UK.

CHOOSING MARKET SEGMENTS

The second step in selecting target markets requires the marketer to critically evaluate the segments identified in Step 1 in order to select those which are most attractive. For small firms this step may not be very involving since they may lack the resources needed to do it effectively. So they are often left with using their own intuition or judgment to determine which segments are the most promising. For companies with the time and money to commit to this step, the results may identify the segments that are primary candidates for current marketing efforts and also present segments that are future targets for the company's offerings.

In determining whether a segment is worthy of being a target market, the marketer needs to address the following questions:

- Is the segment large enough to support the marketer's objectives? This is an especially critical question if the marketer is entering a market served by many competitors.
- Is the segment showing signs of growth? One of the worst situations for a marketer is to enter a market whose growth is flat or declining, especially if competitors already exist.
- Does the company have the necessary skills, knowledge and expertise to service the segment? The company should understand and be able to communicate with the customers in the segment, otherwise they may face a significant learning curve in understanding how to effectively market to a segment.
- Does the segment meet the mission of the company? The segment should not extend too far beyond the direction the company has chosen to take.

Once one or more segments have been identified the marketer must choose the most attractive option(s) for their marketing efforts. At this point the choice becomes the firm's target market(s).

Chapter 7

Plan of Marketing

THE STEPS OF A MARKETING PLAN

The homogeneous mass market, which has dictated the offerings of U. S. producers since the dawn of the industrial revolution, is confronting its demise. At least, that's the word from advertising and marketing experts as we stand at the threshold of the new millennium. If you don't believe it, look no further than assembly-line hamburger maker, Burger King, which was a forerunner in realising that customers want it "their way" and their way is not necessarily everyone else's. As touted in its advertising, Burger King offered "customised" burgers based on a patron's preferences - down to the ketchup - a far cry from the typical one-way-suits-all quarter-pounder. Because the mass market is splintering into fragments, now is an opportune time to figure out which fragments are yours. Writes prophetess of trends Faith Popcorn in her latest version of The Popcorn Report, "Markets are becoming niches and niches are growing smaller. As this market miniaturization occurs, customers gain more stature - and they know it." Reaching those customers requires a new strategy. The scattershot advertising approach, which wasn't necessarily all that effective in the past, will be even less so in the 21st century. The most obvious alternative, shifting to narrower and more specialized markets, is already being tried by many small firms with substantial success.

FIND A NICHE

Atlantic Publication Group in Charleston, South Carolina, spent four years offering broad-based, general interest magazines to a market already saturated with competition. Then in 1989, company president Marvin Jenkins decided it was time to change direction and develop products for specific niches.

Now APG produces 28 publications for many different kinds of organizations. It has grown from four to 11 employees and revenues have tripled. Every APG product is developed in response to a particular need. "Specifically, we search for groups that have a database of readers and are looking for ways to communicate with them," Jenkins explains. APG enters into multi-year contracts to produce publications for groups such as trade associations, economic development entities, municipalities, regulators, architects and others. When a resort needed a services directory for its 40,000 guests, for example, APG produced it.

Clients grant APG exclusive rights to publish the information and sell advertising to defray production charges. The cost to the clients varies with each situation. Sometimes there is no cost at all. For instance, the state of South Carolina annually publishes a book of hunting and fishing regulations, which also carries advertising. The publication used to cost $40,000; now the price tag is zero, thanks to the advertising APG sells.

"Niche marketing is really refinement of product," Jenkins asserts. "The trick is to be open-minded. Look honestly at what you're doing and whether it is working. If not, small companies have the flexibility to change direction." Tapping specific niches can also help small firms stand out from the crowd. "A business must differentiate itself in ways that are important to the customer," notes Philip Kotler, professor of international marketing at Northwestern University.

"Small firms are uniquely positioned for niche marketing. If a small enterprise sits down and follows the principles of targeting, segmenting and differentiating, it doesn't have to collapse to larger companies. "A business can actually be more profitable by going for the niche rather than the volume," he elaborates, "and new technology presents many opportunities for new niches."

RIDING THE SUPERHIGHWAY

Advances in communications technology really do add a valuable new arrow to the small firm's marketing quiver. An increasingly wired population is turning for information to computer online services, cable TV and the information superhighway. Consumers will have a choice not only in the diversions they choose, but also in the method of delivery.

The highly touted and publicized information superhighway, or Internet, may at first glance seem beyond reach to most small companies. But it is probably one of their most effective targeting mediums, and the cost of traveling it may be cheaper than you expect. One pioneering small business, Schoolkids Records in Ann Arbor, Michigan, recently decided to chance the superhighway's uncharted advertising territory. Founded in 1976, Schoolkids operated a main store and two smaller, separate stores devoted to classical music and alternative rock. In November 1994, the record purveyor opened a fourth store, this time on the Internet.

Customers can now read an electronic advertisement that lists the newest releases accompanied by brief reviews. The ad also includes the store's toll-free 800 number and even a map showing how to get there. Customers can order compact discs on line and, if their computers are properly equipped, even listen to samples of the music being offered for sale. "In the first few months alone, we've been receiving 400 to 500 calls a day, and the bottom-line results are very positive," notes founder and owner Steve Bergman. "We're also getting a lot of e-mail messages from Internet users who say they love the visual appearance of our ads. "When you're a small company as we are, you have to be creative," Bergman asserts. "And by being on the Internet, we have an opportunity to impress people the way we impress them in our store. We are convinced this advertising avenue will pay off, and are in it for the long term."

Owners of a tiny Texas company, Id, share Bergman's pioneering spirit. As creators of a computer software game called Doom, they faced a problem typical of software firms, especially small ones: how to advertise and sell Doom to the largest audience at the lowest cost. Id decided to try a technique that is gaining favour with software firms of all sizes. It posted a basic version of Doom on the Internet and let people download it at no charge. The strategy was to get players so hooked on Doom that they would send in $40 for a full version of the game. The plan worked beautifully. Since it was posted on the Internet in December 1993, millions of people have downloaded free versions of Doom and more than 100,000 have paid for a full copy.

"The kind of public recognition we've gotten with Doom - including movie offers and product endorsements - is unheard of," marvels Jay Wilbur, Id's chief executive officer and business manager. "'Shareware' endears us to the public, especially when we tell people who download Doom to play the game even if they don't want to buy it."

MARKET RESEARCH

The Internet is also an effective tool for finding out what your customers want. "More and more companies are using the Internet to communicate with their customers," reports Jane Torbica of CompuServe. "You can go on line to ask customers for product or service ideas or any other input you are seeking."

The Internet also serves as a kind of online Yellow Pages. Firms listed on the Internet are categorized just like the printed version of the Yellow Pages, so it's easy for customers to search for the type of company and product they need.

LOG ON CAREFULLY

While widely acknowledged as the wave of the future, the Internet still poses some challenges for advertisers. Because millions of people can tap into Internet transmissions, for example, it's risky for customers to e-mail their credit card numbers when making a purchase.

Therefore, many companies are waiting for a secure way to exchange financial data and presently use the Internet to advertise while actually selling by phone, mail or in person. Even if online selling is secure, it's not expected to be all that popular in the near future. According to the San Francisco research firm Odyssey, only six per cent of U.S. households currently has any online computer connection. Still, that works out to approximately 5.7 million families nationwide - a market well worth targeting. And the number of subscribers is forecasted to grow steadily.

THE PERSONAL TOUCH

A seemingly contradictory trend will also shape marketing efforts in the next century: that of personal customer service. Claims Faith Popcorn, "'New' will no longer be a compelling selling point, which is an amazing idea in the American marketplace. We've had 'new' all our lives. Now `new' is old. "`New improved' won't do much for consumers, either," she continues, "except make them say out loud what they've always wondered: 'Why didn't you make it good enough in the first place?'

"What will make us buy one product over another is a feeling of partnership with the seller," concludes Popcorn. "Anonymous, impersonal selling is over. We want to buy from a person, a person whom we trust. Trust will be implicit in every purchase." Nancy Ozawa, researcher at the Institute for the Future in Palo Alto, California, agrees. "To succeed in the future, companies will need to focus on their customers and reorganize around their needs.

Once this is accomplished, it's time to get closer to your customers. One way of doing that," she suggests, "is to follow up with customers after transactions to find out if they are satisfied. "And by follow up I don't mean surveys." declares Ozawa. "Pizza Hut, for example, has a toll-free 800 number for complaints and a manager returns a customer's call within 24 hours. The managers are trained to carefully listen to people's voices in order to understand their level of frustration. As a result, customers feel comfortable that their problem is being resolved. Because nine out of 10 people who have problems don't tell you," she emphasizes, "it's important to use that one person who does to uncover the problems of the nine others and fix them."

A MORE EDUCATED CONSUMER

In their book Future Tense, Ozawa's peers at the Institute for the Future, Ian Morrison and Greg Schmid, advise that "anyone connected with the business world must focus time and attention on understanding the driving forces changing today's business environment." Two of those forces are the widening and more proficient use of advanced technology and consumer expectations of more personal service. These two forces also define the 21st century consumer. "Businesses in the next millennium will serve consumers who are more sophisticated and educated," Ozawa predicts. "Well over 50 per cent will have a high school diploma by the year 2000. "Tomorrow's consumers will also be more demanding and vocal, and will expect companies to meet their needs," she adds. "And they will use their wallets to vote for the winners."

STRATEGIES IN THE MARKETPLACE

The three primary strategies followed in the Indian hospitality industry are franchise agreements, marketing alliances, and representations.

Franchise Agreements

The primary motive of a brand franchise agreement is retaining ownership, while receiving a chain advantage. The areas where a company can gain through a franchise agreement is the accessibility of financing, easier start up, existing operating system, business assistance, established customer base, use of nationally recognised name, national marketing, access to discounted vendor relationships, benefit of loyalty programmes worldwide, etc.

Alliances in India are with highly experienced and renowned companies who bring with them management expertise and in-depth knowledge of the industry. They help in operating internally as one integrated hotel company while enhancing the distinct characteristics of each brand in the market. This model can be applied across all verticals with a few alterations. Some of the players dominating the market are

Cendant Corporation, Choice Hotels India, Carlson Hospitality India, Sarovar Park Hotels and Resorts. Another version of this is the management franchise agreement that is increasingly becoming popular today.

Marketing Alliances

These reciprocal relationships are primarily for cross-promotional purposes. It includes joint marketing activities that include joint participation in trade shows, sales events, culinary promotions and niche marketing programmes and sales leads, mutual benefits for loyalty members.

Explaining the rational behind this is Ajoy Misra, senior vice president, of Indian Hotels Company, who says, "With continuous support from either sides, alliances can help us make forays into markets that would otherwise be uneconomical for us to move into, at least in the next five years. Singapore features as one of the top 10 source markets for us while India witnessed about 24,000 arrivals from South Korea in 2005 - an increase by 24 per cent over last year. All these indicators reflect that our alliance is a way forward in getting more business from these markets." He sees global alliances developing in the future with alliance partners having to move towards providing seamless travel and accommodation solution to their customers. "Merging of loyalty programmes and a wider airline route on which the customers can collect loyalty points is the way forward," he concludes.

Representations

Another visible strategy adopted by hotels is an alliance with a company to represent and market the brand internationally, a strategy followed by the Park Hotels with the Design Hotels, and Taj Hotels with the Leading Hotels of the World. V V Giri, associate vice president and general manager of The Park, Chennai cites, "This affiliation takes our company vision and expands it to the world gateways, giving us a place to market the brand internationally.

Our brand mission is to lead by differentiation and Design Hotels fulfills that platform; it helps us reach like-minded travellers who believe in this brand philosophy."

MARKETING PLAN

There are two major components to your marketing strategy:

- How your enterprise will address the competitive marketplace

- How you will implement and support your day to day operations.

In today's very competitive marketplace a strategy that insures a consistent approach to offering your product or service in a way that will outsell the competition is critical. However, in concert with defining the marketing strategy you must also have a well defined methodology for the day to day process of implementing it. It is of little value to have a strategy if you lack either the resources or the expertise to implement it.

In the process of creating a marketing strategy you must consider many factors. Of those many factors, some are more important than others. Because each strategy must address some unique considerations, it is not reasonable to identify 'every' important factor at a generic level. However, many are common to all marketing strategies. Some of the more critical are described below.

You begin the creation of your strategy by deciding what the overall objective of your enterprise should be. In general this falls into one of four categories:

- If the market is very attractive and your enterprise is one of the strongest in the industry you will want to invest your best resources in support of your offering.
- If the market is very attractive but your enterprise is one of the weaker ones in the industry you must concentrate on strengthening the enterprise, using your offering as a stepping stone towards this objective.
- If the market is not especially attractive, but your enterprise is one of the strongest in the industry then an effective marketing and sales effort for your offering will be good for generating near term profits.
- If the market is not especially attractive and your enterprise is one of the weaker ones in the industry you should promote this offering only if it supports a more profitable part of your business or if it absorbs some of the overhead costs of a more profitable segment. Otherwise, you should determine the most cost effective way to divest your enterprise of this offering.

Having selected the direction most beneficial for the overall interests of the enterprise, the next step is to choose a strategy for the offering that will be most effective in the market. This means choosing one of the following 'generic' strategies.

- A Cost Leadership Strategy is based on the concept that you can produce and market a good quality product or service at a lower cost than your competitors. These low costs should translate to profit margins that are higher than the industry average. Some of the conditions that should exist to support a cost leadership strategy include an on-going availability of operating capital, good process engineering skills, close management of labour, products designed for ease of manufacturing and low cost distribution.
- A Differentiation strategy is one of creating a product or service that is perceived as being unique "throughout the industry". The emphasis can be on brand image, proprietary technology, special features, superior service, a strong distributor network or other aspects that might be specific to your industry. This uniqueness should also translate to profit margins that are higher than the industry average. In addition, some of the conditions that should exist to support a differentiation strategy include strong marketing abilities, effective product engineering, creative personnel, the ability to perform basic research and a good reputation.
- A Focus Strategy may be the most sophisticated of the generic strategies, in that it is a more 'intense' form of either the cost leadership or differentiation strategy. It is designed to address a "focused" segment of the marketplace, product form or cost management process and is usually employed when it isn't appropriate to attempt an 'across the board' application of cost leadership or differentiation. It is based on the concept of serving a particular target in such an exceptional manner, that others cannot compete. Usually this means addressing a substantially smaller market segment than others in the industry, but because of minimal competition, profit margins can be very high.

Pricing

Having defined the overall offering objective and selecting the generic strategy you must then decide on a variety of closely related operational strategies. One of these is how you will price the offering. A pricing strategy is mostly influenced by your requirement for net income and your objectives for long term market control. There are three basic strategies you can consider. A Skimming Strategy: If your offering has enough differentiation to justify a high price and you desire quick cash and have minimal desires for significant market penetration and control, then you set your prices very high. A Market Penetration Strategy: If near term income is not so critical and rapid market penetration for eventual market control is desired, then you set your prices very low. A Comparable Pricing Strategy: If you are not the market leader in your industry then the leaders will most likely have created a 'price expectation' in the minds of the marketplace. In this case you can price your offering comparably to those of your competitors.

PROMOTION

To sell an offering you must effectively promote and advertise it. There are two basic promotion strategies, PUSH and PULL.

- The Push Strategy maximizes the use of all available channels of distribution to "push" the offering into the marketplace. This usually requires generous discounts to achieve the objective of giving the channels incentive to promote the offering, thus minimizing your need for advertising.
- The Pull Strategy requires direct interface with the end user of the offering. Use of channels of distribution is minimized during the first stages of promotion and a major commitment to advertising is required. The objective is to "pull" the prospects into the various channel outlets creating a demand the channels cannot ignore.

There are many strategies for advertising an offering. Some of these include:

- *Product Comparison advertising:* In a market where your offering is one of several providing similar capabilities, if your offering stacks up well when comparing features then a product comparison ad can be beneficial.
- *Product Benefits advertising:* When you want to promote your offering without comparison to competitors, the product benefits ad is the correct approach. This is especially beneficial when you have introduced a new approach to solving a user need and comparison to the old approaches is inappropriate.
- *Product Family advertising:* If your offering is part of a group or family of offerings that can be of benefit to the customer as a set, then the product family ad can be of benefit.
- *Corporate advertising*: When you have a variety of offerings and your audience is fairly broad, it is often beneficial to promote your enterprise identity rather than a specific offering.

Distribution

You must also select the distribution method you will use to get the offering into the hands of the customer.

These include:

- On-premise Sales involves the sale of your offering using a field sales organization that visits the prospect's facilities to make the sale.
- Direct Sales involves the sale of your offering using a direct, in-house sales organization that does all selling through the Internet, telephone or mail order contact.
- Wholesale Sales involves the sale of your offering using intermediaries or "middle-men" to distribute your product or service to the retailers.
- Self-service Retail Sales involves the sale of your offering using self service retail methods of distribution.
- Full-service Retail Sales involves the sale of your offering through a full service retail distribution channel.

Of course, making a decision about pricing, promotion and distribution is heavily influenced by some key factors in the industry and marketplace. These factors should be analysed initially to create the strategy and then regularly monitored for changes. If any of them change substantially the strategy should be reevaluated.

The Environment

Environmental factors positively or negatively impact the industry and the market growth potential of your product/service.

Factors to consider include:

- *Government actions*: Government actions can support or detract from your strategy. Consider subsidies, safety, efficacy and operational regulations, licensing requirements, materials access restrictions and price controls.
- *Demographic changes*: Anticipated demographic changes may support or negatively impact the growth potential of your industry and market. This includes factors such as education, age, income and geographic location.
- *Emerging technology:* Technological changes that are occurring may or may not favour the actions of your enterprise.
- *Cultural trends*: Cultural changes such as fashion trends and

life style trends may or may not support your offering's penetration of the market

The Prospect

It is essential to understand the market segment as defined by the prospect characteristics you have selected as the target for your offering.

Factors to consider include:

- The potential for market penetration involves whether you are selling to past customers or a new prospect, how aware the prospects are of what you are offering, competition, growth rate of the industry and demographics.
- The prospect's willingness to pay higher price because your offering provides a better solution to their problem.
- The amount of time it will take the prospect to make a purchase decision is affected by the prospects confidence in your offering, the number and quality of competitive offerings, the number of people involved in the decision, the urgency of the need for your offering and the risk involved in making the purchase decision.
- The prospect's willingness to pay for product value is determined by their knowledge of competitive pricing, their ability to pay and their need for characteristics such as quality, durability, reliability, ease of use, uniformity and dependability.
- Likelihood of adoption by the prospect is based on the criticality of the prospect's need, their attitude about change, the significance of the benefits, barriers that exist to incorporating the offering into daily usage and the credibility of the offering.

The Product/Service

You should be thoroughly familiar with the factors that establish products/services as strong contenders in the marketplace.

Factors to consider include:

- Whether some or all of the technology for the offering is proprietary to the enterprise.
- The benefits the prospect will derive from use of the offering.
- The extent to which the offering is differentiated from the competition.
- The extent to which common introduction problems can be

avoided such as lack of adherence to industry standards, unavailability of materials, poor quality control, regulatory problems and the inability to explain the benefits of the offering to the prospect.

- The potential for product obsolescence as affected by the enterprise's commitment to product development, the product's proximity to physical limits, the ongoing potential for product improvements, the ability of the enterprise to react to technological change and the likelihood of substitute solutions to the prospect's needs.
- Impact on customer's business as measured by costs of trying out your offering, how quickly the customer can realise a return from their investment in your offering, how disruptive the introduction of your offering is to the customer's operations and the costs to switch to your offering.
- The complexity of your offering as measured by the existence of standard interfaces, difficulty of installation, number of options, requirement for support devices, training and technical support and the requirement for complementary product interface.

The Competition

It is essential to know who the competition is and to understand their strengths and weaknesses.

Factors to consider include:

- Each of your competitor's experience, staying power, market position, strength, predictability and freedom to abandon the market must be evaluated.

Your Enterprise

An honest appraisal of the strength of your enterprise is a critical factor in the development of your strategy.

Factors to consider include:

- Enterprise capacity to be leader in low-cost production considering cost control infrastructure, cost of materials, economies of scale, management skills, availability of personnel and compatibility of manufacturing resources with offering requirements.
- The enterprise's ability to construct entry barriers to competition such as the creation of high switching costs,

gaining substantial benefit from economies of scale, exclusive access to or clogging of distribution channels and the ability to clearly differentiate your offering from the competition.

- The enterprise's ability to sustain its market position is determined by the potential for competitive imitation, resistance to inflation, ability to maintain high prices, the potential for product obsolescence and the 'learning curve' faced by the prospect.
- The prominence of the enterprise.
- The competence of the management team.
- The adequacy of the enterprise's infrastructure in terms of organization, recruiting capabilities, employee benefit programmes, customer support facilities and logistical capabilities.
- The freedom of the enterprise to make critical business decisions without undue influence from distributors, suppliers, unions, creditors, investors and other outside influences.
- Freedom from having to deal with legal problems.

Development

A review of the strength and viability of the product/service development Programme will heavily influence the direction of your strategy.

Factors to consider include:

- The strength of the development manager including experience with personnel management, current and new technologies, complex projects and the equipment and tools used by the development personnel.
- Personnel who understand the relevant technologies and are able to perform the tasks necessary to meet the development objectives.
- Adequacy and appropriateness of the development tools and equipment.
- The necessary funding to achieve the development objectives.
- Design specifications that are manageable.

Production

You should review your enterprise's production organization with respect to their ability to cost effectively produce products/services.

The following factors are considered:

- The strength of production manager including experience with personnel management, current and new technologies, complex projects and the equipment and tools used by the manufacturing personnel.
- Economies of scale allowing the sharing of operations, sharing of production and the potential for vertical integration.
- Technology and production experience
- The necessary production personnel skill level and/or the enterprise's ability to hire or train qualified personnel.
- The ability of the enterprise to limit suppliers bargaining power.
- The ability of the enterprise to control the quality of raw materials and production.
- Adequate access to raw materials and sub-assembly production.

Marketing/Sales

The marketing and sales organization is analysed for its strengths and current activities.

Factors to consider include:

- Experience of Marketing/Sales manager including contacts in the industry familiarity with advertising and promotion, personal selling capabilities, general management skills and a history of profit and loss responsibilities.
- The ability to generate good publicity as measured by past successes, contacts in the press, quality of promotional literature and market education capabilities.
- Sales promotion techniques such as trade allowances, special pricing and contests.
- The effectiveness of your distribution channels as measured by history of relations, the extent of channel utilization, financial stability, reputation, access to prospects and familiarity with your offering.
- Advertising capabilities including media relationships, advertising budget, past experience, how easily the offering can be advertised and commitment to advertising.
- Sales capabilities including availability of personnel, quality of personnel, location of sales outlets, ability to generate sales leads, relationship with distributors, ability to demonstrate the benefits of the offering and necessary sales support capabilities.

- The appropriateness of the pricing of your offering as it relates to competition, price sensitivity of the prospect, prospect's familiarity with the offering and the current market life cycle stage.

Customer Services

The strength of the customer service function has a strong influence on long term market success.

Factors to consider include:

- Experience of the Customer Service manager in the areas of similar offerings and customers, quality control, technical support, product documentation, sales and marketing.
- The availability of technical support to service your offering after it is purchased.
- One or more factors that causes your customer support to stand out as unique in the eyes of the customer.
- Accessibility of service outlets for the customer.
- The reputation of the enterprise for customer service.

After defining your strategy you must use the information you have gathered to determine whether this strategy will achieve the objective of making your enterprise competitive in the marketplace. Two of the most important assessments are described below.

Cost to Enter Market

This is an analysis of the factors that will influence your costs to achieve significant market penetration.

Factors to consider include:

- Your marketing strength.
- Access to low cost materials and effective production.
- The experience of your enterprise.
- The complexity of introduction problems such as lack of adherence to industry standards, unavailability of materials, poor quality control, regulatory problems and the inability to explain the benefits of the offering to the prospect.
- The effectiveness of the enterprise infrastructure in terms of organization, recruiting capabilities, employee benefit Programmes, customer support facilities and logistical capabilities.

- Distribution effectiveness as measured by history of relations, the extent of channel utilization, financial stability, reputation, access to prospects and familiarity with your offering.
- Technological efforts likely to be successful as measured by the strength of the development organization.
- The availability of adequate operating capital.

Profit Potential

This is an analysis of the factors that could influence the potential for generating and maintaining profits over an extended period.

Factors to consider include:

- Potential for competitive retaliation is based on the competitors resources, commitment to the industry, cash position and predictability as well as the status of the market.
- The enterprise's ability to construct entry barriers to competition such as the creation of high switching costs, gaining substantial benefit from economies of scale, exclusive access to or clogging of distribution channels and the ability to clearly differentiate your offering from the competition.
- The intensity of competitive rivalry as measured by the size and number of competitors, limitations on exiting the market, differentiation between offerings and the rapidity of market growth.
- The ability of the enterprise to limit suppliers bargaining power.
- The enterprise's ability to sustain its market position is determined by the potential for competitive imitation, resistance to inflation, ability to maintain high prices, the potential for product obsolescence and the 'learning curve' faced by the prospect.
- The availability of substitute solutions to the prospect's need.
- The prospect's bargaining power as measured by the ease of switching to an alternative, the cost to look at alternatives, the cost of the offering, the differentiation between your offering and the competition and the degree of the prospect's need.
- Market potential for new products considering market growth, prospect's need for your offering, the benefits of the offering, the number of barriers to immediate use, the credibility of the offering and the impact on the customer's daily operations.

- The freedom of the enterprise to make critical business decisions without undue influence from distributors, suppliers, unions, investors and other outside influences.

PARTNERS

Fluidly interlocking into the fabric of business, alliances are indispensable drivers of growth in the hospitality industry. "The forces of a powerful ally can be useful and good to those who have recourse to them...but are perilous to those who become dependent on them." Niccolo Machiavelli, political genius and commentator, penned the aforementioned somewhat sinister version of alliances in his epochal 'The Prince'. While Machiavellianism alludes to alliances amongst unequals, the end justifying the means, in the realms of commerce it refers to a symbiotic relationship for mutual benefit between likeminded partners, equals in their own stead.

Historically, alliances resulted from spontaneous cooperation between people. The resultant synergies and innate power of a massive, yet heterogeneous body, with a unified objective furthered the interest of its constituent members. This flagged off its initial popularity in tourism, in a fragmented marketplace where resources were limited and the industry - heavily regulated.

The composite benefits of these associations weren't always visible to the end consumer and government. Having been perceived as a threat to a free economy as cartels, they resulted in taking recourse to anti-trust immunity in extreme cases, an attempt to prove them as pro-consumer and pro-competition. The scenario here is now replicating global patterns.

India, since independence, followed the socialist ideal with state control on resources, both natural and manmade. Most tourism policies were grounded in socio-political leanings and macro economic connotations with development restricted by the license-permit Raj. A tourism policy came into the picture as late as 1982 and a national Action Plan for Tourism, just 10 years later. An isolationist approach followed by the democratic government, a crippling paucity of funds to fuel growth, and an absence of infrastructure kept demand to the minimal. This somewhat bleak and regulated landscape drove strategic alliances to the forefront, with partners leveraging benefits of access to additional resources and a strong brand to increase network. This was primarily outward, be it airlines through code-sharing or hotels through marketing and franchise agreements, and much later in the day, through tactical alliances.

The opening of the economy stimulated tourism, which was growing till then in spurts and gasps. Today, the world's eyes are focused on India, and rightly so. The World Travel and Tourism Council's projection of travel and tourism growth for 2006-2015 in India is a staggering annualised rate of 8.6 per cent. Logically, the scenario impels one to capitalise on and leverage the strength of a partner, before the dust settles.

The Fundamentals of Alliances

Alliances fall in the category of either strategic alliances at one end of the spectrum or a time-bound tactical promotion at the other end. Each segment has a valid reason for an alliance, objectives being clearly etched out by the partners, benefiting consumers and bringing economic benefits to the parties.

A critical aspect of an alliance is the partner. Most organisations have a diktat to affiliate with the right partner, a brand which is the right fit with their own growth as well as the time frame to meet mutual objectives, taking cognisance of investments. For a successful alliance, you look for a like-minded business for a partner along with a value proposition to the customer, and the speed and readiness for rolling out to retain competitive edge, so that both sides gain, with measurability of the campaign's outcome.

Alliance partners within tourism share a symbiotic relationship with each key player working in tandem with the other, either within the same vertical or outside. No single supplier can be a claimant of success without an alliance, strategic or otherwise due to co-dependency. But were alliances the mainstay of all promotional activities and growth strategies? Not necessarily. They came into the picture only when the perceived success rate and profitability of the venture were compelling factors to cement their position.

Hotels traditionally looked at alliances to leverage a brand name. The examples of this were Holiday Inn franchisees or marketing franchise agreements in India, Taj Hotels and Shilla Hotels based in Korea - one of the oldest alliances being the marketing franchise between ITC-Welcome group with the Sheraton Corporation that lasted 30 years.

Each homegrown player strengthened its reach across borders, primed to capture a slice of the high spend market - primarily through the franchise route. This has been effectively employed by brands choosing to enter India, without taking recourse to sizeable investments. This strategy is not only popular with hotels but with other segments as well.

Choice Hotels India franchises its Quality Inn and Comfort Inn brands across India with the benefits of a chain affiliation accruing to partners, leveraging the brand's international reservations and optimising their yields. Vilas Pawar, CEO, Choice Hotels India, says, "Today it is difficult to create a brand. Establishing an identity needs a gestation period of about 50-60 years."

In such a scenario, a strategic brand partnership has found its roots within the segment, a popular recourse followed by many realtors foraying into the segment. But for the established brands, strategic marketing alliances with the additional bait of loyalty programmes are the preferred approach. For instance, Bharat Hotel's marketing alliances with the Intercontinental Hotel Group, such as Priority Club Rewards and the Ambassador Programme has ensured an increase in occupancy F&B revenues.

But it stretches to consumer goods too. Hyatt International has developed a strategic marketing partnership with Porsche that encompasses a range of joint marketing activities, in addition to one with Bang and Olufsen to specially design products and provide expertise to Hyatt, reveals Ratnesh Verma. Such alliances create an inspirational value to customers, and invariably, a brand connect and loyalty.

TYPES OF ALLIANCES

There are different objectives for forging an alliance with another partner, but they could be broadly categorised into the following: Strategic alliances are long-term associations with a higher commitment of resources.

It is essentially forged to build a long-term competitive advantage in the current business environment that is more global than regional, has more discerning and demanding consumers and is more dynamic than ever. Examples of this could be to launch a co-branded product, have a common loyalty programme or have a long-term joint marketing programme due to consonance between two brands in terms of customer demographics and image.

Tactical alliances are short-term associations, addressing short term needs. Examples could include sales promotion to boost sales in a lean period, acquire more customers into a loyalty programme or partner an event. It is also pertinent to mention that advances in technology and the evolution of the Internet have opened up new dimensions in this area.

Benefits of an Alliance

- Leverage of each other's brands through positive brand association
- Reach to a larger slice of their target audience through partner's database
- Gain competitive advantage by offering their customers more choices
- Stretch the marketing rupees
- Increased market share, revenues and incremental revenue earned
- Enhanced image and perception of the alliance partner
- Increased share of mind space with end customers

INDIAN HOSPITALITY

In 2004-05, Visakhapatnam was the market leader in terms of occupancy, registering occupancy of 80.6 per cent. Bangalore achieved the second-highest occupancy at 79.8 per cent. It also had the highest across all categories among the 30 cities, with an ARR of Rs 6,762. New Delhi was the second highest, registering an ARR of Rs 5,498. All India average occupancy was 63.6 per cent, an increase of 3.9 per cent occupancy points the previous year's level, or 6.5 per cent in real terms. All India ARR increased by 26.9 per cent over the previous year.

Star category-wise occupancies ranged between 46.3 per cent to 72.1 per cent. Average rates showed a much greater spread, from Rs 5,499 for five-star deluxe hotels to Rs 643 for one-star hotels, an increase of Rs 1,052 and Rs 140, respectively, from the previous year. The All India average revenue per available room increased substantially, from Rs 1,605 in 2003-04 to Rs 2,170 in 2004-05, reflecting an increase of 35.2 per cent. In the eight years of the survey, this has been the second-highest RevPAR growth.

Rooms revenue, generally considered being the most important source of a hotel's overall profitability, was 57.7 per cent of total revenue for five-star deluxe hotels, 60.1 per cent of total revenue for five-star hotels and 56.6 per cent for four-star hotels. Overall it represented 57.3 per cent of total revenue. Food and Beverage revenue represented 28.3 per cent of total revenue across all hotels, a decrease of 4.6 per cent from last year. The all India average of Rooms department expense as a percentage of Rooms revenue declined further from 17.8 per cent in 2003-04 to 14.7 per cent in 2004-05.

Similarly, the all India average Food and Beverage department expense as a percentage of Food and Beverage revenue declined from 55.9 per cent in 2003-04 to 53.9 per cent in 2004-05. Minor Operated department expense as a percentage of Minor Operated department revenue registered an increase from 53.7 per cent in 2003-04 to 58.8 per cent in 2004-05. Telephone and other department expense, at 64.3 per cent of total revenue, was the highest departmental expense. Total departmental expense as a percentage of total departmental revenue reflected a further decline, from 37.4 per cent in 2002-03 and 33.7 per cent in 2003-04 to 30.9 per cent in 2004-05. This is partly owing to higher ARRs. Percentage of foreign guests increased to 28.3 per cent in 2004-05, compared to 25.0 per cent in 2003-04, primarily as the percentage of foreign business travellers grew. Of the foreign guests, the UK provided the largest demand, at 16.2 per cent, followed by USA, at 12.8 per cent, and France at 7.2 per cent. Domestic guests continue to be the most important segment for the Indian hotel industry, accounting for 71.7 per cent of all guests in 2004-05, though this has decreased marginally from 75 per cent in 2003-04 and 76.9 per cent in 2002-03.

All India average stay of a business traveller has increased from two days to 2.4 days. There is an increase in foreign business travellers utilising five-star deluxe, five-star, four-star hotels and heritage hotels from 27 per cent, 18.6 per cent, 11.4 per cent and 11.7 per cent, respectively, in 2003-04 to 28.1 per cent, 21.4 per cent, 13.7 per cent and 14.1 per cent, respectively, in 2004-05.

Owing to all India increased occupancy, property operations and maintenance expenses per available room has increased from Rs 69,735 in 2003-04 to Rs 91,981 in 2004-05. Average monthly occupancy was highest in December, followed by November and January, February. Direct enquiry and advance reservations by travel agents and tour operators cumulatively comprise 75.9 per cent of reservation source for the Indian hotel industry.

Five-star deluxe hotels are making the best use of GDS as 8.1 per cent of the total reservations for five-star deluxe hotels come from GDS, against the all India average of 1.7 per cent. GDS reservations generally provide higher room rates compared to the other channels. Print advertising is the most popular medium used by the Indian hotel industry with the all India average at 92.2 per cent of hotels using it, followed by 82.5 per cent using direct mails.

Radio advertising features as the least utilised marketing media at 8.4 per cent, followed by merchandising at 24.5 per cent, by the Indian hotel industry in 2004-05. All five-star deluxe hotels used the hotel website at 100 per cent as a marketing medium in 2004-05. Credit cards as a mode of transaction increased from 27.7 per cent and 30.4 per cent in 2002-03 and 2003-04, respectively to 32.5 per cent in 2004-05. Credit cards remained the most popular method of payment at five-star deluxe hotels at 47.4 per cent. Visa was the most widely used credit card by hotel guests in 2004-05, followed by Mastercard. American Express charged the highest credit card commission at 2.9 per cent against 1.7 per cent by Visa and Mastercard.

Comparison with the results of the survey in 2004-05 with the previous year, shows that nearly all categories saw an increase in occupancy and a significant increase in average rate. This resulted in a major increase in RevPAR across all categories with the highest RevPAR growth in four-star hotels at 41.9 per cent and an all India RevPAR growth at 35.2 per cent. The demand for rooms has been positive and owing to lack of adequate new supply, hotels in nearly all categories have managed to simultaneously increase the occupancy and average rates.

Among environmental issues, electricity consumption is the most monitored attribute, followed by water consumption. Five-star deluxe and five-star hotels continue to monitor environmental issues most closely. Energy expenses accounted for 8.9 per cent of total revenue in 2004-05 against 10.5 per cent of total revenue in 2003-04 and 12.3 per cent in 2002-03. This may be partly attributed to rising revenues and partly to the increase in efforts made to conserve energy by the industry in India.

Other Significant Trends

All India average revenue per hotel has grown significantly, from Rs 9.15 crore during 2003-04 to Rs 11.49 crore during 2004-05, and is expected to see further improvement in the next few years owing to an increase in occupancy and average rate.

House Profit as a percentage of revenue increased from 34.8 per cent in 2003-04 to 40.7 per cent in 2004-05. The all India average net income per hotel also increased, from Rs 2.80 crore in 2003-04 to Rs 4.08 crore in 2004-05, reflecting the overall health of the industry. July has the lowest monthly occupancy in the year. However, occupancy for all months was higher in 2004-05 compared to the last five years. The year 2004-05 saw a continuation of the growth momentum experience by the hotel industry in 2003-04. Most cities saw occupancy levels improve over the previous year and, consecutively for two years, both occupancy and average room rates have improved.

City Trends

The following paragraphs detail the expectations of new supply and performance for 19 important hotel markets, based on research undertaken and forecasts made by HVS International.

New Delhi

Occupancy witnessed a growth of 10.82 per cent in 2004-05. Average rates registered an increase of 29.43 per cent. The National Capital Region is expected to see an estimated 27 new hotels, serviced apartments and mixed-use developments with approximately 4,900 rooms in various categories over the next three to four years, with nearly 20 new hotels to be in Gurgaon alone. The new supply will start entering the market in 2007-08. This growth will be supported by significantly improved road and transport infrastructure, privatisation of the Delhi airport and demand induced by the Commonwealth Games, to be held in Delhi in 2010. There will be further increase in hotel activity, especially in the mid-market and budget segment, after the much-awaited auction of sites by the Delhi Development Authority.

Mumbai

Citywide occupancy in Mumbai increased by 13.0 per cent and average rate witnessed an increase of 40.6 per cent in 2004-05. Mumbai is expected to see 19 new hotels, serviced apartments and mixed-use developments with approximately 4,950 rooms in various categories over the next three to four years. The bulk of the new supply will enter the Mumbai market by 2008-09. Most companies setting up operations in Mumbai now prefer to locate to new commercial districts in the suburbs like Andheri, Bandra-Kurla and Malad, and other periphery areas like Navi-Mumbai and Mulund; and, hotel development has shifted to these areas. Now, with availability of commercial space in the mills area, places like Parel, Lower Parel, Worli and Mahalaxmi will see increased hotel development activity. This is more so with the proposed development of Bandra-Worli Sea Link, which will significantly reduce the travel time between Bandra and central Mumbai.

Kolkata

Kolkata is expected to see 12 new hotels, serviced apartments and mixed-use developments with approximately 2,000 rooms entering the market in various categories over the next few years. The city is becoming a preferred location for conferences and seminars due to the relatively easy availability of space and at a lower cost as compared to other metros. It is also the commercial capital of the northeast region, with most companies basing their headquarters in the city.

Pune

Pune is expected to see 11 new hotels, serviced apartments and mixed-use developments with approximately 1,600 rooms in various categories over the next three to four years. The addition to supply, although quite high, is likely to be successfully absorbed, taking into account Pune's low room base of approximately 800 rooms and a continuous growth in the city's IT, ITeS, BPO and manufacturing industries.

Chennai

Chennai witnessed an occupancy increase of 15.7 per cent, following a decline for two consecutive years. The city saw a simultaneous increase in average rate by approximately 15.6 per cent. Chennai is expected to see 14 new hotels, serviced apartments and mixed-use developments with approximately 2,900 rooms in various categories over the next few years. The Old Mahabalipuram Road connecting Chennai with Mahabalipuram is being developed as an IT corridor to house various IT and ITeS companies. As existing tech parks are full to capacity, software companies are also looking at sick industrial unit areas such as Guindy, Taramani, Ambattur and Padi, which are being converted into software technology parks. We see Chennai as a stable market and expect it to continue to show improvements in occupancy and average rate in the next few years.

Bengaluru

Bangalore's hotel market grew marginally in terms of occupancy and by approximately 64.5 per cent in terms of the average room rate. This is on the back of very high demand and lack of new supply. Approximately 7.0 million square feet of commercial space is likely to be absorbed this fiscal year . Bangalore is expected to see, at last count, 27 new hotels, serviced apartments and mixed-use developments with approximately 6,100 rooms in various categories over the next few years. With work on the international airport having commenced the northern areas of the city will see pronounced commercial and hotel development activity. The first phase of the airport is estimated to open by October

2008. Road infrastructure, however, remains the biggest challenge for the city.

Goa

Goa is expected to see development of eight new hotels with approximately 1,200 rooms in various categories over the next 2-3 years. Goa is an extremely promising market with the highest average length of stay by both foreign and domestic guests. The proposed Mopa airport is anticipated to witness much higher traffic flow than the airport at Dabolim. Accompanying the airport project will be a new ground transportation system, which will benefit the whole of Goa.

Agra

Agra has seen an increase in occupancy of 22.9 per cent. Average rates have decreased marginally by 1.4 per cent. This may be partly attributed to a higher base surveyed in 2003-04 and an increase in smaller hotels participating in the survey. Tourists typically make a day trip to Agra from Delhi; the increase in occupancy is owing to the meetings and conference segment, which has seen a significant growth for two consecutive years.

Ahmedabad

The survey indicates an occupancy decline of 7.7 per cent and a decrease in average rate by 8.9 per cent. This may again be due to change in composition of hotels participating in the survey.

However, HVS's independent research indicates an estimated 15.0 per cent increase in both occupancy and average rate. Hotel activity will increase in the city owing to expected commercial growth on CG Road, Ashram Road, Satellite Road and SG Highway-particularly from the pharma, financial sector, telecom, retail, textiles, BPO and IT services.

Kochi

The survey indicates a decrease in occupancy of 4.2 per cent and a decrease in average rate by 22.3 per cent. This may be partly attributed to a variation in the hotels participating in the survey and does not reflect the true market condition. The city's hotel demand generators are mainly tourism related, with commercial demand borne out of shipping, Kochi Port, Cochin Shipyard, oil refineries and marine and agro export industries based in the city. Banking, financial services, insurance and the telecom sectors have seen growth over the past two years.

Hyderabad

In Hyderabad, overall occupancy increased by 3.3 per cent. Average rates registered an increase of 13.4 per cent over the previous year. HITEC City, HITEX, Genome Valley and ICICI Knowledge Park demonstrate the state's commitment to create world class infrastructure. The convention centre opening in 2006, with approximately 75,000 square feet of conferencing facility and 55 break-out rooms, is the first of its kind in South Asia. The convention centre will induce substantial demand for rooms in the city. The Hyderabad market will continue to witness a strong increase in occupancy and average rate in the next few years.

Jaipur

Occupancy levels increased by 14.2 per cent in 2004-05 and average rates increased by 10.0 per cent over the previous year. Besides being a preferred tourist and wedding destination, the city of Jaipur is gaining prominence as a commercial destination as well. This is owing to increased travel by buyers for gems, jewellery and textiles. With the proposal for a Jaipur special economic zone, an international airport and an ethnic village, the city will see development of new hotel projects. There is a chance of Jaipur facing an oversupply of rooms in 3-4 years.

Lucknow

Occupancy levels increased marginally by 0.6 per cent in 2004-05 and average rates increased by 10.0 per cent over the previous year. Lucknow has been a very stable market and is witnessing a rise in average rate for the last two years. Lately, Lucknow has also seen increased retail activity.

Nagpur

Nagpur witnessed a decline in occupancy by 10.1 per cent and a decrease in average rates by 5.5 per cent from the previous year. The Nagpur market has now declined for two years consecutively.

Thiruvananthapuram

The city witnessed a decrease in occupancy of 7.0 per cent, and a growth in average room rate of 38.6 per cent. Being the state capital, the city is a hub of political activity. Moreover, Thiruvananthapuram, with its famous beaches, is among the top tourist destinations in India. The city has grown as a tourist and commercial centre, with the international airport being one of the gateways into Kerala.

Udagamandalam

Ooty city has seen a decline in occupancy by 9.0 per cent and an increase in average rate by 15.6 per cent. Mainly a tourist destination, Ooty is known for its picturesque locales. The city is unlikely to see any major hotel activity in the next 2-3 years.

Udaipur

Citywide occupancy increased by 19.25 per cent in 2004-05. Average rate showed a steep increase of 53.65 per cent. The increase in the average rate may be partly attributed to the inclusion of luxury/heritage hotels in the survey. Udaipur has lately seen an increase in international events and is attracting many domestic off-site meetings, conferences and weddings as well.

Vadodara

Citywide occupancy increased marginally from 62.5 per cent in 2003-04 to 62.6 per cent in 2004-05. Similarly, the average rate increased from Rs 458 in 2003-04 to Rs467 in 2004-05. The Gujarat government has also been promoting the state as a commercial destination and is giving incentives to various companies.

Visakhapatnam

Visakhapatnam witnessed a steep increase in occupancy by 15.0 per cent in 2004-05 and an increase in average rates by 18.4 per cent. In the past, the city experienced rapid industrialization with the onset of major industries: an oil refinery, a large fertilizer factory, the Hindustan Zinc smelter and the Visakhapatnam steel plant.

INDIA LACKS INFRASTRUCTURE

Even as the city of Bangalore witnesses domestic and international visitors in equal measure, much like any other international metropolitan, it is still lacking in the most basic of amenities - infrastructure. We have vehicles that ply the city with registrations from across the country and the city's inhabitants speak more than four or five regional languages. We have the best specialty restaurants. Despite this, the existing facilities don't even meet national standards, forget international proportions. While she admits that there have been new hoteliers in the city most of whom are foreign brands, Marshall feels that all of this is sometimes a huge myth.

"I believe in construction!" She adds, "Sometimes, projects remain on paper, barring a few projects. I do hear from industry sources and read in print that a certain player is in a management tie-up with someone and certain realtors are venturing into the project. But there has not been one stone turned in the name of construction." While the international business travellers and domestic tourists who visit the city come looking for five-star properties, they all need to maneuver through potholes on bumpy roads.

Marshall believes that unless basic infrastructure is not taken care of with immediate effect, things might worsen. She says, "Infrastructure is mandatory. However, it is amazing to see how the city is still thriving with business travellers despite everything. Sadly the supply of quality hospitality services still continues to be in short supply. But hopefully things will improve in future both for the city and the travellers."

Right in the Eleventh Try

Hosting five million visitors from abroad has been the tourism industry's dream for well over a decade and a half. In the quest for this magic number a dream paper was drawn up in the early 1990s by the then cabinet secretary - an unusual level of initiative. That paper had envisaged an investment of Rs 36,000 crore from both the public and private sectors and a whole list of actions were listed to build the infrastructure to service that many tourists.

The move caused a lot of excitement among trade associations, a few ripples in the national media and received accolades from travel journals. As is the case with such grandiose ideas, industry leaders stopped talking about it. But the dream of five million arrivals somehow sustained itself as a reference point in any discussion on infrastructural requirements. Then came a new tourism secretary. He revived the 'strategy paper' in his own name with a few changes in the previous draft, and it received the same interest from national and trade media as well as trade conventions as before. The next step of implementation was neither demanded nor taken. But the dream of five million tourists persisted. Then there was a change of government. Tourism success stories from our neighbourhood had already made some dent on the socialism-stung leadership and the spirit of economic reforms wafted over the tourism sector as well. The prime minister's reference to the importance of tourism from the ramparts of the Red Fort on Independence Day confirmed that the sector was now on the national agenda. The Planning Commission made a five-fold increase in the allocation for tourism in the Tenth Plan. Aviation stepped out from darkness into brilliant sunshine. The rest is history.

This trip down memory lane was caused by the latest arrival statistics circulated by the tourism ministry. In the first nine months of this year, 3.06 million visitors came to India - an increase of 13.1 per cent over the same period in 2005. On the basis of this growth rate we should close the year with a count of 4.40 million, just 6,00,000 short of the coveted five million. And so 2006 will be remembered as the year in which we crossed the four-million mark. But wait; with a sustained growth of some 13 per cent in 2005 and 2006 so far, India can be sure of welcoming the five millionth visitor before 2007.

Interestingly, one entity to which the dream coming true will be no surprise is the Planning Commission. In its Tenth Plan projections, it had set a target of raising India's share of the world market from 0.39 per cent to 0.62 which many had thought was ambitious. Translated into numbers, the Commission's target would come to 5.6 million. Arrivals now projected would come pretty close to the Commission's calculations for which it deserves the industry's applause.

The Million Time-line

The country's march towards the five-million mark is also interesting. The first million was achieved in 1980. The second, fifteen years later, in 1995. It took another decade to reach three million in 2004 and only two years to get to four million in 2006. Hopefully, it will just take a year for its fifth million. Tourism ministry mandarins would like us to believe that it is all thanks to the Incredible India campaign. Some analysts would give a fair share of the credit to economic reforms and the burgeoning corporate traffic from abroad. Industry doyens would hasten to remind you that this is all fine. Indian tourism is definitely on the upswing but in the global context it has miles to go. Look at China's 37 million arrivals and well over 10 million counts of smaller countries like Malaysia and Thailand.

Tourism ministry mandarins would like us to believe that it is all thanks to the Incredible India campaign. Some analysts would give a fair share of the credit to economic reforms and the burgeoning corporate traffic from abroad. We are in the final year of the Tenth Plan and the approach to the Eleventh Plan scheduled to begin in April 2007 is now under discussion. Here is what the draft approach paper says on tourism: 'The contribution of tourism services in the GDP for 2002-03 is estimated at 5.83 per cent including direct and indirect effects. Tourism, as the third largest net earner of foreign exchange, earned some US $6 billion in 2005. Total employment, direct and indirect, generated by the sector is estimated at 38.6 million for 2002-03 constituting 8.27 per cent of the total employment in the country.

During the Eleventh Plan period, there is potential to generate 27 million additional jobs due to tourism. To fully benefit from natural, cultural, business, leisure, spiritual, religious, ecological, adventure and medical tourism, the Eleventh Plan should focus on creation of adequate tourism infrastructure like modernisation and expansion of airports, increase in accommodation facilities under star and budget category and improved road connectivity to tourist destinations.' Industry's lobbying for tourism's needs, it would seem, has reached the right address. A robust economy, growing businesses, greater purchasing power, and surge in business and leisure travel has resulted in a flourishing and booming hospitality industry. But with the opportunity comes difficult challenges. Mounting competition and rising guest expectations are compelling the industry to take a fresh look at their businesses. The emerging technologies, capabilities and supporting infrastructure are 'must have' tools to overcome these challenges and ensure a better tomorrow. Integration of the latest technologies in hospitality are fast becoming the cornerstone of delivery for profitability, guest satisfaction, and most importantly, a differentiating factor.

Chapter 8

Effects and Impacts of Internal Marketing and Sales

INTERNAL MARKETING

Internal marketing is an ongoing process that occurs strictly within a company or organization whereby the functional process aligns, motivates and empowers employees at all management levels to consistently deliver a satisfying customer experience. Relationship marketing stresses what it calls internal marketing. This refers to using marketing techniques within the organization itself. It is claimed that many of the traditional marketing concepts can be used to determine what the needs of "internal customers" are. According to this theory, every employee, team, or department in the company is simultaneously a supplier and a customer of services and products.

An employee obtains a service at a point in the value chain and then provides a service to another employee further along the value chain. If internal marketing is effective, every employee will both provide and receive exceptional service from and to other employees. It also helps employees understand the significance of their roles and how their roles relate to others'. If implemented well, it can also encourage every employee to see the process in terms of the customer's perception of value added, and the organization's strategic mission. Further it is claimed that an effective internal marketing Programme is a prerequisite for effective external marketing efforts. Key concepts of internal marketing include:

- IM functioning as a continual internal 'upskilling' process.
- Alignment of the organization's purpose with employee behaviour.

- Employees internalizing the core values of the organization.
- Motivation, reframing and empowerment of employee attitude.
- Inside-out management approach.
- Retaining a positive customer experience throughout the business objectives

Internal marketing used to be such a simple thing: an occasional product training day, a product launch at the annual sales conference, and a few memos to staff. Today's internal marketer faces a sterner, and much more crucial, task – driving and even changing organisational culture to ensure a business both survives and thrives. The Australian Marketing Institute's May webinar, 'Internal marketing', presented two case studies of internal marketing success, one which saved an Australian icon from oblivion and another that brought discipline and focus to a fragmented, uncoordinated recruitment operation.

The AMI webinar series is conducted through the online technology of Premier Global Services, which sponsors these professional development events. Members can participate in webinars from their home or work computer from any location in the world via the Internet and a standard telephone voice line. The first presenter was Maree Howard, head of HR, product manufacturing, AMP Financial Services who told of how the company had recovered from a near-death experience that began in 2002. Its biggest business had breached its minimum regulatory solvency level, precipating a public crisis that quickly cost the jobs of the CEO, most of the senior management, the chairman, most of the board, and 500 employees. "It was really quite a bewildering time for the employees," Howard said. "AMP was still basking in the glow from the Olympics and they still thought everything was great. All the messages that had been given to them by senior management was that we were a company with a grand vision for global expansion. "The organisation had to change very quickly and the existing culture that we had just wasn't going to help the process. The new senior management team was passionate about tackling really deep-seated cultural issues." Howard said AMP quickly had to become a nimble and commercial organisation.

This started with job and cost cutting, and then moved into remaking the culture. "We got through this period largely thanks to our senior leaders displaying absolute passion and commitment and integrity for our company, and they took the rest of us with them for the ride," Howard said. AMP realised that its culture was not as performance focused as it needed to be, and that there were several strong internal beliefs that would inhibit the necessary changes. These were:

Inhibiting belief	Reframed belief
Big is safe	High performance is our only security
Low cost means low quality	Examples of where this is not so, such as Toyota
Low performance is tolerated	There are adverse consequences for low performance and higher performance gets higher rewards
Risk and control are boring	Risk management is about business survivaland high performance
I need to be involved in everything	I trust those with the accountability

Howard said that the key message was "only high performance will give us security". "That was a very confronting message for our employees," she said. "What it was really talking about was that nobody owes us a living and that our heritage counts for very little on its own. "It also gave us a very measurable goal for our employees.

It allowed us to continually send a message to our staff that we need to raise the bar and that staying as we are, it's just not an option. We were trying to align our high performers and challenge our low performers, to say 'Is this still really the right place for you because this organisation is changing'." AMP chose a 'back to basics' approach to communicate its cultural change. It eschewed the glossy brochures, coffee cups and abseiling-type options and instead relied on the passion and personal integrity of its senior leaders to transmit the messages, consistently and repeatedly. The message became 'The AFS story'. "We used story telling as our platform for delivering our message," Howard said. "It's quite a personal message, and we made our leaders use their own personal credibility and put their own reputations on the line for the way they delivered the story.

"Our leaders talk about what makes them get up and come to work each morning. Why they are staying with AMP. What do they see the future actually holding. The beauty of it was that it allowed the message to be personalised in a way from that leader and not as some glossy corporate message that was delivered without adequate content."

Reinforcing the New Messages

The AFS Story was launched at "town hall sessions", where the managing director talked about his belief in and passion for AMP and what could be achieved. Leaders in each part of the business supported and emphasised the core messages, making all employees think about how they could align with the new AMP. To reinforce the new cultural messages, AMP moved quickly to make changes to its structure, which was highly symbolic within AMP. "We moved our business to bring accountability closer to the individual, and not just held at a senior level," Howard said. "We tried to engage everybody into the new vision for the business."

AMP also reset the levers of its performance management systems. Misaligned benefits and handouts that sent the wrong messages were eliminated to get people thinking the new way. "We wanted to send the message that high performers in AMP will receive higher awards," Howard said. "We clearly focused on *how* people achieve the goals within their business line and their business strategy." Howard said that one of the important lessons AMP learnt was that for messages to produce sustainable change, they had to be repeated continuously. "We repeat them on a number of levels and using a number of mediums," she said, from the managing director through to the local team leader. AMP has now moved its 'burning platform' from survival mode into 'burning ambition'. "So the goals are clearly aspirational; we are still on the journey," she said. "We have moved from 'high performance is our only security' to 'high performance is our best shot at winning'. We are trying to move people's mindsets around wanting to be part of a winning team, that AMP can actually be a winning team. Who is it that we aspire to be? What is it that AMP could be for Australia in the future?"

AMP conducted testing during the cultural change process to check that it was working, using direct staff polling via telephone contact. As the changes were realigning the staff to business results, financial indicators were also used a measure of success. "What our results tell us is that it does feel like quite a different place," Howard said. "We have moved on very much from 2002. People are choosing to stay with AMP in a very hot employment market, and we're finding that as people leave the business it's not because of the way that we have moved the culture, it's for other reasons."

Howard said the key message from the AMP journey was to "create a burning platform. That's always the most powerful driver of change, it just feels quite painful when you are going through it. Create really simple messages. And when you are in a time of crisis, I think the integrity and commitment of the leaders is the key way to deliver it".

The Search for Best Practice

The marketing team identified and reviewed the best practices among units to ensure they were in line with brand integrity and DFR outcomes, with the aim of building standardised procedures and processes for the recruitment of new ADF personnel. The result was the *Regional Marketing Guide*, which was tested with Tasmanian units in 2003, modified, and rolled out Australia wide during 2004 through launch workshops. The Regional Marketing Guide is a paper-based manual that contains target marketing information: unit-specific demographic information; planners; activity guides; proven marketing and recruitment activities with step-by-step guidelines, artwork and tools; a full suite of advertising artwork and collateral; and reporting functions and evaluation tools.

"We were not talking about coming up with complex modelling or anything; we were just talking about standardising the simple approaches to local marketing, which include activity guides and how to run an information session, and so on," Crosbie said. The key part of the Regional Marketing Guide strategy was that it was not sent out to the units unsupported. A purpose-built call centre contacted every unit across Australia, once a fortnight, every fortnight – in the process discovering an additional 30-40 reserve units!

The call centre has accumulated a huge amount of information about the reserve units and has ended up being a key source of Army Reserve information. The call centre staff check how each unit is going with its marketing and advertising, and keys the units into the 'how to' resources available in the Regional Marketing Guide. The guide is also complemented by a bi-monthly, hard-copy newsletter, as many of the units do not have access to good-quality technology and downloading large PDFs is not possible.

Evaluation Results were Positive

The marketing team conducted an evaluation of the Regional Marketing Guide strategy.

The outcomes showed that:

- At the launch workshops, 98% of participants believed the guide would meet their objectives.
- The guide was adopted by 100% of Army Reserve units.
- A satisfaction survey achieved a 100% rating for the guide as meeting unit requirements.
- The achievement of the DFR's recruitment target rose from 66% to 90%.
- Relations between DFR and the reserve units improved considerably, as the units could see that DFR was adding to the value of their business.

- Awareness of national DFR marketing campaigns rose from 15% to 80%, as the units had media plans for across Australia and could see the creative that was being sent out nationally.
- There was more efficient allocation of budget and resources for marketing.
- There was more consistent brand execution at local levels.
- Units came to understand the importance of evaluating their campaigns, and to feel that they were actually part of a larger organisation.

RELATIONSHIP MARKETING

Relationship marketing is a form of marketing that evolved from direct response marketing in the 1960s and emerged in the 1980s, in which emphasis is placed on building longer term relationships with customers rather than on individual transactions. It involves understanding the customer's needs as they go through their life cycles. It emphasizes providing a range of products or services to existing customers as they need them.

Development of Relationship Marketing

The origins of relationship marketing observes: "What is surprising is that researchers and businessmen have concentrated far more on how to attract customers to products and services than on how to retain customers". The initial research was done by Leonard Berry at Texas A&M and Jag Sheth at Emory, both of whom were early users of the term "Relationship Marketing", and by marketing theorist Theodore Levitt at Harvard who broadened the scope of marketing beyond individual transactions.

In practice, relationship marketing originated in industrial and B2B markets where long-term contracts have been quite common for many years. Academics like Barbara Bund Jackson at Harvard re-examined these industrial marketing practices and applied them to marketing proper. According to Leonard Berry, relationship marketing can be applied: when there are alternatives to choose from; when the customer makes the selection decision; and when there is an ongoing and periodic desire for the product or service. Fornell and Wernerfet used the term "defensive marketing" to describe attempts to reduce customer turnover and increase customer loyalty. This customer-retention approach was contrasted with "offensive marketing" which involved obtaining new customers and increasing customers' purchase frequency. Defensive marketing focused on reducing or managing the dissatisfaction of your customers, while offensive marketing focused on "liberating" dissatisfied customers from your competition and generating new customers. There are two components to defensive marketing: increasing customer satisfaction and increasing switching barriers.

Traditional marketing originated in the 1960s and 1970s as companies found it more difficult to sell consumer products. Its consumer market origins molded traditional marketing into a system suitable for selling relatively low-value products to masses of customers. Over the decades, attempts have been made to broaden the scope of marketing, relationship marketing being one of these attempts. Marketing has been greatly enriched by these contributions.

The practice of relationship marketing has been greatly facilitated by several generations of customer relationship management software that allow tracking and analysing of each customer's preferences, activities, tastes, likes, dislikes, and complaints. This a powerful tool in any company's marketing strategy. For example, an automobile manufacturer maintaining a database of when and how repeat customers buy their products, the options they choose, the way they finance the purchase etc., is in a powerful position to custom target sales material. In return, the customer benefits from the company tracking service schedules and communicating directly on issues like product recalls.

Customer Retention

At the core of relationship marketing is the notion of customer retention. According to Gordon, relationship marketing involves the creation of new and mutual value between a supplier and individual customer. Novelty and mutuality deepen, extend and prolong relationships, creating yet more opportunities for customer and supplier to benefit one another. Studies in several industries have shown that the cost of retaining an existing customer is only about 10% of the cost of acquiring a new customer so it can often make economic sense to pay more attention to existing customers.

It is claimed by Reichheld and Sasser that a 5% improvement in customer retention can cause an increase in profitability of between 25 and 85 per cent depending on the industry. However Carrol, P. and Reichheld, F. dispute these calculations, claiming they result from faulty cross-sectional analysis.

According to Buchanan and Gilles, the increased profitability associated with customer retention efforts occurs because:

- The cost of acquisition occur only at the beginning of a relationship, so the longer the relationship, the lower the amortized cost.
- Account maintenance costs decline as a percentage of total costs.
- Long-term customers tend to be less inclined to switch, and also tend to be less price sensitive. This can result in stable unit sales volume and increases in dollar-sales volume.
- Long-term customers may initiate free word of mouth promotions and referrals.
- Long-term customers are more likely to purchase ancillary products and high margin supplemental products.
- Customers that stay with you tend to be satisfied with the relationship and are less likely to switch to competitors, making it difficult for competitors to enter the market or gain market share.
- Regular customers tend to be less expensive to service because they are familiar with the process, require less "education", and are consistent in their order placement.
- Increased customer retention and loyalty makes the employees' jobs easier and more satisfying. In turn, happy employees feed back into better customer satisfaction in a virtuous circle.

Relationship marketers speak of the "relationship ladder of customer loyalty". It groups types of customers according to their level of loyalty. The ladder's first rung consists of "prospects", that is, people that have not purchased yet but are likely to in the future. This is followed by the successive rungs of "customer", "client", "supporter", "advocate", and "partner". The relationship marketer's objective is to "help" customers get as high up the ladder as possible. This usually involves providing more personalized service and providing service quality that exceeds expectations at each step.

Customer retention efforts involve considerations such as the following:

1. Customer valuation - Gordon describes how to value customers and categorize them according to their financial and strategic value so that companies can decide where to invest for deeper relationships and which relationships need to be served differently or even terminated.
2. Customer retention measurement - Dawkins and Reichheld calculated a company's "customer retention rate". This is simply

the percentage of customers at the beginning of the year that are still customers by the end of the year. In accordance with this statistic, an increase in retention rate from 80% to 90% is associated with a doubling of the average life of a customer relationship from 5 to 10 years. This ratio can be used to make comparisons between products, between market segments, and over time.

3. Determine reasons for defection - Look for the root causes, not mere symptoms. This involves probing for details when talking to former customers. Other techniques include the analysis of customers' complaints and competitive benchmarking.
4. Develop and implement a corrective plan - This could involve actions to improve employee practices, using benchmarking to determine best corrective practices, visible endorsement of top management, adjustments to the company's reward and recognition systems, and the use of "recovery teams" to eliminate the causes of defections.

A technique to calculate the value to a firm of a sustained customer relationship has been developed. This calculation is typically called customer lifetime value. Retention strategies also build barriers to customer switching. This can be done by product bundling, cross selling, cross promotions, loyalty Programmes, increasing switching costs, and integrating computer systems of multiple organizations. Many relationship marketers use a team-based approach. The rationale is that the more points of contact between the organization and customer, the stronger will be the bond, and the more secure the relationship.

The Broad Scope of Relationship Marketing

Relationship marketing has been strongly influenced by re-engineering. According to re-engineering theory, organizations should be structured according to complete tasks and processes rather than functions. That is, cross-functional teams should be responsible for a whole process, from beginning to end, rather than having the work go from one functional department to another. Traditional marketing is said to use the functional department approach.

This can be seen in the traditional four P's of the marketing mix. Pricing, product management, promotion, and placement are claimed to be functional silos that must be accessed by the marketer if she is going to perform her task. According to Gordon, the marketing mix approach is too limited to provide a usable framework for assessing and developing customer relationships in many industries and should be replaced by an alternative model where the focus is on customers and relationships rather than markets and products. In contrast, relationship marketing is cross-functional marketing. It is organized around processes that involve all aspects of the organization. In fact, some commentators prefer to call relationship marketing "relationship management" in recognition of the fact that it involves much more than that which is normally included in marketing. Martin Christopher, Adrian Payne, and David Ballantyne at the Cranfield Graduate school of Management claim that relationship marketing has the potential to forge a new synthesis between quality management, customer service management, and marketing. They see marketing and customer service as inseparable.

In spite of this broad scope, relationship marketing has not lost its core marketing orientation though. It involves the application of the marketing philosophy to all parts of the organization. Every employee is said to be a "part-time marketer". The way Regis McKenna puts it: "Marketing is not a function, it is a way of doing business marketing has to be all pervasive, part of everyone's job description, from the receptionist to the board of directors." Because of this, it is claimed that relationship marketing is a more pure form of marketing than traditional marketing.

The Six Markets Model

Adrian Payne from Cranfield University goes further. He identifies six markets which he claims are central to relationship marketing. They are: internal markets, supplier markets, recruitment markets, referral markets, influence markets, and customer markets.

Referral marketing is developing and implementing a marketing plan to stimulate referrals. Although it may take months before you see the effect of referral marketing, this is often the most effective part of an overall marketing plan and the best use of resources.

Marketing to suppliers is aimed at ensuring a long-term conflict-free relationship in which all parties understand each other's needs and exceed each other's expectations. Such a strategy can reduce costs and improve quality. Influence markets involve a wide range of sub-markets including: government regulators, standards bodies, lobbyists, stockholders, bankers, venture capitalists, financial analysts, stockbrokers, consumer associations, environmental associations, and labour associations. These activities are typically carried out by the public relations department, but relationship marketers feel that marketing to all six markets is the responsibility of everyone in the organization. At times Payne sub-divides customer markets into existing customers and potential customer, yielding seven rather than six markets. He claims that each market will require its own strategies and recommends separate marketing mixes for each of the seven.

When to Use Relationship Marketing

Relationship marketing and transactional marketing are not mutually exclusive and there is no need for a conflict between them. However, one approach may be more suitable in some situations than in others. Transactional marketing is most appropriate when marketing relatively low value consumer products, when the product is a commodity, when switching costs are low, when customers prefer single transactions to relationships, and when customer involvement in production is low.

When the reverse of all the is true, as in typical industrial and service markets, then relationship marketing can be more appropriate. Most firms should be blending the two approaches to match their portfolio of products and services. Virtually all products have a service component to them and this service component has been getting larger in recent decades.

Criticisms of Relationship Marketing

Internal marketing and the six markets model has been criticised as not really being marketing at all. At the core of marketing is the marketing philosophy of first determining what the market wants, then providing it. It is doubtful that this is what is occurring in influence markets, supplier markets, recruitment markets, or internal markets. What is occurring is closer to public relations, persuasion, and management. It appears to be marketing because it uses some marketing techniques, but it would more accurately be described as salesmanship. Relationship theorists tend to compare themselves to traditional marketing. In doing so they frequently present traditional marketing in an unfavourable light. For example, Adrian Payne claims that traditional marketing concentrates on product features, has minimal interest in customer service, limited customer contact, and quality is primarily a concern of production. Although there may still be some marketers that think this way, these statements have not reflected marketing best practices for more than three decades.

THE ROLE OF THE EMPLOYEES IN INTERNAL SALES

As an Internal Sales Executive, you will be responsible for generating new business for hospitality. New business will be generated via outgoing telephone calls only, on the back of product evaluations, marketing campaigns and general sales enquiries.

Main Duties

- Call on opportunities generated from specific marketing campaigns, procured databases, reseller databases and incoming evaluations
- Make 60 dials, with 20 contacts per day
- Work with Channel Managers and their resellers in joint marketing campaigns, giving input into the creation of data lists, agreeing timescales/dates of campaigns and agreeing on a mechanism for feedback of information to the account manager and the reseller
- Accurately update in-house database information
- Support other sales teams on specific campaigns and ensure that accurate and complete information is passed to the appropriate account manager on time
- Conduct both specific and general awareness campaigns to promote hotel facilities and products within targeted markets, as directed by Manager, Marketing or Channel Partners
- Develop and maintain detailed knowledge of both hotels and competitor products and services

EMPLOYEE EMPOWERMENT

People are firm's most underutilized resource. In the new knowledge economy, independent entrepreneurship and initiative is needed throughout the ranks of the organization. Involvement in an organization is no longer a one-way street. In today's corporate environment a manager must work towards engaging organization forcefully enough to achieve its objectives. New knowledge-based enterprises are characterized by flat hierarchical structures and multi-skilled workforce. Managers assume more leadership and coaching tasks and work hard to provide employees with resources and working conditions they need to accomplish the goals they've agreed to. In brief, managers work for their staff, and not the reverse.

Empowerment is the oil that lubricates the exercise of learning. Talented and empowered human capital is becoming the prime ingredient of organizational success. A critical feature of successful teams, especially in knowledge-based enterprises, is that they are invested with a significant degree of empowerment, or decision-making authority.

Equally important, employee empowerment changes the managers' mind-set and leaves them with more time to engage in broad-based thinking, visioning, and nurturing.

This intelligent and productive division of duties between visionary leaders, focusing on emerging opportunities, and empowered employees, running the business unit day to day provides for a well-managed enterprise with strong growth potential. Employee empowerment is a two sided coin. For employees to be empowered the management leadership must want and believe that employee empowerment makes good business sense and employees must act.

Let us be clear about one thing immediately, employee empowerment does not mean that management no longer has the responsibility to lead the organization and is not responsible for performance. If anything the opposite is true. Stronger leadership and accountability is demanded in an organization that seeks to empower employees. This starts with the executive leadership, through all management levels and includes front line supervisors. It is only when the entire organization is willing to work as a team that the real benefits of employee empowerment are realised.

For an organization to practice and foster employee empowerment the management must trust and communicate with employees. Employee communication is one of the strongest signs of employee empowerment. Honest and repeated communication from elements of the strategic plan, key performance indicators, financial performance, down to daily decision making. If an organization has not be actively cultivating employee empowerment, it may take considerable time and effort before employees start to respond. Often the first efforts and communications are met with employee derision and mockery. Those who are only interested in trying the latest management fad will give up when met with this response. A good rule of thumb for communications to employees is to enumerate what management considers adequate and then multiple by a factor of ten.

When considering employee understanding and acceptance of decisions consider how long it takes for the management team to discuss and then make a decision. Allow several multiples of this time for employees to think about the issue. For management wanting employee empowerment the evidence will not come across the board with wide spread acceptance. A small number will accept the invitation to become more involved, say 3-5 per cent. The rest will be watching every move to see what happens. Every communication, decision and action by management will be viewed as either supporting a move to employee empowerment or not. Probably nothing demonstrates the commitment or lack of commitment to employee empowerment more than promotions and selection for leadership positions. Employees know those that attempt to "shine up while dumping down". For an organization to enjoy the returns from employee empowerment the leadership must diligently work to create the work environment where it is obvious to all that employee empowerment is desired, wanted and cultivated. Management's responsibility is to create the environment for employee empowerment. When organizational leadership has started to take actions to encourage employee empowerment it is then up to the employees to decided if they wish to take advantage of the opportunity or not. It is not unusual for only a small minority to accept the challenge initially. Also it is very likely that some fraction will never respond. It is the large middle group that must be convinced to practice employee empowerment.

It is our conviction that most organizations have exactly the level of employee empowerment the management wants. This is demonstrated by the amount of communications, level of training provided employees, opportunities for personal growth, the solicitation and implementation of ideas, the recognition and reward system, promotion and advancement criteria, and uncountable little signals from management that demonstrate whether employees are valued or not. When Six Sigma is deployed in an organization employees have numerous opportunities to demonstrate that they are empowered. Unless there is employee motivation to accept and act on the opportunities little will change. Employee empowerment is evidenced by working with a six sigma project team to understand the changes coming out of the project. Being a participant using improvements found by others is a form of empowerment. Employee can demonstrate empowerment by suggesting areas or processes that might be candidates for a six sigma project. Part of employee empowerment is the recognition by management that often people who most know of pressing needs for improvement are those who have to work in the process.

Employee empowerment can take the form of being asked to bring expert knowledge to six sigma projects. Even if not a full time member of the project team the fact that competence and first hand experience are valued and an employee is willing to help demonstrates a level of empowerment. The employee can volunteer to serve on a project team as a Green Belt. This usually means that the employee has some subject matter expertise in the process scoped for a project. By completing the Green Belt training the employees will learn the Fundamental Improvement tools and will learn how to use the Define Measure

Analyse Improve and Control steps as part of problem solving. With this additional skill sets the empowerment of the employee is increased, they are able to work more effectively and efficiently in solving problems and providing potential solutions. Employees can make it know that they would like to become Black Belts. This form of employee empowerment assumes that the employee has the necessary skills and ability to complete the Black Belt training. Usually this means a college level education with comfort in mathematics and if not some statistical understanding a willingness to learn. One of the strongest signs from employees is when they take the lead to advance their skills and knowledge with education and training either provided by the organization or out side the organization. Management has the obligation to create the environment that fosters employee empowerment, employees have the duty to accept the opportunity and demonstrate they are willing and capable.

INTERNAL MERCHANDISING

Many marketing efforts that should be assigned to specific people for coordination sometimes fall between the cracks. The great majority of hotels have a basic problem that makes it difficult to be as successful as they could be. The problem is that many of the marketing responsibilities are ignored or not given the attention they require. It all starts with the definition of marketing. To understand the problem, we must look at the definition of marketing. Here's one definition: Marketing is the blending and controlled supervision of all efforts that affect the sale of your product. What are these efforts? There are a number of separate but related efforts that affect the sale of a hotel product.

- Research
- Public relations, including relations with the community, prospects, present customers and employees
- Product design
- Pricing
- Selling
- Yield/revenue management
- Media advertising
- Packaging
- Direct mail
- Planning/evaluation

- Internet marketing
- Internet merchandising

So what's the problem? When hotel general managers are asked as to who is responsible for their marketing, they often say, "We have a director of sales who handles that." Then later, when the directors of sales are asked to define their responsibilities, they usually include the following: all groups requiring sleeping rooms, plus corporate and government transient business.

Going back to the list of marketing efforts, who then is handling such efforts as public relations, packaging, internal merchandising, pricing, Internet marketing, and food and beverage marketing? The conclusion is always the same. Many of the efforts that should be assigned to specific people for coordination have fallen between the cracks and are handled on a piecemeal basis as the need arises. Even in large hotels, where marketing staffs are larger and the responsibilities a little better defined, some efforts still fall between the cracks. For example, seldom does one find a hotel that has a well-thought-out annual plan for internal merchandising. If you ask what tent card will be featured in the sleeping rooms next month, you get lots of blank stares.

Many hotels that are members of national brands leave it up to the brand to do all of the internal merchandising without thinking about how this medium can be used to promote local restaurants and packages that would benefit greatly from this simple marketing effort. As far as pricing is concerned, seldom does a marketing plan indicate that a specific package will go up in price by $10 on a specific date. The reason usually is that no one person takes responsibility to give pricing the attention it deserves throughout the year, rather than just during the week that budgets are submitted for the coming year.

How to Pull it Together

What is needed is that close looks is taken at all of the responsibilities and establish a marketing committee chaired by your general manager to coordinate all of these activities? Spread the responsibilities throughout the hotel so several of your people will be responsible to the marketing committee for every aspect of the plan. This concept involves getting more employees involved in the marketing of the hotel and encourages advance planning to replace the old "next Sunday is Mother's Day and we have to get an ad in the paper by 2 this afternoon" concept of marketing, a practice that wastes money and drives us to complete frustration. Planning your marketing in an orderly fashion will build a positive team spirit that will motivate your people as never before.

Producing Effective Materials

Generally customers don't want to read a lot of information before they find something interesting. Customers need to be inspired to 'try and buy'. Use words that are descriptive and eye catching.

Describe the freshness of the product:

- Pure
- Real
- Hand picked each day
- Free range
- Natural
- Freshly squeezed
- Fresh

Describe the environment:

- Corn fed
- From our local market
- 'Happy animals'
- A herd name
- Home grown

Describe the overall product:

- Local flavour
- Inventive use of ingredients
- Ask your supplier what words they would use!
- Traditional
- House speciality
- Chilled

Bibliography

Airey, D.: *Tourism Education*, New Delhi: Oxford University Press, 2011.

Ankomah, P.: *Education Tourism: A Strategy to Sustainable Tourism Development*, Philippines: Oxford University Press, 2006.

Charles, K.: *Progress in Tourism and Hospitality*, New Delhi: Oxford University Press, 2011.

Hall, C. M.: *Trends and Issues in Tertiary Tourism Education*, England: University of New England, 2009.

Hegarty, J.A.: *Ethics in Tourism and Hospitality Education*, Kolkata: Allied, 2004.

Jafari, J.: *Towards a Framework for Tourism Education*, Princeton: Princeton University Press, 2008.

Kasper, C.: *Tourism Marketing and Management Handbook*, New York: Prentice Hall, 2007.

Ketyer, E.: *Tourism Education in Formal Education*, New Delhi: Oxford University Press, 2008.

Lam, T.: *International Journal of Contemporary Hospitality Management*, New Delhi: Oxford University Press, 2004.

Lavery, P.: *Tourism Marketing and Management Handbook*, New York, Prentice Hall, 2012.

Moilliet, D.: *Hospitality Research Journal*, London: Macmillan, 2011.

Moscardo, G.: *The Journal of Tourism Studies*, New Delhi: Penguin Books, 2010.

Payne, K.: *Tourism and Hospitality Research*, Guwahati: United Publishers, 2008.

Pearce, P.: *Locating Tourism Studies in the Landscape of Knowledge*, Calgary: University of Calgary, 2007.

Shea, L. J.: *Journal of Hospitality and Tourism Education*, Kolkata: ICSP Publication, 2011.

Sheldon, P. J.: *Training Needs Assessment in the Travel Industry*, Mumbai: Sabrang Publications, 2010.

Tao, H.: *The Development and Construction of Tourism Personnel*, London: Yale University Press, 2003.

Tribe, J.: *The Tourism Curriculum*, London: Yale University Press, 1998.

Umbreit, T.: *The Role of Education in the Tourist Industry*, Salt Lake City: University of Utah, 2002.

Vroom, J. A.: *Tourism Education: A Model Program*, New Delhi: Manas Publications, 2014.

Walle, A.H.: *Journal of Hospitality and Tourism Education*, New Delhi: Indian Institute of Public Administration, 2010.

Walsh, M. E.: *Tourism Management*, New Delhi: Government of India Press, 2007.

Watson, J.: *Developing Tourism Managers*, New Delhi: Government of India Press, 2005.

Xiao, H.: *Annals of Tourism Marketing*, New Delhi: Oxford University Press, 2004.

Xiao, Q. H.: *Tourism and Hospitality Education*, New Delhi: Planning Commission, 2005.

Youell, R.: *Tourism Education Handbook*, London: The Tourism Society, 2006.

Zhao, J. L.: *International Journal of Hospitality Management*, New York: HRW, 2008.

Index